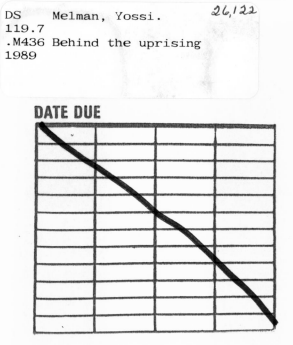

Behind the Uprising

Recent Titles in
Contributions in Political Science

Behind the Uprising

Israelis, Jordanians, and Palestinians

**Yossi Melman
and
Dan Raviv**

CONTRIBUTIONS IN POLITICAL SCIENCE, NUMBER 238

GREENWOOD PRESS

New York • Westport, Connecticut • London

Library of Congress Cataloging-in-Publication Data

Melman, Yossi.
    Behind the uprising : Israelis, Jordanians, and Palestinians /
Yossi Melman and Dan Raviv.
    p.   cm.—(Contributions in political science, ISSN 0147–1066 ;
    no. 238)
    Bibliography: p.
    Includes index.
    ISBN 0–313–26787–1 (lib. bdg. : alk. paper)
    1. Jewish-Arab relations—1949– 2. Israel—Foreign relations—
Jordan.   3. Jordan—Foreign relations—Israel.   I. Raviv, Daniel.
II. Title.   III. Series.
DS119.7.M436   1989
956.04—dc20   89–7486

British Library Cataloguing in Publication Data is available.

Library of Congress Catalog Card Number: 89–7486
ISBN: 0–313–26787–1
ISSN: 0147–1066

First published in 1989

Greenwood Press, Inc.
88 Post Road West, Westport, Connecticut 06881

Printed in the United States of America

∞™

The paper used in this book complies with the
Permanent Paper Standard issued by the National
Information Standards Organization (Z39.48–1984).

10 9 8 7 6 5 4 3 2 1

To our parents,
Anna and Yitzhak Melman
and
Esther and Benjamin Raviv

Contents

Preface

This book was born, but not yet written, some 6 miles over the North Sea in January 1986. As working journalists, we were both flying aboard the official jet of Israel's Prime Minister Shimon Peres, covering his tour of Western Europe. The itinerary included meetings with Premier Ruud Lubbers of the Netherlands, Britain's formidable Prime Minister Margaret Thatcher, and West German Chancellor Helmut Kohl. Only with time did we realize that behind the scenes, Peres was engaged in even more fascinating and vital diplomacy.

Israel's prime minister was meeting his nation's formal enemy to the east, Jordan's King Hussein ibn-Talal.

There were a few clues for the attentive. Without explanation, the United States ambassador to Israel, Thomas Pickering, accompanied Peres on his flight from Tel Aviv to The Hague. There, the U.S. Middle East envoy, Richard Murphy, appeared without fanfare or comment for late-night talks with Peres.

The prime minister's official daytime schedule was busy enough; at night Peres seemed to revert from Dr. Jekyll to Mr. Hyde, with nonstop meetings with his aides and with the Americans. People and documents were sneaking in and out of back doors in the Dutch darkness.

Hussein, we discovered, was visiting London at the time. And the American diplomats were on a shuttle mission, taking one-hour flights between London and The Hague in hopes of furthering the cause of peace.

The Palestinians in the West Bank and Gaza were quiet, awaiting developments and hoping to be brought into the nighttime U.S.-Israeli-Jordanian diplomacy. They were, as so often before, disappointed.

The book that has finally sprung forth from our curiosity as journalists took on a sudden urgency when, on December 9, 1987, the Palestinians living under occupation rose up against the Israelis. It was the start of the *intifadda,* the "uprising."

We have found that the recent history of the Middle East conflict can better be understood by focusing on an unacknowledged, but powerful partnership among three key parties in the dispute: the Israelis, the Jordanians, and the Palestinians. It is generally a hostile partnership, to be sure, but the three sides are locked together in a relationship they cannot control, but also cannot escape.

Americans and others who are concerned about the region have, for too long, ignored the Palestinians. In the *intifadda,* however, youngsters armed with slogans, rocks, and bottles had the mighty Israeli army on the run and shattered the confidence of the Israeli people in their ability to maintain the occupation of the lands captured in 1967. Among other effects, the United States responded to the new, moderate diplomacy of the Palestine Liberation Organization by opening a dialogue with Yasser Arafat's PLO.

Even as Jordan's King Hussein lost the central role he used to have, he remained definitely in the picture. He has become expert in delicately balancing his relationships with Israel and with the Palestinians. Western diplomats have affectionately dubbed him PLK—the "plucky little king" who has become the Middle East's longest surviving ruler against many odds and doomful predictions.

The PLO has good reason to hate Hussein, but still it would be very difficult to achieve lasting peace in the region without taking the Hashemite Kingdom of Jordan's interests into consideration.

Our aim, then, is to examine closely the troubled triangle of Israel, Jordan, and the Palestinians. The research for this volume began in early 1986 and extended to Washington, London, Paris, Amman, Cairo, Jerusalem, and the West Bank. We cannot claim to have discovered the whole truth, and we offer detailed descriptions of Hussein's meetings with Israeli leaders only where we are certain of our material. There were more encounters, dating back to 1963, but we believe we learned of the most significant ones.

We had valuable cooperation from firsthand sources: individuals who personally took part in the secret meetings and who have finally decided to tell— almost—all. In the world of shadowy diplomacy and espionage, there were many sources who insisted on anonymity but a surprising number who shared their memories on the record. To them, we are especially grateful.

Our thanks go also to Peter Snow, the BBC broadcaster who granted us permission to use his excellent 1972 biography of Hussein as the basis for our description of the king's youth; to the staff at the Israel State Archives who provided significant documents; to the talented journalists Meir Bleich and Dan Avidan; to archivist Shaika Zilberman of the newspaper *Davar;* to Herzl Hamush and Larry Miller for valuable advice; and to Norman Frankel whose help guided this book into print.

Our highest gratitude is reserved for our wives, Billie Melman and Dori Phaff, whose patience, counsel, and assistance seem boundless.

Introduction

If the king of Jordan were an impolite man, which he certainly is not, he would have ignored or even laughed at the question put to him by his American hosts. But they received a direct and serious answer.

It was May 1985, and Hussein was visiting Washington. Secretary of State George Shultz asked him, bluntly and almost innocently, why Jordan refused to enter into direct peace negotiations with Israel.

Hussein smiled for a moment as he replied, in the deep voice that surprises those who expect frailty from a monarch so lacking in physical stature. He said he had had over 150 "discussion hours" with Israel's leaders. It was a measure only a professional pilot would use, and Hussein, a talented flyer, spoke as though he were clocking his flight hours in a challenging aircraft.

Informed of the conversation, senior Israeli officials did their own calculations and found the king had been too conservative. The secret discussions totaled over two hundred hours.

Either way, it is a fact—however hidden and denied—that Hussein has met with Israeli representatives more than any other Arab leader. This includes even the late President Anwar Sadat of Egypt, who openly negotiated a peace treaty with Israel, and Morocco's King Hassan. Since his first meeting with an Israeli official in 1963, Hussein has had over twenty encounters with the Jewish state's leadership, ranging from four prime ministers through the highest defense and diplomatic echelons of Israel.

The talks were long on content, but also on tension and other emotions. The locations of the meetings were interesting, too. For the sake of security, the king and the Israelis chose sites ranging from the relatively ordinary mansion and clinic of an extraordinary doctor in London, to a missile boat in the Gulf of 'Aqaba, to a tent amid the desert sands, to a closely guarded house in a Tel Aviv suburb.

Some of the steps taken to keep the contacts clandestine could have been adopted from a cheap detective novel, but others were staged by the Israeli intelligence agencies, which were widely judged to be the best in the world. In any event, the secret diplomacy became rather an open secret in the Middle East. Perhaps it was simply the highly visible results: tacit cooperation between Israel and Jordan in administering the West Bank of the Jordan, captured by the Israelis in 1967, and the de facto peace since that year. There was also the fact that some Israeli politicians, motivated by self-interest, leaked selected details of the talks to the press.

The aim of the discussions between the Israelis and the Jordanians—the king, his brother Crown Prince Hassan, his military officers and senior ministers—was a peace treaty. After years of arguments, however, the notion of a formal peace without an overall settlement for the Middle East dispute was put aside. Instead, verbal understandings were reached on a wide range of issues, "from anti-terrorism to anti-mosquito tactics," in the words of one official. Eventually, there were even some written agreements. These were kept secret and shared, if at all, only with the United States and Britain.

The true aim, even more deeply hidden, of the Israeli and Jordanian dialogue was to prevent the birth of a Palestinian state. Despite the unremitting efforts of the two established powers along the banks of the Jordan River, the Palestinian people caught in the middle did not surrender. Their nationalist movement, both within the occupied West Bank and Gaza Strip and outside in the umbrella structure of the Palestine Liberation Organization (PLO), became even stronger. As their uprising, which began in 1987, showed, they want a state of their own between Israel and Jordan, rather than being carved up between the Zionists and the Hashemites.

The cooperation began even before the State of Israel was born in May 1948. The Zionist leadership recognized the common interests it had with the Hashemite Kingdom of Transjordan ruled by Hussein's grandfather, Abdullah. Neither side wanted what it saw as an angry, radical Palestinian Arab state between them in an already volatile region. Both sides were, and still are, scared to death of the notion.

Shared interests resulted from Middle East history. The borders of Jordan, before 1967 and more confined since then, did not result from ancient settlement patterns or geographic imperatives. Jordan's shape, and the very existence of the kingdom, were a product of spheres of influence carved out by European imperialist powers after the First World War.

Israel has far-deeper roots in the region than the modern state's birth date of 1948 would indicate. The Jews considered the land their home long after they were driven into exile by the Roman imperialists, who burned Jerusalem's Holy Temple in the first century after Christ. King David and his Israelites ruled Jerusalem a thousand years earlier.

The Jews, in exile, yearned for their historic homeland. It became known, under Rome's rule, as Palaestina and was named for the Philistines, one of the tribes that had sailed there from elsewhere around the Mediterranean.

The Prophet Muhammad brought a new, vibrant religion to the region in the seventh century, converting the mainly pagan peoples to Islam across a huge area from Mecca in Arabia to the Mediterranean Coast and beyond. The coastal strip lost its Latin name in favor of the Arabic *Falastin*, "Palestine." Jerusalem was a holy city for the Muslims, too, and on the same small mountain where the Jews had had their temple, overlooking Christian shrines such as the Gardens of Gethsemene where Judas betrayed Jesus, the Muslims built one of their most important mosques, calling it *Al-Aqsa*, "The Last." They believed that Muhammad was elevated to heaven from that spot.

Jerusalem and, more broadly, Palestine were, therefore, holy to three religions. The Holy Land was also a great crossroads for commercial, political, and military interests.

As should seem obvious from the name itself, this land was inhabited by people who considered themselves, with the rise of Arab nationalism standing against European imperialism, to be Palestinians, a true nation. For them, the Zionists were foreign intruders serving the interests of the west; but the Hashemites, too, came from far off and were not welcome.

For the Hashemite ancestors of King Hussein, Jordan was a gift. Hussein's grandfather Abdullah came from the Arabian Peninsula where he had been an anti-Turkish ally to the British. They showed their gratitude in 1921 by giving him two-thirds of their Palestine mandate. They called the Arabian emir's new emirate Transjordan, and it was a valuable buffer separating the French mandate in Syria from British Palestine and the British protectorate of Iraq.

Abdullah and Hussein, the only two long-ruling kings Jordan has known in nearly seventy years, proved themselves to be more than mere figureheads. They depended for support on Britain and more recently on the United States, but they were not puppets. Surviving in the face of powerful radical trends in the Arab world, Jordan's monarchs concocted a combination of moderation and patriotism devoted to the government in Amman more than to the wider Arab nation of nations.

The contacts with the Zionist movement began in the first years of Abdullah's rule over Transjordan. In the 1920s, Abdullah's family had lost control of the sacred mosques in Mecca and Medina, and the emir naturally cast his eye on the holy places in Jerusalem. He sought influence, if not physical custody, over the ancient city.

The Zionists, meanwhile, concluded that the Palestinian Arabs in the largely barren country they were settling would never welcome a Jewish nation in their midst. The Zionist leadership saw Abdullah as the gateway to acceptance and legitimacy in the region.

In 1947, when the United Nations (UN) approved a partition plan for what was then a British mandate, the Zionists realized that they had gambled on the right horse. The Jews would have their state.

The Palestinians, under their leader Hajj Amin el-Husseini, rejected the UN plan. They believed the entire land belonged to them and could not see any justification for sharing it with a usurper from abroad. They managed to drag the neighboring Arab states into the caldron, only to realize, too late, what a mistake they made. The Palestinians lost their land and the chance they had had no longer to be a stateless people.

The war of 1948 became the finest hour for the Zionists and the Hashemites. Both sides achieved their most important aims in May, when the State of Israel was born and withstood a joint Arab invasion that included Jordan's impressive, British-led Arab Legion. Abdullah's legionnaires, although fighting through the year, had tacit limits to their ambitions and were truly interested only in the Arab sector of Palestine as delineated by the UN. They made no serious effort, unlike the other Arab armies, to seize the land apportioned to the Jews.

By the time the smoke cleared and the truces were signed, Transjordan had seized the West Bank and East Jerusalem. The holy places were Abdullah's. He changed his expanded kingdom's name to Jordan, and he prepared a nonaggression treaty with Israel. He paid with his life, as a Palestinian assassin cut him down at the Al-Aqsa Mosque.

So as to avoid a similar fate, the grandson, King Hussein, did not talk to Israel at first and insisted on secrecy and slow progress when he later did so. His loss of the West Bank and his half of Jerusalem in 1967 prompted him to deepen his contacts with the Israelis, so as to maintain some Jordanian influence in the occupied territories. Once again, the Palestinians found themselves, as they did nineteen years earlier, squeezed in the middle.

Despite Hussein's announcement in 1988, as a response to the Palestinian uprising, that he was dropping all claims to the West Bank, he does want the land back—especially the mosques in Jerusalem.

The peace process, however, needs a major push. Once the PLO recognized Israel, renounced terrorism, and accepted all UN resolutions, the decision of the United States to talk to the organization was a step in the right direction. There is talk of convening an international conference, to bring all parties in the conflict to the negotiating table. There is the rapid growth in Palestinian nationalism growing to a crescendo, which Israel and Jordan ignore at their peril.

The true requirements are face-to-face negotiations between Israelis and Palestinians, with Jordanian participation, to find a *modus vivendi* to live together in whatever agreed structure may emerge. It could be a Jewish state alongside an Arab confederation, or even three independent states if that is the wish of the parties involved. Direct negotiation is preferable, but if another forum for discussion is needed—with the involvement of the two superpowers or other international sponsors—let it be. Security guarantees, the main Israeli demand, should not be impossible to devise, especially in light of what Israel and Jordan have already accomplished in their secret diplomacy.

This, then, is the story of the contacts between the two states, and how they formed a partnership aimed at boxing out the Palestinians. Israel, Jordan, and the Palestinians are three sides of a triangle, and their people and the outside world should know the details of the relationship. They must better understand the limitations of de facto peace and the challenge of reaching comprehensive peace. Without knowledge, and without peace, the alternatives are ignorance and war—a conflict that could spread from the Middle East to the rest of the globe.

Chapter 1

The Territories Explode

The rumor spread as would fire on a sea of petroleum. From the narrow alleyways of the shantytown known as the Jibalyah refugee camp in the northern Gaza Strip, to the equally poor, but less-crowded, town of Rafah on Gaza's border with Egypt, word that "the Jews have killed in cold blood" was whispered and even shouted.

The occupation forces who have held this unhappy parcel of land since the Six Day War in 1967 are rarely known as "the Israelis" to the locals. On December 8, 1987, the Palestinians of Gaza were saying that the deaths of four Arabs, run down by a truck, was "the revenge of the Jews." On that Tuesday, on the main road that leads from Jibalyah Junction to the refugee center at Bayt Hanoun, the Israeli driver lost control of his heavy truck and plowed into a crowd of civilians. In addition to the four who were killed, seven Jibalyah camp residents were injured. Hundreds of Palestinians, on their way home from their jobs in Israel, witnessed the incident and were convinced it was murder.

The driver was detained for questioning by the Israeli-controlled Gaza police. Witnesses came forward, swearing by the name of Allah that he had intentionally steered off the road, probably as an act of vengeance for the murder of an Israeli, two days earlier, by a Palestinian guerrilla squad.

In crowded conditions, rumors are passed through the population with surprising speed, and the 650,000 Arabs of the Gaza Strip were willing to believe the worst. A simple road accident, in their view, was most unlikely. It is a general, if not universal, attribute of the Levantine people that they perceive an organized conspiracy behind even the most fortuitous acts of nature. Some 400,000 of the Arabs who had the misfortune to live under Egyptian rule until 1967 and Israeli administration since, found their homes in ten refugee camps built in 1948, when Israel won its war of independence. Palestinian Arabs found they could not return to their former towns and villages. More explosive human material is unlikely to be found anywhere.

The belief that the Israelis were now going too far made December 8 the beginning of *el-intifadda,* Arabic for "the uprising," that continued, into 1988 and beyond, to change the Middle East conflict. The competition between two peoples, the Jews and the Palestinian Arabs, for the same lands now known as "Israel and the territories," erupted into prolonged, violent, civil strife that limited the diplomatic options to find a peaceful solution.

Until that day, politicians on both sides of the Jordan River had generally acted on the conviction that two parties, Jordan and Israel, could make peace in the area formerly known as Palestine. The neighboring states were certainly not friends or allies—far from it, considering the bloody wars of 1948 and 1967. But in the twenty-five years before the Palestinian uprising, they had conducted secret diplomacy and had reached a network of understandings constituting a de facto peace settlement without telling anyone about it.

As the million and more people of the occupied territories learned the details, through hints and leaks over the years, they found little to please the Palestinians. In December 1987, the last straws of their patience were broken.

On the ninth day of the month, less than twenty-four hours after the fatal crash of the truck, a morning patrol of Israeli reservists driving through Gaza became the target of stones thrown by teenagers and children of the Jibalyah camp. The officer in charge left the personnel carrier behind with one soldier but took the others to pursue the Arab youths on foot. The stone throwers simply dissolved into the dusty alleys.

By the time the officer returned to his vehicle, by now with reinforcements who had joined the fruitless chase, the Israelis were surrounded by dozens of angry young people. The "kids of the gutter" were rising, in rebellion, as they never had before. Some of them were trying to grab a rifle from the lone soldier who had been left on guard. Rocks, pieces of brick, and glass bottles began to rain down ferociously, and within minutes the bottles were filled with petrol and these Molotov cocktails were lit before being thrown by the young Palestinians.

The officer did not even have to make a conscious decision that his men's lives were in danger. Their predicament, on the receiving end of a violent attack by ordinary civilians, was almost unprecedented, but it was clear. He gave the order to open fire, as the Israeli army—the unchallenged masters of the Middle East military scene—had to use bullets to fight its way out of a crowd of youngsters.

A Palestinian, seventeen years old, was killed instantly. Sixteen of his fellow rioters were wounded, and one of them later died of his wounds. The patrol managed to get away, of course, with no serious injuries to the Israelis.

A crowd of Jibalyah refugees, by now swollen to several hundred, marched to the camp hospital. They seized the dead youth's body and, holding it high above their heads, embarked on a massive parade of mourning through the unpaved roads.

Israeli soldiers based in the heart of the refugee camp, most of them serving their unliked but mandatory thirty-five days or more of annual reserve duty, were taken by surprise: untrained and unsure how to confront an uncontrolled mob, which by the afternoon numbered in the thousands. They emptied their riot control arsenals, but the tear-gas canisters and large rubber bullets they fired to disperse the crowds were met only by defiant cries of *"Itbah el-Yahud!"* and most of the soldiers knew enough Arabic to understand "Butcher the Jews!"

The army chief of the southern command, General Yitzhak Mordecai, imposed a curfew on the Jibalyah camp and attempted to cut it off from the rest of the Gaza Strip so that the unrest would not spread.

That was only the first day, and only the first death, of the uprising that could not so easily be nipped in its budding stages. General Mordecai would learn that the contagion of anger, combined with desperation, was not quarantined by any of the methods previously developed to control civil unrest in the occupied territories.

Demonstrations, featuring the worst rock and bottle throwing Israel's army had faced in many years, spread throughout the Gaza Strip, and within two days the focus of the fledgling *intifadda* had shifted from Gaza to the much larger West Bank, also captured by Israel in 1967 but from Jordan rather than Egypt.

West Bank radicals were inspired by news reports from Gaza, and the Israelis immediately found that censorship of the press was useless when radio and television from surrounding nations could easily be received. Trouble broke out at the Balata refugee camp near Nablus, the largest town in the West Bank's northern half, the sector that Jewish nationalists call Samaria.

Whoever was organizing the demonstrations, and the Israelis were at a loss to identify them, managed to add the power of Islamic fervor to the usual cries for Palestinian independence. Some 1,500 Balata residents, fired up by the weekly prayers on Friday, poured out of their mosques declaring their solidarity with the rioters of the Gaza Strip. They attacked a unit of Israel's paramilitary border police, which is often assigned to duty in the West Bank.

The officers fired back, with little hesitation, and three Arabs were killed and another eleven wounded. That night, huge crowds of Palestinians converged on the Itihad Hospital in Nablus, declaring that they were the friends, relatives, and ultimately the avengers of the casualties. The demonstrators, feeling safety in numbers and a rare sense of cockiness in the face of Israeli forces, shouted anti-Zionist slogans, and many wrapped their faces in the traditional Arab scarf called the *kefiyya,* but in the revolutionary Palestinian colors of red and black. The protesters blocked the main streets of the West Bank's main town with makeshift barricades of burning tires. Among their prime targets were Arabs suspected of collaborating with Israeli intelligence. Dozens were lynched, stabbed, or shot to death by fellow Palestinians. The liquidation of the informers touched the very heart of Israel's system of control in the occupied territories.

Inflamed passions grew red-hot from town to village throughout the occupied lands, and even to East Jerusalem, which the Israelis had captured in 1967 and promptly annexed as part of the nation's newly united capital city. The Old City, with its Muslim, Christian, Armenian, and Jewish quarters, was again divided in the sense that protest strikes closed Muslim and other shops, and Jews felt there were "no go" areas in Jerusalem for the first time in over twenty years.

During one of the worst sorts of rainstorms that Jerusalemites ever have to suffer, a new neighborhood of the ancient city was rocked by the most frightening sort of sectarian violence. It was December 19, a Saturday, and Jews were quietly celebrating their sabbath day in the newly constructed Jewish area on the hilltop where the British high commissioner had his headquarters until Britain's rule over Palestine ended in 1948. The neighborhood was a symbol of Israel's determination to dominate all the high ground around Jerusalem, to build densely populated Jewish settlements on former Arab lands for the sake of strategic advantage.

On that Saturday, dozens of young Palestinians made their way to this area known as the "Commissioner's Palace" and hurled rocks at a well-known Jewish restaurant, finally setting it ablaze.

A few hours later, an even larger crowd of Arab teenagers physically took over Saladin Street, the main thoroughfare for business, shopping, and traffic in East Jerusalem. They broke shop windows and set fire to branch offices of Israeli banks, leaving a trail of shattered glass and Israeli police, who never felt so powerless.

Teddy Kollek, the elderly but energetic mayor, had to admit that twenty years of efforts to unite the ancient city through the peaceful coexistence and commerce between Arabs and Jews were being destroyed.

Even within the pre–1967 borders of Israel itself, seven hundred thousand Arab citizens, who had usually felt some sympathy with their Palestinian brethren in the occupied lands but rarely any necessity to actively protest on their behalf, were undergoing a sea change of attitude. Young or old, the Israeli Arabs had been living their lives with a split personality: they were ethnically and unavoidably Palestinians, but they had democratic rights of citizenship in a nation established for world Jewry, while enjoying one of the highest standards of living in the Middle East.

In the Jewish state as in the West Bank and Gaza, nationalism and even religious fundamentalism were reawakened among the Palestinians. Led again by the teenagers, Arabs in the nominally Israeli cities of Nazareth and Acre to the north, in Arab villages in the Galilee region, and even in the old Jaffa section of Tel Aviv joined demonstrations to protest on behalf of "our brothers in the occupied territories." Stones were thrown at cars known to be driven by Jews, and for one day there was a successful general strike by Arab workers and students.

One Arab member of parliament resigned from the Labor party, no longer feeling he could be in the same political party as Defense Minister Yitzhak Rabin, who was responsible for army tactics in the occupied territories. The dilemma of the Israeli Arabs did not quite erupt in an uncontrollable manner, but it was no longer so acceptable for a Palestinian, even with an Israeli passport, to think of himself as Israeli.

Israel's police and army cracked down as hard as they ever had in the occupied territories, arresting thousands of alleged rioters and organizers of the violence. But still the trouble continued. Israeli security agents proudly announced they had raided and shut down a clandestine printing press that had distributed instructions to the mobs, but still these newsletters of the uprising continued to appear in the Arab streets.

Attacking the army became a daily occupation, even a game, for young Palestinians. There was no shortage of rocks, bottles, and stones. The Palestine Liberation Organization (PLO) had not initiated the *intifadda,* but PLO propagandists outside the territories jumped on the bandwagon and proudly told the people living under occupation that their primitive weapons were accomplishing more than guerrilla guns and rockets ever had.

By April 1988, however, Israel sent a commando squad over 1,500 miles to Tunisia to kill Khalil el-Wazir, the military commander of the PLO also known as Abu Jihad, charging that he was plotting the continuing violence in the territories and that he was also planning to step up terrorism from outside to add further pressure on Israel. He was blamed for a bus hijack in southern Israel during the early stages of the uprising in which three Israelis were killed.

The short-term effect of Abu Jihad's assassination, never formally acknowledged by Jerusalem as an Israeli deed, was a large outpouring of protesters in the West Bank and Gaza, and the deaths of seventeen in a hail of Israeli gunfire on the day the news came from Tunis.

The worldwide media featured the uprising at the top of front pages and television news bulletins for months, giving the Palestinian issue more prominence than it had for years. The rioting and the Israeli response—exaggerated beatings replacing live ammunition for a while—eventually became almost routine, however. The young protesters who apparently had unlimited time to take part in defiant marches, burn tires, and throw stones began to slip from the headlines.

The occasional shocking incident would again focus attention on the situation, however. Angry crowds lynched a Palestinian who was known to be an informer for the Israelis. Most of the 1,000 Arab policemen working for the Israelis in the occupied territories resigned. The border police were seen swinging their clubs and firing tear gas outside one of Islam's holiest mosques, the Dome of the Rock atop Jerusalem's Old City. Israeli troops were seen confronting Arab women who mounted their own protest gatherings, and proud Palestinians spoke of their ''mothers of the revolution.'' The death toll in the first year of the *intifadda* exceeded 330, mainly unarmed Palestinians, but also 6 Israelis.

Even in the months before the uprising, a brew likely to be violent could be seen fermenting in the Gaza Strip. Israeli troops battled new Arab guerrilla groups, which were small but significant in that they were obviously inspired by the Islamic fundamentalism of Iran's ayatollahs. Ironically, Israel's occupation authorities had originally encouraged the religious revival among the Palestinians, hoping that prayer would be less dangerous than the stubborn nationalist demands of the PLO and its leader, Yasser Arafat.

At the same time that the military government took action to stop the flow of cash from abroad to local pro-PLO activists, the authorities turned a blind eye to the huge "contributions" reaching Gaza from Arab states such as Saudi Arabia. These funds were used to build new mosques, religious schools and an Islamic college. Within a few years, the college became a hotbed of radical activism, as secular nationalists who yearned for a PLO state found common cause with Muslim fundamentalists who prayed for a place in heaven.

The poverty and population density of Gaza, among the world's worst, also contributed to the dangerous discontent. Most jobs, for those Arabs who have them rather than depending only on handouts from the United Nations (UN) are in Israel rather than in Gaza, and the trip to employment in construction, factory assembly lines, trash collection, and similar work usually entails a crowded ride in the back of a truck and humiliating security searches by the border police when crossing the pre–1967 border known as the "Green Line."

Palestinian workers coming from Gaza and the West Bank require special permits to spend the night in Israel itself, but there is plenty of daytime in which to compare their own living standards with those of the Israelis for whom they are laboring. They see wealthy Jews enjoying the riches of their independent state, including freedom and democracy, while the Palestinians earn much less and sleep illegally in the basement of the building they are constructing or in the kitchen of the restaurant in which they wash the dishes.

Even before the *intifadda* broke into the open, the rumblings had begun. Defense Minister Rabin made an official visit to the occupied West Bank in early September 1987, and in Nablus he asked the local commanders who accompanied him, "Are we going into Balata?" Rabin did not really want to know what Israeli administrators were beginning to realize about the West Bank's largest refugee camp: it was, for quite a few months, under the nearly total control of the *Shebiba,* the "Gang" of young Palestinian radicals who defiantly waved the banned PLO flag and beat up Arabs who collaborated with the Israelis in any way.

As a center of activism and rebellion, Balata was to the West Bank what Jibalyah was to the Gaza Strip. Jibalyah, however, was both energized and tempered by the fervor of Islamic fundamentalism. Balata was out-and-out, 100 percent political. The youths of the *Shebiba* were in charge of daily life in the camp, and they even declared Balata a tiny first chunk of "liberated Palestine."

Alongside their declared but not yet violent battle against the Israeli authorities, the *Shebiba* also declared all-out war on drug abuse, prostitution, and crime. Youths volunteered to clean the alleyways of Balata, to repair neglected buildings, and to organize social events.

Camp residents passed the word to Arab police officers and employees of the civil administration, both employed by the Israelis, not to enter the camp. Their functions were carried out, quite successfully, by the young men of *Shebiba.*

So when Defense Minister Rabin visited the area, three months before the Palestinian uprising began, his escort officers urged him not to enter the camp, saying, "The kids there throw stones." Rabin heeded the advice, and instead the senior cabinet member charged with ruling the occupied territories stood on a rooftop and took in the view of the rundown Balata houses through military field glasses. He chose a safe distance, and it was part of the growing realization, certainly among most soldiers serving in the West Bank, that "this is not Israel."

The Israeli leadership was receiving many signals from the Palestinians that, even after more than two decades of Israeli rule, they were unwilling to accept the ongoing situation. The writing was on the wall, but Israelis of various political shades would read it based mostly on what they would like to see.

For many, a clearheaded analysis of the occupation as a seemingly permanent institution would be too painful. Idealistic Zionists whose dreams of a Jewish state had been fulfilled knew that the early, optimistic and uplifting plans for Israel had never included military rule over an Arab minority. Worse still were the demographic predictions that with their greater birthrate, Arabs could out-number Jews in Israel and the occupied territories soon after the beginning of the twenty-first century.

The government in Jerusalem, since the deadlocked national election of 1984, had been hopelessly divided on issues of war and peace. It was not precisely lions and lambs lying together, but the hawkish Likud bloc under Yitzhak Shamir was sharing power with the relatively flexible Labor party led by Shimon Peres. The political archrivals were taking turns as prime minister, and for four years the cabinet would be divided into two halves sitting as a National Unity Coalition.

Shamir's reading of the writing on the wall could be simply summarized as: "I don't read such messages in Arabic, and we didn't fight for a state in the Middle East in order to let our hostile neighbors, who are out to kill us, dictate our policies. We must remain strong and patient. If the Palestinian Arabs will not accept the situation today, then they will accept it sooner or later, because Judea and Samaria are part of historic Israel."

Peres, however, sees some urgency in reaching a peace settlement in the region, and his point of view would say: "We cannot afford to waste any opportunities to reach understandings with any of our neighbors, be they Arab governments or Palestinians if they accept Israel's existence and do not support terrorism. We have a formal peace treaty with Egypt, which eases our security concerns on that front. Now we must redouble our efforts for an agreement, to include an acceptable status for the West Bank and Gaza, with King Hussein of Jordan."

The Israeli public, in 1987, appeared to be tiring of the issue. Almost all of the nation's men put in annual reserve duty, and this was often in the occupied territories, but they felt that the less they heard about the West Bank in their civilian life, the better. The Israeli press published many thousands of words on the occupation and what it means, on the twentieth anniversary of the Six Day War victory in June, but as one senior editor put it, "Nobody wants to read about it."

There were, of course, the several thousand Jews in a population of nearly four million who were so strongly nationalistic that they resided in the farming, industrial, and paramilitary settlements dotted throughout Gaza and the West Bank, or Judea and Samaria as the biblically minded would prefer.

But the typical Israeli, if such an animal exists, was sharply changed from his counterpart of 1948 when his nation was a newborn. Back then, he was most likely to be a European socialist who had moved to Palestine to escape the Nazi Holocaust, and other persecutions, and had fought with determination and courage to win an independent homeland for the Jews after two thousand years of wandering the earth in exile.

Now, he might be of European origin, but more likely his family came from a Middle Eastern country where Jews were persecuted and, naturally, he took a hard line when it came to Arabs. Israel still had its idealists, to be sure, but for most citizens there seemed to be little time for political handwringing and debates about social justice in Israel's "go-go" economy and society. To stand still was to fall behind, and the successful Israeli added to his hard work and military service a busy schedule of shopping for luxuries, traveling abroad at least once a year, eating in restaurants, and laughing with friends while sitting in outdoor cafés.

It was full steam ahead for the pursuit of affluence, built largely on borrowing. Each year, there were more and more automobiles of the latest model, despite the import taxes, which at least doubled the prices when compared with Europe. As though to sharpen the heaven and hell, paradise and desert contrast with the refugee camps of Gaza, the fashionable Tel Aviv boardwalk on the Mediterranean was packed with restaurants always filled to capacity with revelers.

Perhaps in Israel more than in any other nation, the army and the people are one. The soldiers are ordinary citizens, and with few exceptions they were as hedonistic as anyone else. Sympathy with the downtrodden Arabs who had lost the war was distinctly unfashionable. The politicians most in favor were those who reminded their nation and the world that the declared policy of most Arab nations and certainly of the PLO was to wipe the Jewish state off the face of the earth.

Only a few days before the *intifadda* began in December 1987, a warning to Israel's leaders was issued by the General Security Service, the domestic intelligence agency better known by its Hebrew initials Shin Bet. The confidential report predicted that major disturbances were likely, soon, in the occupied territories. The indications, however, were of "disturbances to order," and there was no mention of a mass uprising.

Shin Bet was established shortly after Israel's independence and had become the most important arm of government for maintaining internal security, comparable with Britain's MI5 and America's Federal Bureau of Investigation (FBI). In its first twenty years of life, Shin Bet was a small agency that made its reputation by smashing foreign espionage rings in Israel, notably Arab and Soviet bloc spies, while also keeping track of the nation's Arab minority.

After the Six Day War, however, Shin Bet's assignments drastically changed, when the agency was put in charge of monitoring the activities of the Palestinians now under Israeli jurisdiction. Shin Bet was expanded, and new agents were hired.

The attempt by the PLO and similar groups to wage a guerrilla war against the occupation forces immediately after 1967 and the wider terrorist campaign in Israel's cities and against Israeli interests in Europe posed additional, previously unknown, challenges to Shin Bet. The agency's chiefs were forced to compile a list of priorities, and foremost among them was to put a stop to the bombings and other attacks in Israel and the occupied territories. Impressive manpower was mobilized to find the terrorists and their caches of arms and explosives. Of secondary importance was the mission to combat political activists who were fighting for a Palestinian revolution.

Shin Bet agents became known, locally, as "kings of the territory." In almost feudal fashion, each Israeli operative was assigned a specific area. His responsibility was to ensure that no one should depart or arrive in his sector without his knowing about it.

If a Palestinian applied for a construction permit, the civil authorities within the military government would consult the local Shin Bet man before responding. An Arab merchant who wished to export olive oil or vegetables would similarly receive the necessary papers only with Shin Bet's approval. It seemed that every minute of every day was either scheduled or at least monitored by Israel's spies, including a network of Arab informers within the West Bank and Gaza.

Dozens of alleged terrorist rings were unveiled and arrested each year. For the Arabs of the territories, Shin Bet's power was often frightening. For the Israeli public, Shin Bet's successes were awesome and the object of general gratitude. The agency prevented the establishment of any organized Palestinian underground and the spread of terrorist activity into Israel itself.

In their obsessive eagerness to eliminate the threat of Arab terror, Shin Bet's chiefs ignored other tasks. Agents regularly met with their sources, who were mainly Palestinian collaborators and paid informers. The security service failed, however, to learn all there was to know about the political and economic trends of the Palestinian community and of their rituals and habits.

It was as though in refusing to see the Palestinians as people constituting an unlanded nation, the peculiarities of their nationality were allowed to go unnoticed. Shin Bet seemed to be a success in capturing and locking up those who strayed into violence, but it failed to know its enemy well enough.

Israeli intelligence officers recall with some bitterness a study file prepared by their instructors a few years before the *intifadda* began. It contained a large caricature that had appeared in an Arab magazine. The cartoonist, referring apparently to the blindness displayed by Arab armies, portrayed military scouts pacing through the desert, in a wide-eyed search for their enemy's trail. Just a short distance ahead of them, a huge armored column emerged. The scouts were practically in the shadow of the tanks but did not even lift their eyes from the sand and did not see the danger before them.

Intelligence chiefs were thus warning their men and women not to be complacent and not to miss the big picture. Shin Bet failed to draw the conclusions, however, for it maintained its gaze so intently on Palestinian terrorism that the agency entirely missed the growing organization and threat of Palestinian nationalism in the occupied territories.

A few weeks after the *intifadda* began, the controversial General Ariel Sharon and other cabinet ministers of the right-wing Likud bloc accused Shin Bet of an intelligence failure. Indeed, the agency failed to see the uprising coming. It had spoken of the likelihood of Palestinian demonstrations and protests, but it had confidently stated that these could quickly be suppressed as had occurred before. Several ministers made a comparison with the intelligence debacle of 1973, when Israeli agencies felt any Arab invasion could be repulsed and failed to predict the joint Egyptian and Syrian attack on Yom Kippur, Judaism's holiest day.

The truth, in 1987, was that the Shin Bet was only one part of Israel's failure. Even greater responsibility lies with the concepts that dominated official Israeli thinking. The leading exponent of the flawed thinking was Shmuel Goren, who had the title of coordinator of government activities in the territories. He left a secret job with the foreign intelligence agency, the Mossad, in 1984 to take up his post in the Defense Military building in the center of Tel Aviv.

Three years later, Goren found himself in a long conversation at the wedding of the daughter of Yaakov Nimrodi, a former Mossad operative who had become an international businessman and was involved in the Iran-Contra scandal, which included the sale of U.S. and Israeli weapons to Iran in exchange for U.S. hostages held in Lebanon by pro-Iranian terrorists. It was Israel's "wedding of the year," and a veritable who's who in the financial, political, media, intelligence, and defense establishments attended.

One of the veteran officers chatting with Goren asked him, "Well, when will the rebellion in the territories begin?"

The senior official was clearly taken aback, and he snapped, "No rebellion, not ever."

"Are you sure about what you're saying?" the officer persisted.

Goren's macho answer was, "You want to bet?"

The so-called coordinator had settled comfortably into his job. He enjoyed the complete confidence of his boss, Defense Minister Rabin, and had a practically free hand in administering the occupied territories. Goren had become "the emperor of the territories," and even had the nerve to impose censorship on government ministers. When "Minister-Without-Portfolio" Ezer Weizman, a retired air force general, who now flew politically as a dove, wished to confer with Palestinian notables in the West Bank, Goren used his military authority to ban such a meeting.

Israel's policy, as developed by Goren, was simple: all-out war against the PLO and its sympathizers in the occupied lands, suppression of any attempt by the Arabs to form a local leadership, and the development of fruitful relations with the government of Jordan across the river.

Approximately a year after the conversation in the garden of Nimrodi's grand house in Tel Aviv's wealthy suburb Savyon, the Israeli concept collapsed. The theory had been that despite the frustration, despair, bitterness, and anger of the Palestinians under occupation in the face of a barely improved quality of life and the lack of any hope for a political settlement in the region, Israel could continue to rule the territories without great difficulty and without draining vital military resources.

From time to time, of course, there came a wave of demonstrations, perhaps even riots and terrorist attacks, but the Israelis were confident that they could always overcome such challenges. Overconfidence was at the root of the Israeli decision makers' painful error.

The Israelis were not, however, the only ones surprised by the Palestinian uprising and its strength. Yasser Arafat, at the PLO's distant headquarters in Tunis, clearly had no idea the *intifadda* was coming. The month before, in November 1987, the guerrilla leader had concluded that the Arab world was ignoring the plight of his people and focusing only on the dangers posed by the Gulf War between Iran and Iraq. Arafat attempted to demonstrate that the Israeli-occupied territories were still, in a sense, his.

He issued a call to the Palestinians in the West Bank and Gaza Strip to fill the streets and protest against Israeli occupation. Arafat hoped that the leaders of the twenty-one Arab states and the news media of the world would then give the Palestinians some attention. Arafat's call to action, broadcast by various Arab radio stations and distributed through PLO supporters who dared to be activists, failed dismally. No one poured into the streets. No slogans were shouted. No headlines were made.

In the first week of the uprising, which did start from within, in December, Arafat was as convinced as were his Israeli enemies that the stone throwing and the angry assaults by Palestinian youths were phenomena that would soon pass into the minor footnotes of history.

After a second week of protests and violent Israeli attempts to suppress the crowds, Arafat realized the truth that the Israelis were still attempting to deny: something new, deeper, and more powerful than anything in the past, had broken out.

Around the same time in Israel, the military chief of staff General Dan Shomron told a closed-door meeting of the government's inner cabinet, "In a short while, tempers will cool."

Defense minister Rabin was repeatedly asked to explain the unrest to fellow cabinet members and publicly to the hundreds of news reporters flying in from all corners of the globe to cover the story of the year. At first, he blamed Iran's influence on Muslim fundamentalists. Then, he pointed his finger at incitement by Syria, and indeed there was a clandestine radio station operating from Syria and broadcasting suggestions and instructions to the Palestinian rioters. And later, Rabin blamed the PLO.

Arafat and his top aides, however, recognized that some of the million and more Palestinians they had promised to liberate were now rising up impatiently and spontaneously. The civil disorder began without orders from outside or any warning from within, without setting any schedule, without choosing leaders and without weapons. The incitement came from the "children of the occupation," the youths of *Shebiba* and similar spirit who had never known any other government but the Israeli.

The young people were mainly high-school students or graduates, and some were even educated at the universities that were established in the West Bank only in the years under Israeli rule. A shortage of jobs, especially for intellectuals, meant that many hundreds of bright and able Palestinians were unemployed or, at best, hauling boxes of citrus fruit at the port of Haifa or sweeping up after restaurant customers in Tel Aviv. Their view of Israeli society was dominated by jealousy and hatred.

Some of their elders were wealthy farmers with fine villas dotting the West Bank, but most of the young Palestinians deeply resented the clean and obviously wealthy Jewish settlements that sat astride the strategic heights throughout the occupied territory. Those who had the menial jobs in the cities of Israel returned home to underdeveloped Arab villages, on roads that passed the settlements. The hardy settlers were blamed for using huge government grants to seize Arab lands and usurp precious water supplies.

The gloomy view they had of their own lives made it easy to summon the youthful masses into the streets once the angry explosion of the *intifadda* began. The uprising did not need an organized headquarters to fill its ranks on the battlefield. The teenagers were on the front lines with an inner conviction that said to them, "We have nothing to lose. We are already standing with our backs to the wall. Things could not be worse."

The better-educated youngsters realized, after the initial populist release of energy, that some direction was required to give the uprising a durable life of its own. The foundation for some local leadership already existed, in the Balata refugee camp as an example, and in other camps and villages local management committees sprouted from the invisible underground.

These were political beasts, however, fed primarily by allegiance to one or another faction of complicated Palestinian politics. The existing groups felt themselves linked to either the mainstream Fatah wing of the PLO, the more radical and Marxist Popular Front for the Liberation of Palestine, the Communist party, or an Islamic faction. Coordination among the activists was poor, and in the past they had clashed and even had killed each other. These divisions were among the reasons that Israel's Shin Bet was so convinced that a long and powerful uprising was impossible.

With the outbreak of unrest in December 1987, however, an amazing truce developed among the bitterly competitive factions. By telephone and in person, communicating between and throughout the West Bank and Gaza, Palestinians who had waited for their chance to lead a revolt against the Israelis decided to cooperate and coordinate. A new, underground body was formed, calling itself "the United National Command of the Uprising," or "the Command."

The organization exercised its influence and ability to direct events by publishing declarations and instructions in the form of handbills, clandestinely printed and quickly disseminated to every town and village in the occupied territories. The Command leaders did not panic when the Israeli authorities, led by the Shin Bet, proudly announced they had raided an Arab printing press, confiscating the equipment that included computerized word processors. Other publishing facilities were brought into action, and the contents of each declaration were broadcast over the new Voice of Jerusalem radio station in Syria. When the Israelis jammed the radio station, known to the Arabs as *al-Quds* ("the Holy," the Arabic name for Jerusalem), the Command newsletters were read instead over far-off Radio Monte Carlo, the pro-PLO station broadcasting in Arabic and heard throughout the Mediterranean.

From the early stages of the *intifadda*, the secret leaders set its tactics and its strategic goals. The eventual aim was to establish an independent Palestinian state. The method: systematically nibbling away the authority and functions of the Israeli occupation forces. The resignations of the Arab police officers, after one was murdered in Jericho, were part of the strategy, as was the refusal of any Arabs to take part in the Israeli-appointed local councils in the West Bank.

Palestinians refused, in massive numbers, to pay the taxes collected by Israel to finance the occupation. Commercial strikes effectively shut most of the West Bank and Gaza shops as and when the Command instructed, despite efforts by Israeli soldiers to pry open the locked shutters. Arabs refused to purchase Israeli products in what had been a captive export market for Israel. For weeks at a time, Palestinian workers refused to travel to their jobs in Israel, in the hope that the Jewish state's economy would be damaged. Most alarming to the Israeli authorities were the continuing attacks by stones, firebombs, and occasionally knives on soldiers, settlers, and Arabs who had collaborated with the Israelis.

In addition, the secret Command structure took steps to establish an alternative, autonomous Palestinian administration. The banned Palestinian flag flew over local council buildings in many of the 530 Arab municipalities, towns, and villages in the West Bank.

In Israel, the few intellectuals and left-wing writers who had long warned of such developments had been unheard voices in the wilderness, lost in the hubbub of an optimistic and overly confident nation.

There was Lord Winchilsea, the peer from Britain's minor Liberal party, who visited the occupied territories in late November 1987 and wrote a strong letter to the pro-Israeli Prime Minister Margaret Thatcher to say that he felt an unarmed, civilian uprising would soon begin and would lead to terrible casualties. Little attention was paid.

Only after the *intifadda* began, and the international media—led by television news—brought the violence into hundreds of millions of homes worldwide, did the leaders of the great powers realize that something had to be done. The United States, committed to Israel's existence and security, quickly developed a new peace plan to attempt to sell to political leaders in the Middle East.

U.S. Secretary of State George Shultz failed, in several tours of the region, to enlist significant support for his peace plan. Israel's Prime Minister Shamir would not agree to the principle of withdrawing from parts of the West Bank in exchange for peace with Jordan and the Palestinians. None of the Arabs would agree to sit at the negotiating table with Israel, unless there were a prior commitment to withdraw from all the occupied territories. The PLO was excluded from the Shultz plan.

Shultz pressed the PLO even harder, refusing in November 1988 to grant Arafat a visa to speak to the UN General Assembly in New York. Shultz still branded the Palestinian leader a terrorist.

Arafat cut no ice with the Americans by staging a dramatic declaration of independence for "Palestine," in Algiers that month, an event clearly modeled on David Ben-Gurion's declaration of the modern State of Israel in 1948.

Within weeks, however, the United States made a dramatic U-turn, after Arafat repeatedly declared that he accepted the three conditions set by the Americans: recognition of Israel, renunciation of terrorism, and acceptance of UN resolutions guaranteeing the security of all states in the region.

American and PLO officials held an open political dialogue, for the first time, aimed to bring the Palestinians into direct peace talks with Israel. Israeli leaders, under a new national unity government formed after a second, deadlocked national election in November, refused. Regardless of party label, the Israeli politicians still believed in the old historical ties with King Hussein.

Hussein, however, was as stung as anyone by the uprising. It was most obviously directed against the Israelis, but it was aimed against him, too. The king, as the PLO's Arafat had done, tried to clamber aboard the *intifadda* bandwagon. He announced that he would donate a month's salary for the support of Palestinians detained, injured, or left bereaved by the Israelis. Hussein instructed Jordan's civil servants to donate a day's wages to the cause.

The Command leaders in the occupied territories, however, expressed no interest in Hussein's overtures. Their clandestine handbills declared that the king was not their leader. They called for a boycott of the newspaper *An-Nahar*, which clearly supported Hussein, and one of its distributors was firebombed. Another two Molotov cocktails were thrown at the West Bank home of a Palestinian member of Jordan's Parliament Musa Abu Ghosh. Pro-Jordan mayors were told by the Command to resign.

West Bank journalist Ibrahim Karaeen justified the hopes he and his neighbors had for a state of their own, "If we were a flock of sheep, then you might ask who is our shepherd—Israel or Jordan. But if we are human beings, then our right of decision should be respected."

The general populace in the West Bank, however, harbored no affection for the king. The older Palestinians recalled that he had harshly suppressed their nationalist leaders betwen 1948 and 1967, when the territory was part of Jordan. The younger Arabs had a natural antipathy toward royal dictators. All residents were aware of the early failure of a five-year development plan announced by Hussein in 1987, ostensibly designed to bring prosperity to the West Bank but obviously aimed at boosting Hussein's influence in the area.

Hussein was in the worldwide spotlight, but he showed little concern for the Palestinians and their denied rights. The majority in the West Bank and Gaza would not forgive Hussein for ignoring them. They assumed that he was far too busy conducting secret and friendly diplomacy with the Israelis. And they were right.[1]

Chapter 2

Abdullah of Arabia

There never would have been a Kingdom of Jordan, if not for a visit to Cairo by Hussein's grandfather Abdullah shortly before the First World War. Then a young prince from Mecca, under Turkish rule, Abdullah traveled nearly a thousand miles to tell the British Empire's chief representative in the Middle East, Lord Kitchener, that "the Hashemite branch of the Prophet Muhammad's family" would side with the British if war against the Turks were to break out.

Kitchener, who held the grand titles of His Majesty's Consul General and Agent in Egypt, took careful note of the conversation, for Abdullah's father was Sharif Hussein ibn-Ali, guardian of the Muslim shrines in Mecca and Medina and king of the Hejaz region in Arabia. The Hashemites' influence would be useful.[1]

Sharif Hussein had recognized the fragility of Turkey's Ottoman Empire and had decided that his family could benefit from joint planning of the future with the British in Egypt. Abdullah, then thirty-four years old, told Kitchener that the people of Arabia would, sooner or later, rebel against the Turks. The prince asked the British to help the Arabs mount a revolt and to pledge in advance that London would recognize a new Arab Empire under Hashemite rule.

The British Consul declined to promise military aid, and Abdullah returned home to Mecca, disappointed. The British had useful contacts with other nationalist groups that might be expected to be antiroyalist, and Kitchener was still exploring various routes to oust the Turks. He was reluctant to promise all-out support for exclusive authority over Arabia by the Hashemite family.[2]

With the beginning of the world war in August 1914, the facts on the ground dictated policy. The British were suddenly enthusiastic about pursuing close relations with Sharif Hussein. He, however, delayed a declaration of revolt against the Ottoman Empire and announced only that the Hashemites had rejected the Turkish sultan's call for a Muslim *jihad,* or holy war, against Britain.

Kitchener had returned to London to serve as secretary of war, and now it was his turn to be disappointed. His officials in Egypt made it clear that they frowned on Hussein ibn-Ali's passivity. British military commanders applied heavy pressure on Mecca and the people of the entire Hejaz region by threatening to cut off shipments of all the various goods normally supplied from Cairo.[3]

The pressure and the threats prompted the sharif to enter into negotiations with Kitchener's successor in Egypt, General Sir Henry McMahon. Hussein, still vigorous in his early sixties, offered to mobilize the Arab peoples on the side of Britain and her allies in the war against Turkey, Germany, and Austria-Hungary. In exchange, Hussein requested a declaration of support from Britain for the nationalist demands of the Arabs with Hussein—a descendant of the Holy Prophet of Islam—as their leader.

There was a double meaning to Hussein's desires: the transfer of authority from the Ottoman crown to the shield of the Hashemites, and the establishment of a new empire in the lands of the Arabian Peninsula and the fertile crescent. The negotiations led to an exchange of correspondence with Sharif Hussein known as "the McMahon letters."

Standing against the hopes and dreams of Arab nationalism was the beginning of an organized Jewish demand for a homeland in Palestine. The movement's impact began to be felt in 1897 with the First Zionist Congress in Basel, Switzerland. Its leader, Theodore Herzl, declared that organizations would be formed to work, under international law, for a national home for the Jews in the ancient lands of the Bible.

At the time, Palestine was under Ottoman rule and had only fifty thousand Jewish residents, compared with half a million Arabs living between the Mediterranean and the Jordan River.

Perhaps surprisingly, the Zionist movement was not met in its first years by howls of protest from Arab leaders, who above all appeared concerned with gaining their own independence. As for the sovereign of the territory, Sultan Abdul Hamid of Turkey even granted Herzl an audience and discussed with him the proposals of the Basel Congress.

The efforts of the new Zionist diplomacy to win a "charter" from the sultan to establish a new state did not, however, succeed. The despair of the Jewish campaigners was so deep that some of the Zionists, including Herzl himself, were willing in 1903 to consider accepting an African alternative. There was talk of persuading the British to grant the Jews a state of their own in Uganda.

Only the First World War kept the focus on Palestine, known as *Falastin* to the Arabs and at times labeled *Palestina* in Hebrew but much more widely referred to by the Jews as *Eretz Yisrael*, a biblical term for the Land of Israel. The Ottoman Empire sealed its own fate by joining Germany's alliance known as the Central Powers in an unprecedentedly bloody war against the so-called Allies led by Britain, France, Russia, and later the United States. The Middle East, conquered by the British and French armies, was very much involved in the new international order imposed by the victors.

Even before the war ended, the British officer T. E. Lawrence stirred the long-awaited Arab revolt against the Turks, and the Ottoman Empire was driven out of Jerusalem and Baghdad in 1917. The Arabs thus achieved important gains on the ground, but the Zionist campaigners in Europe accomplished feats of their own. Led in London by Dr. Chaim Weizmann, the Zionists pressed for British approval of a Jewish state in Palestine.

Success for Weizmann, successor to Herzl who had died thirteen years earlier, came on the second day of November 1917, when the British government published a letter by Foreign Secretary Arthur James Balfour, which was bland in its content but historic in its impact. It was addressed to the president of the British Zionist Federation, Lord Rothschild, and said the entire cabinet had approved "the following declaration of sympathy with Jewish Zionist aspirations . . . :'His Majesty's Government view with favor the establishment in Palestine of a national home for the Jewish people . . . it being clearly understood that nothing shall be done which may prejudice the civil and religious rights of existing non-Jewish communities.' "[4]

It did not come from Constantinople, after all, but this was the charter that the late Herzl had been seeking.

With the end of the war, the other Allies implicitly accepted the Balfour Declaration by agreeing that Britain would have a mandate over all of Palestine. The area was to have been under shared control with France, under the 1916 agreement between British diplomat Sir Mark Sykes and a French envoy Charles François Georges-Picot, which carved the Middle East into zones of influence.

Arab nationalists, including historians of today, see the Balfour Declaration as the principle trigger of the Arab-Israeli dispute. November 2 continues to be the date of annual protest conferences in a host of Arab nations, and demonstrations by Palestinians in the occupied territories have marked the anniversary every year, even before widespread rioting began in December 1987. From the viewpoint of Palestinians, their own rights were negated on the day the British recognized those of the Jews.

When the Balfour Declaration was issued, an Arab nationalist movement was just blossoming with the intention of wresting from the Turks authority over Arab-populated areas. In other words, the new nationalists were seeking control over most of the Middle East.

Sir Henry McMahon and the intelligence officer already dubbed Lawrence of Arabia had pledged British support for Arab nationalism. Thus it was that Sir Henry sent his letters of endorsement to the Hashemites Sharif Hussein and his son the Emir Faisal. The fact that they were guardians of the Moslem holy places made them Arab nationalist leaders as far as the British in Cairo were concerned.

In exchange for their enlistment on the British side and their willingness to lead a revolt against Turkey in the Arabian Peninsula, the Hashemite family was granted British support for "the independence of the Arabs in all the region within the limits demanded by the Sharif." McMahon's crucial commitment, in a letter dated October 24, 1915, applied not only to Arabia but also to Mesopotamia (later Iraq) and to Syria. Specifically excluded were territories claimed by Britain's French allies along the Mediterranean coast (parts of Syria and the future Lebanon).[5]

Today's legacy of bitterness stems in part from turning back the pages to the explosive second decade of the twentieth century. Arab historians claim that the McMahon letters, pre-dating the Balfour Declaration by two years, in effect promised that Palestine, too, would be under Arab control. Analysts continue to debate the borders that the British might have envisioned in McMahon's concept of 1915 and Balfour's of 1917.

Although the letters from Cairo did not constitute a binding contract, Sharif Hussein felt he had sufficient backing from the British to declare the birth of the Arab revolt against the Ottoman Empire on June 5, 1916, in his kingdom of Hejaz. The sharif organized his forces in Arabia, and his son Faisal launched military operations against the Turkish army in distant Syria.

The Hashemite forces coordinated their campaign with Britain's "Egyptian Expeditionary Force" under General Sir Edmund Allenby, and Faisal was in especially close contact with Colonel Lawrence.

In July 1917, Faisal conquered the port of 'Aqaba at the Northern tip of the Red Sea, and in October 1918, his forces entered Damascus where he set up an Arab government. A gathering calling itself the Syrian National Congress elected Faisal the King of Syria in March 1920. This was formal endorsement of the situation that already existed in effect, except that the congress had a greater Syria in mind, which would include the holy city of Jerusalem and all of Palestine.

Around the same time, a group of Iraqi politicians and dignitaries was summoned to elect Faisal's brother Prince Abdullah of Hejaz as their king. The difference, however, was that Abdullah was not in Iraq at all at the time of the Arab victory and did not have the opportunity to take power in Baghdad.

Abdullah had been the original Hashemite envoy to see Lord Kitchener, but he barely had any role in the military campaign against the Turks. His role was close to the family home in Mecca, helping to plan attacks aimed at liberating Medina and Taif in Arabia, but Lawrence's memoirs portray Abdullah as an unremarkable soldier who was "not serious enough for leadership."[6]

The Iraqis in the ancient lands of Mesopotamia were similarly not enthusiastic about the Arabian prince, but his brother and the British advised Abdullah to be patient.

The Hashemites had reason to feel, at the end of the four-year conflict known as the Great War, that they were on the verge of realizing their great dream: to rule over the Arabian Peninsula and the two most important capitals in the ancient fertile crescent, Baghdad and Damascus. This could clearly be the basis for a new Arab empire.

They failed, however, to take into account that their British benefactors were caught in a web of conflicting promises and secret agreements they had made in order to win the war against Turkey. Britain had gained international Jewish support for the Allies by issuing the Balfour Declaration, and there was the

Sykes-Picot Agreement with France, which mapped out zones of influence without ever informing the Hashemites.

The victorious powers conferred in San Remo in April 1920, and endorsed the Sykes-Picot maps, which put Syria and Lebanon in French hands. The Arabian king of Syria's election was ignored. British rule over Palestine was confirmed, and both arrangements became official mandates of the League of Nations in 1922.[7]

On July 25, 1920, the French army overthrew King Faisal and expelled him from Damascus. The British, to the utter shock of the Hashemites, did not lift a finger to help their Arabian wartime ally.

Abdullah, meanwhile, continued to wait in Medina for a call to come and take the throne in Baghdad. Of equal importance was Abdullah's failure to suppress the ultrareligious Wahhabi sect, which declared a revolt in Arabia against his father Sharif Hussein. Still hearing no news from Iraq, Abdullah resigned from his post as foreign minister to the sharif and took the title of field marshall instead. His father sent him north to restore the pride of the Hashemites.

Abdullah took two thousand armed men on the rickety Turkish railway from Medina to Ma'ān in the southern part of Transjordan, an area administered loosely by the British who had no particular plans for the quiet Christian and Muslim villages and Beduin tribes who generally minded their own business on the eastern side of the river, as the name of the territory suggests, across ("trans") from Palestine.

In the days of the Roman Empire, towns in the region developed thanks to the Roman trade with desert tribes. The capital now known as Amman was then called Philadelphia, and it was one of many fortress cities in Rome's Middle East.

Under the Ottoman Empire, from 1516 until the First World War, Transjordan was part of the province of *el-Sham,* the Arabic name for Damascus. The area was, as now, some 90,000 square kilometers, or 35,000 square miles. It was never densely populated and throughout history has been considered a neglected sector of an exciting, vital region. During the war, Transjordan was one of the most primitive and least-developed parts of the entire Middle East, where the level of western-style civilization was extremely low in any case.

The area had strategic value, to be sure, but mainly because of the railway that connected Damascus with Arabia. The stations along the way were in an exceedingly poor country, with almost no natural resources to sustain its 350,000 people. Trade and agriculture were not well developed, the farmers having a tough time in the Jordan Valley and the traders little to do in the hills where Irbid, Ajlun, Salt, Jarash, and Amman were the small towns.[8]

In the deserts to the east and south wandered Beduin, tending their herds of camel, clinging with ferocious loyalty to their own extended families, but otherwise avoiding each other. There were no fixed boundaries, neither of family grazing grounds nor of the country itself. Highway robberies were common.

When the Emir Faisal captured Damascus from the Turks, it was natural that his new kingdom of Syria would include Transjordan. Nature and tradition dictated that the ruler of one would have the other, too, but the Sykes-Picot Agreement suggested otherwise.

Even the British, however, knew not what to do with their Transjordan. The first high commissioner of the British mandate in Palestine, Viscount Herbert Samuel, hurriedly sent telegrams to London asking that the other side of the river be merged into his area of authority. The Foreign Office decided, however, that Transjordan could best be governed, or at least supervised, as it had been, in small administrative sectors based in part on tribal lines. Samuel was permitted to send a political officer to be stationed in each locality, but there was no true responsibility or accountability to any central regime.[9]

Prince Abdullah, frustrated in his ambitions for many years, was heading all the way to Damascus in 1920, planning to ride the rails that were usually used to bring Muslim pilgrims south on their pilgrimages to Medina and Mecca. How he could possibly capture Syria from the French was an unanswered question.

Abdullah arrived in Ma'ān, just over halfway on his intended journey, on November 11, 1920. He immediately declared his intentions, much to the embarrassment of local British officials who had no instructions from London for such an eventuality, but who immediately recognized that this prince from afar was threatening to upset the peaceful status quo. On the other hand, Transjordan did need a leader.[10]

The British representative in Karak, in the heart of Transjordan, was Alec Kirkbride, and he had the task of greeting Abdullah as the prince advanced through the country, apparently gaining a taste for it. Abdullah asked politely about the international status of Transjordan and how it was governed, and the Briton replied that no one was absolutely certain. Kirkbride added that no one would care, now that Abdullah had arrived.

The Arabian newcomer was delighted. "I was sure we would understand each other," he said with a smile. He had decided to stay.[11]

Abdullah got along handsomely for the rest of his life with Kirkbride, who was promptly named by London to serve as British "resident" in Transjordan and then ambassador to Jordan. He was the chief foreign influence in Amman for many years.

In London, Foreign Secretary Lord Curzon did not seem to take Abdullah's stated intention of recapturing Damascus for the Hashemites seriously, but the British security chief in Transjordan Colonel F. G. Peake felt there was a danger of an embarrassing clash with the French in Syria. Peake urged the Foreign Office not to allow Abdullah to turn Transjordan into a base for military action against Syria.

When Abdullah's army did attack French forces in the border town Dar'ā and took it over for a few days, the British understood that they appeared to be sponsoring an uncontrollable potentate. The government in London decided to protect itself from any wild behavior by Abdullah and began applying pressure on the Hashemite family. Messages from the Foreign Office called on his brother Faisal and their father Sharif Hussein to restrain the rebellious ruler of Amman.

When no change was apparent, the British attempted a new approach, coincidentally during the upheaval of a bureaucratic reorganization. The Middle East Department was transferred from the Foreign Office to the Colonial Office. The new team, having seen that Abdullah would not silence himself over the Syrian issue, decided on a policy that amounted to: "If you cannot beat him, join him."

The news of aggressive plans being laid by Transjordan reached the British around the same time as word of trouble came from Palestine and Iraq. Then colonial secretary, Winston Churchill was in Cairo chairing a conference on the Middle East, and he decided to attack some of the empire's problems head on, face-to-face, before they became worse.

Churchill invited Abdullah to meet him in Jerusalem and attempt to agree on a role for the Hashemites in the region. Encouraged by Colonel Lawrence, who continued to wield decisive influence on Britain's Middle East policy, Churchill and Abdullah reached agreement on May 27, 1921.[12]

The British minister agreed to recognize Abdullah's government as the Emirate of Transjordan, with a budget from London of £5,000 a month. The British would send advisers to conduct military training, and Churchill promised that full independence would follow in due course.

Abdullah pledged that he would not attack the French and would permanently put aside his claims on Syria. He also renounced his claim on the proposed Kingdom of Iraq, ceding that theoretical throne to his brother Faisal as compensation for what he had lost in Damascus. Faisal did finally rule as Iraqi monarch.

The agreement, which plainly delighted Churchill, began with a six-month trial period during which Transjordan and Abdullah were officially under the authority of High Commissioner Samuel in Palestine. A British envoy was assigned to Abdullah's royal court: an assimilated Jew named Abramson. After proving himself a failure in Amman, he was transferred to a post as lands administrator for the mandate government in Palestine.[13]

At the end of the six-month trial, Churchill sent Lawrence to Transjordan to report on any changes and progress toward orderly rule. The famous colonel sent a positive summary to London, and the colonial secretary accepted the advice to move toward independence for Abdullah.

The government archives in Kew, England, known as the Public Records Office, contain the full report by a senior official of the Colonial Office who took charge of the Transjordan file. At the beginning of the report is the question: "Do we wish for Abdullah to implant himself in Transjordan—yes or no?" And alongside the printed question, there is a handwritten, even scribbled, reply:

"Yes!" It is initialed "W.C.," suggesting the enthusiasm of the colonial secretary himself. This is the dramatic birth certificate of the Hashemite Kingdom
of Jordan.[14]

For the next year, until the fall of the Lloyd George government in London
in October 1922, Churchill worked quickly to turn Abdullah's shaky regime into
a solid reality. The allowance from the British was raised to £150,000 a month,
and the new emir was using the money to buy the cooperation of local sheikhs
throughout his territory. The League of Nations, meanwhile, agreed that as the
mandate authority in Palestine, Great Britain should be allowed to resolve Transjordan's problems as it saw fit.

Abdullah was greatly relieved that his new homeland would not be part of
the planned "national home for the Jewish people." As he wrote in his memoirs,
"Allah granted me success in creating the Government of Transjordan by having
it separated from the Balfour Declaration which had included it since the Sykes-
Picot Agreement assigned it to the British zone of influence."[15]

When Abdullah visited London in November, he received the further pleasure
of a binding pledge that Britain would recognize an independent nation of Jordan
under the Emir Abdullah ibn-Hussein. The promise was kept secret for a further
half a year but was published on May 25, 1923. That date is the Kingdom of
Jordan's official independence day, celebrated annually in Amman.[16]

Zionist historians recall the event as the "tearing" of the eastern lands of
ancient Palestine away from the remainder. There are right-wing elements still,
in the modern-day State of Israel, who see Jordan as part of a greater land of
Israel and dream of the reunification of the biblical birthright of the Jews.

The Zionists of the 1920s, however, had expressed only passing interest in
Transjordan, and they did not mount a strong protest against Abdullah's independence.

There is no question that Jordan, as a sovereign state, is an artificial creation
by an outside, imperial power. Britain created the emirate to fulfill a wartime
commitment to the Hashemite family, which in turn was desperate to set up a
throne somewhere. If a government can be said to have a troubled conscience,
the British authorities were trying to do some good for both the Hashemites and
for the Jews.

Sharif Hussein's family, after all, was not doing nearly as well as it might
have expected during the successful campaign to evict the Turks. Britain's French
allies had ousted the sharif's son Faisal from Damascus, and the Hashemites
were later forced out of their home base in Arabia when they were defeated in
1925 by the religiously fervent Wahhabi sect led by the House of Saud. If Jordan
has a raison d'être, therefore, it is the lack of any other place for the Hashemites
to lead a kingdom, combined with Britain's geopolitical interests in the days
when London still controlled an empire.

Abdullah was a fairly typical Arab ruler, in that he rewarded loyalty with
impressive generosity but could be very cruel in crushing any opposition. He

suppressed several revolts in his first year in Amman, and twice called in Britain's Royal Air Force to help subdue his enemies.[17] One of these occasions was an assault by the Wahhabis from the south. After the Wahhabi takeover in Mecca and Medina, the British compensated Abdullah by transferring to Transjordan the Ma'ān sector of Sharif Hussein's former Kingdom of Hejaz. This gave Jordan, as the nation came to be known, its only outlet to the sea, 'Aqaba.

By the end of the 1920s, Abdullah led an established government making its own mark on the region. His was a tribal autocracy, its defense and very existence dependent on his British sponsors. The emir, soon calling himself a king, did not have time for any pretence of democracy. There was an elected council, but it had no power. Britain tolerated the situation, and the relationship flourished. Abdullah sent his son Talal, the heir to the throne, to be educated at the upper-class British boarding school Harrow.[18]

The Hashemites, as guardians of the holy places, although deposed from Mecca and Medina in 1925, had some religious and historical legitimacy, which eased their acceptance by the Beduin tribes who were the dominant power in the deserts and many villages of Jordan.

Abdullah declared that the gates of his palace were always open to the Beduin, and as a former man of the desert himself he well understood their concerns and their etiquette. When forming his army, Abdullah first and foremost chose Beduin officers. He named his troops "the Arab Legion," successor to his brother Faisal's forces in the First World War. Their loyalty through the decades kept Abdullah and more recently his grandson Hussein in power.

A British man of the desert named John B. Glubb was transferred to Jordan from Iraq in 1930 to help turn the Beduin force into a modern, disciplined army. Like Kirkbride, Glubb soon had a passionate love affair with the Kingdom of Jordan, although Glubb was expelled by Hussein twenty-six years later.

Abdullah enjoyed his formal independence, codified in the signed agreement of 1928, which recognized his emirate. Britain, however, retained in the country an army of both soldiers and political advisers, led by Resident Kirkbride. No important legislation or finance bill became binding law without the British resident's consent.

Only after the Second World War, when Abdullah's self-confidence appeared to be well founded, was Jordan granted true independence. The king, who had never truly given up his desire to rule over Syria and to unite his government with his brother's kingdom in Iraq, issued a call in 1944 for the formation of "Natural Syria." Again, as after the First World War, Britain felt compelled to mediate and was trying to avoid an embarrassing clash of interests with its ally France, just as the Allies in Europe were liberating Paris and defeating the Nazis.

The British, in March 1945, were instrumental in founding the Arab League, which would impose responsibilities of peaceful coexistence on Jordan as a member.[19]

On March 22, 1946, another treaty was signed between Great Britain and Transjordan, still the nation's official name. Sovereignty was granted to the emirate, but in a manner that kept financial decision making and all military matters in the hands of the British.

Approximately two months later, on May 25, Abdullah celebrated his twenty-third independence day by crowning himself king. The emirate formally became a kingdom.

In fact, the kingdom was ruled by a triumvirate: the king; Sir John Bagot Glubb, as the British commander of his army; and the British Ambassador Kirkbride. There were, however, the standard trappings of a government: the Majlis or parliament, prime ministers who were hired and fired by the king at an astounding pace, and ostensibly free elections in which the king's candidates always won.

The apparently representative institutions did not, in any way, infringe on the power of the triumvirate. There were very few matters on which the three men could not reach full agreement. Glubb and Kirkbride learned that the secret of getting along with Abdullah was never to utter the word no. Instead, the king would have to be told, "Yes, Your Majesty, but . . . ."

Although the monarch officially had absolute power after 1946, the two British advisers learned how to guide him in the directions they or London wished.

There is no doubt that Abdullah was powerful in his ambitions, well schooled in the conspiracies of government, yet known for enjoying a good joke. He lived life enthusiastically and gained a reputation as a lover of both women and money. The cash was not for himself, but to spend on his loyal friends.

The king made up for his lack of military prowess with decisiveness when it was needed, political realism and impressive patience no doubt born of the disappointments he suffered in the 1920s. He was a crafty man who, as they say in the Middle East, might fail to reach his destination by going through the door, but would surely get there by entering through the window instead.

Abdullah's attributes came to the fore in his complicated, sometimes clandestine relationships with the leaders of the Zionist movement and later with the State of Israel, just across the Jordan River.

Chapter 3

"Meir"

"My situation is always difficult, and you Jews must remember it." Those blunt words came from the Emir Abdullah, on November 24, 1936, in a secret meeting he had with Moshe Shertok, one of the senior diplomats of the Zionist movement before the State of Israel was born.[1] The bluntness aside, Abdullah's statement summed up in one sentence the entire relationship that the former Arabian, now Transjordanian leader established with his Jewish neighbors to the west.

Even at the beginning of his efforts to set up a government in Amman, Abdullah sought to reach understandings with the Zionist leaders. He was always willing to talk to them, although only in secret, and he was clearly a moderate among Arabs when it came to Jews and Zionists.

The emir was, however, unwilling to overcome his fears of how other Arab leaders would react to his contacts with the Jews. Abdullah would enter discussions ostensibly aimed at formal accords or even treaties, but he would always withdraw at the last moment. He certainly knew how to demand as much in the way of concessions as anyone could from the Zionist leadership.

The roots and the nature of the present-day relationship between Israel and Abdullah's grandson King Hussein can clearly be seen in the sporadic attempts to reach understandings fifty years earlier when the political map was entirely different.

The long-standing, secret link over the Jordan River between the two nominally warring nations is part of the network forming—contrary to the more common view of the Arab-Israeli dispute as having two sides—a three-way game: Israel, Jordan, and the Palestinians.

The Zionist leaders, for their part, well understood Abdullah's problems and were prepared to accept his rules for the game. In their foreign and defense policies, they gambled—at a very early stage, even before they had their own state—on "the Jordanian option." This policy path can be traced as a scarlet thread running through the six decades of the Arab-Israeli conflict.

The source of the eastern-looking orientation of many early Zionists can be seen in a combination of *Realpolitik* and personal sentiments.

The history of the region's conflict, in its various forms, is marked by sporadic attempts at dialogue between the leaders of the two nationalist movements: Zionism, representing the renaissance of the Jewish people as a nation; and the national Arab movement, as the achievement of the Muslim peoples' longing to rule themselves. Unfortunately, both movements had designs on the same land: the Zionists were committed to settling the world's Jews in Palestine, and the Arab nationalists included Palestine and especially Jerusalem in their concept of the greater Arab nation.

The Arab nationalists within Palestine itself saw their dispute from the beginning as a "zero sum game," in that every inch of territory that the Jews might gain would necessarily be at the expense of the Arabs. Every aspect of the dispute is then seen as a life or death struggle, and a small victory of one's opponent seems a total defeat. In such a view, there is no room for compromise.

Palestinian nationalism owes its very existence to the appearance of Zionism. The local Arab movement rose as an antithesis to the settlements and diplomatic efforts of the Jews. The danger was seen by the Palestinian Arabs as so great that the only possible response was to attempt the complete uprooting and removal of the Jewish nationalist movement. Anything less, any compromise at all, would seem a betrayal of the simple faith that "Palestine is Arab" and would undermine one of the bases of the struggle for Arab independence.[2] The Palestinian Arab national movement, also acting at an early stage, made a vital political decision: total war against Zionism.

The inconsistencies of the British and their spurious promises to both Jews and Arabs did not escape the attention of the Zionists. They sought methods to exploit the internal contradictions as a bridge toward dialogue with the Arab nationalists. When the Zionist leaders saw that they simply were not getting through with any positive effect, they decided to search for some other partner for discussions and negotiations. The Zionists found that partner in King Abdullah.

This was not simply a decision based on a cold analysis of the political situation. The Zionist leadership was also acting on emotions, on a heartfelt desire in the early ideology of the movement to maintain dialogue and seek understanding with the inhabitants of Palestine.

Dr. Chaim Weizmann turned to the task immediately after the First World War. He had a fruitless meeting in the summer of 1918 with a group of Syrians who were living in London. They were not willing to entertain the notion of a Jewish-dominated state in the Middle East. Quite disappointed, Weizmann made a difficult ten-day trip to 'Aqaba, the Red Sea port that the British would later transfer to the Hashemites, which was then a small village. The Emir Faisal, son of Sharif Hussein, came north from Arabia for the meeting, which the Arab started on a positive note with a lavish banquet.[3]

The Zionist leader told Faisal that there was plenty of room in Palestine for both Arabs and Jews, "and that the lot of the Arabs would be greatly improved through our work there."[4] The emir seemed to have no trouble with this, and the two men signed a formal agreement on January 4, 1919. The accord set out a joint Arab-Jewish position for the international conferences settling territorial and other problems after the world war. The treaty, for that is what it was, envisioned that negotiations would lead to secure borders for Arab and Jewish states. Its opening words reflected a spirit of cooperation:

His Royal Highness the Emir Faisal, representing and acting on behalf of the Arab Kingdom of Hejaz, and Dr. Chaim Weizmann, representing and acting on behalf of the Zionist Organization, mindful of the racial kinship and ancient bonds existing between the Arabs and the Jewish people, and realizing that the surest means of working out the consummation of their national aspirations is through the closest possible collaboration in the development of the Arab State and Palestine.[5]

The document then affirmed the right of Jewish immigrants to settle in Palestine. On the Arabic-language version, however, Faisal attached a note below the signatures that said, "Provided the Arabs obtain their independence as demanded in my Memorandum dated January 4, 1919, to the Foreign Office of the Government of Great Britain."[6]

Faisal seemed, at that time, very friendly to the Jewish cause. He even went so far as to go on the record, to the Reuter news agency on December 12, 1918, before his meeting with Weizmann, "The two principal wings of the Semitic family, the Arabs and the Jews, understand one another, and I hope that after an exchange of views at the Peace Conference which will be directed by the ideas of national self-determination, both nations will progress successfully toward their goals." Faisal said that Arabs and Jews were promising to be "fair" to each other in their respective territories.[7]

After a few years, however, the leaders of the Jewish settlement movement in Palestine had to acknowledge that the historic treaty had no real value. Arab leaders in Palestine, and in other countries—even in Iraq, which was Faisal's kingdom—either forgot the agreement or treated it as an unimportant slip of paper that represented no commitment by anyone.

Weizmann and the other leaders had to base their case, instead, on the Balfour Declaration and on the British mandate, the very existence of which provided legitimacy for the case that Palestine was separate from the rest of the Middle East. In constructing a powerful diplomatic campaign, the Zionists concentrated on Great Britain, relegating to a secondary priority the pursuit of diplomacy with the Arabs in the so-called Promised Land itself.

There were no serious attempts by the Zionist leadership in the 1920s to talk to the Arabs of Palestine, even in the face of bloody rioting that broke out in May 1921. The two peoples fighting for the one land—the Jews and the Arabs— were kept from killing each other only by the British police and army, although even then dozens from each side did lose their lives.

The violence had begun in Jaffa, the ancient Arab port alongside the new Jewish town of Tel Aviv. A local dispute grew, within a week, into a widespread Arab protest against the growing presence of the Jews and against the British mandate, which the Arabs saw, since the Balfour Declaration, as the protector of the Jews.

Many of the Arabs believed that the British must have made an error. In granting the Jews a homeland, they thought, the British must have mistakenly believed that the Jews were a majority in Palestine. Eventually, the British would recognize they were wrong.

Other Arabs claimed there was a clear, internal contradiction in the Balfour Declaration. It favored "a national home for the Jewish people," but it said this must not "prejudice the civil and religious rights" of the Arab community. Inevitably, it was claimed, a Jewish home would harm Arab rights.

Later when it became clear to the Palestinian leaders, notably the mufti of Jerusalem, Hajj Amin el-Husseini, that the Balfour Declaration would not be canceled by London, the Arabs presented new arguments. These focused on the supposed dangers that Jewish settlement posed to the land of Palestine itself. The territory, they claimed, was simply not large enough for the two peoples. They pointed to the aggressive purchases of land from Arabs by the Jewish National Fund (JNF), but the almost absolute refusal of Jews to sell any land to Arabs. The Arabs insisted that the British place strict limits on Jewish immigration and on the JNF and Jewish Agency's continuing construction of new settlements.

Some Arab spokesmen warned the British that the Jewish immigrants were Bolsheviks attempting to bring communism to the Middle East. On the other hand, some of the Arab propaganda described the Jews as the "avant-garde of Western imperialism."

The British seemed to lean back and forth, sympathizing, in turns, with the Jews at times and with the Arabs on other occasions. The result was a sloppy patchwork quilt of policies. The Zionist leadership confidently continued to build and to invest in Palestine, and Britain's indecisiveness often encouraged the Jews to believe that the Arabs would gradually learn to accept them. They pointed to the fact that Jews and Arabs had good social ties and worked peacefully side by side in cities with mixed populations, Jerusalem and Haifa.

The Zionists were also encouraged by a more cynical analysis of the divisions within the Arab community: between various families and clans, such as the radical Husseinis and the moderate Nashashibis.

The next serious outbreak of rioting, in 1929, shook all the comforting conclusions and assumptions. It began as a dispute over the rights to pray in Jerusalem: at the Al-Aqsa Mosque, for the Muslims, and the Western or "Wailing" Wall just below, for the Jews. It spread to all corners of Palestine, and in five days of bloodshed 133 Jews and 87 Arabs were dead and more than twice as many were wounded.

A further shock for the Zionists came in 1930 when the British began to take a firm hand in limiting how many Jews could arrive on Palestine's shores. Jewish Agency chief David Ben-Gurion conceded, for the first time, that an "Arab national movement" was confronting Zionism. Two nations were in conflict.

The 1930s saw some efforts by the Zionists to conduct discussions with the Arab nationalists in Palestine. Ben-Gurion wished to consolidate his absolute leadership of the Jews, as he was worried about the growing power of a hard-line, right-wing Zionism called revisionism, under Vladimir Zeev Jabotinsky, whose concept of a Jewish state covered all of Palestine and most of Transjordan, too.

After fruitless and brief talks with Arab politicians, such as George Antonius, the theoretician behind pan-Arabism—the belief in a united Arab nation—and his Syrian, Lebanese, and Saudi followers, Ben-Gurion managed to make a connection with the Husseini wing of Palestinian politics. He and Moshe Shertok met in 1933 and 1934 with Musa el-Alami, an adviser both to the mufti and to the British authorities. They probed the possibility of gaining Arab recognition of an independent Jewish state. Ben-Gurion hoped eventually to meet the Mufti el-Husseini himself, but the Arabs continued to see the Zionists as dangerous expansionists, and no goodwill was created.

The Arabs rose up in anger again in 1936, and in a six-month uprising of strikes and guerrilla attacks, eighty Jews were killed but even more—around two hundred—Arabs died, as British troops fought to quell the unrest. Nearly thirty Britons were killed. The unrest resembled the so-called *intifadda* of fifty-one years later, in that it included commercial and work stoppages and Arab barricades blocking major roads. The fighting was renewed in 1937 and 1938, swelling the casualty figures into the thousands.

The British, in 1936, established the Royal Commission of Inquiry under Lord Robert Peel, and after detailed hearings, a plan to partition Palestine into Jewish and Arab states emerged. The Peel Commission would actually have created three entities in Palestine: the two independent states, plus a "Mandated Enclave," which would continue to be governed by Britain. The zone that the British would retain for themselves, for the sake of peace, Christianity, and the interests of their empire, included Jerusalem, Bethlehem, and Nazareth.

The Zionists had a huge internal debate, but Ben-Gurion had his way and the Jews officially declared that they would accept the partition plan and the tiny and strangely shaped state it would grant to the Jews. The mufti of Jerusalem was in no way satisfied, however, so the official response from the Arabs of Palestine was no to the partition plan.

Ben-Gurion had tried to gain the recognition of the Palestinian Arabs for the Jews' right to a homeland. The Zionists, and later the Israelis, would never seriously try again.

These, then, were the factors that led to the special, secret relationship between the Zionists and the Emir Abdullah of Transjordan: the hard-line stand of Palestinian Arabs based on the principle of not losing an inch, the Zionists' lack of trust in the Palestinian Arabs, the dependence of all parties on British goodwill, and Britain's positive sentiments toward the Hashemites.

Even though the Zionist leaders saw Abdullah as a usurper, ruling a country that was his for no good reason at all, they also saw his authority as an accomplished fact, and they were willing to live with it. The sense of realism on this particular point was shared by the centrist and left-wing elements of the Zionist movement, led respectively by Weizmann and by David Ben-Gurion, and they were stronger than the right-wing Herut group led by Menachem Begin's predecessor and role model, Zeev Jabotinsky. Relations with Transjordan were an excellent first step in the Zionist diplomatic drive for recognition from the Arabs.

The Zionist leaders believed they could detect in Abdullah the two characteristics that they sought, but failed to find, in any Palestinian Arab leader: trustworthiness and moderation. The Zionists expected that Abdullah could be counted on to negotiate with them. They also believed that if Abdullah's moderation bore fruit for him, then with Britain's encouragement he would somehow develop the authority to speak on behalf of the Arabs of Palestine.

Abdullah, for his part, hoped his Jewish partners in dialogue would grant him full recognition, because his authority over Transjordan was of questionable legitimacy. The Jews might not approve fully of his plans and policies, but he hoped they would at least recognize he was king. Otherwise it would be extremely difficult to achieve his ambitious program: to establish solid authority over all of the East Bank, to be followed by gaining control over parts of Palestine to the west of the Jordan River.

Abdullah saw the Jews as a powerful force, and he took a positive view of their determination to challenge Palestinian Arab nationalists. The Jews might even save him the trouble of defeating the Palestinians. The parallels with the situation of the late 1980s are stunning.

The emir was able to see that he shared many of the Zionists' interests, and he keenly felt the need to reach some kind of agreement with them. Abdullah attempted to persuade them to endorse his notion of a "Greater Syria," with a guarantee of broad autonomy for the Jews within a large Arab kingdom.[8] It was similar to a plan unsuccessfully outlined to the Zionist leadership by Abdullah's brother Faisal back in 1919.[9]

In 1922, Abdullah sought Zionist support for his pitch to the British to be named not only leader of Transjordan, but emir of Palestine as well. Meeting that year with Weizmann, Abdullah said he could guarantee the Balfour Declaration's promise of a national home for the Jews, if the matter were left in the hands of an Arab government named by the British to rule Palestine. The British, however, rejected the plan.[10]

Some two years later, when Sharif Hussein, the father of the Hashemite dynasty, visited his son in Amman, he met with a delegation of Jewish settlers in Palestine. Abdullah continued to emphasize his desire for a peaceful arrangement between himself and the Jews. He preferred, after all, that they not reach any accords with the local Palestinian Arabs who might rule out any chances of rule from Amman.

"Palestine is one indivisible unit," Abdullah said to a Jewish nationalist he met in 1926. "Dividing the land into two sides of the Jordan would be artificial."

The emir added, "We, Jews and Arabs, can converse between ourselves to live a life of peace on the undivided soil. We are poor, you are rich. Please consent to come across the Jordan. I guarantee your safety. Together we shall work for the good of the land."[11]

From 1932 to 1934, when Transjordan was going through a severe economic crisis, Abdullah proposed an economic arrangement with the Jews: lands in exchange for investments. He opened intensive negotiations with the Zionist leadership and suggested allowing them to purchase land and settle Jews on the eastern side of the Jordan River, if the Jews would invest financially in Transjordan as a whole. The cash, Abdullah hoped, could rescue his country from economic stagnation.

In March 1933, Abdullah said, "The Jews in all the world will find in me a new Lord Balfour; and even more than this, Balfour gave the Jews a land which was not his to give, and I pledge my own land."[12]

The exchange that the king had in mind, which could be called land for loot, never became reality. It became impossible because among the activists who were working against Abdullah were not only Palestinian Arabs, but the British government. Officials in London took an interest in the failure of the emir's proposal for a Jordanian-Zionist entity.

In 1931, for instance, Weizmann was set to arrive for a meeting with Abdullah in his capital, Amman. On the eve of his journey, the Zionist leader was warned by British officials that they could not guarantee his security and that they recommended cancellation. The meetings continued however, despite several attempts to sabotage them, and the secret contacts extended through the 1930s.

Abdullah was seen by the Zionists as an important and intimate source of information on events and attitudes in the Arab world, and on the political relations between the Arabs and Britain. In exchange, they paid him from time to time, to cover some of his personal expenses. The Zionists lavished gifts, including furniture, on the emir to help decorate his palace.

Abdullah hired a Jewish carpenter to construct and maintain the royal residences. The carpenter, Mendel Cohen, also performed a valuable service for the Jewish Agency: providing credible intelligence on events, behind the scenes, in the Transjordanian royal court.[13]

The Agency had a code name for Abdullah in its internal documents. It called him *Meir*, Hebrew for "illuminator." It was one of the most simple intelligence codes: simply scrambling the letters of *emir* to conceal his identity. Based on all these facts, the king of the Arab nation to the east might be seen to have acted as a spy for the Zionists, casting light for the Jews onto the shadowy politics of the Arab-dominated region. It might be more proper to describe him as "an agent of influence," a senior personality who based his actions on his own interests and how to advance them by all possible routes. Abdullah had obviously concluded that his interests in many ways coincided with those of the Zionist leadership.[14]

The cooperation and the regular contacts also grew from shared economic interests, specifically the two biggest and most important industrial plants in Palestine: the potash factory on the shores of the Dead Sea, and the electricity plant built, with Abdullah's consent, at Naharayim, which is in fact on the East Bank of the Jordan. For many years, the king maintained a special relationship with the Jewish managers of both facilities, most strongly with Pinhas Rotenberg, the director of the Electricity Company of Palestine and later of Israel.

World War II put a brief halt to the secret connection between Abdullah and the Zionists. As the war ended, and the British granted Transjordan more complete independence, the contacts were renewed, and even more intensively, against the background of increased hostility within Palestine between Jews and Arabs.

The relationship between the Zionist movement and the Hashemites reached its climax in the years from 1947 to 1951. The well-established orientation toward cooperation became the basis of a political concept, which was naturally leading toward a strategic alliance. Occasional contacts gave way to serious negotiations that could yield a formal accord.

Four basic facts shaped Abdullah's policy toward the Jews of Palestine:

1. His hostility toward the Palestinian Arab leaders, led by the mufti of Jerusalem, Hajj Amin el-Husseini, and Abdullah's shaky relations with the other Arab states, notably Saudi Arabia led by the Hashemite family's old enemies, and Egypt and Syria.

2. His desire to regain the prestige of the Hashemites by reunifying Arab lands, even after the proposal for a "Greater Syria" led nowhere, so that Abdullah renewed his efforts to spread his authority to Palestine while offering autonomy to the Jews.

3. His military and economic dependence on and his traditional loyalty to Great Britain, which at times put London's interests ahead of his own, meaning that Arab unity and the avoidance of instability must be major goals.

4. His willingness to treat with respect the Zionist campaign for a Jewish national home, without the almost automatic hostility engendered in most Arab leaders.[15]

As early as August 1946, Abdullah said privately to Eliyahu Sassoon, one of the senior diplomats of the Jewish Agency, that his goal is a division of Palestine aimed at preventing the establishment of a separate Arab state. Abdullah wanted, in effect, to conquer not only most of Palestine—the Arab-populated areas—but also certain strategic sections that were dominated by Jews. Among the latter were the port of Haifa, so that the one large Arab nation would enjoy access to the Mediterranean, and the Negev Desert, which was mainly uninhabited.

Abdullah would then, it seemed, be willing to reach political agreements with a Jewish state on the remaining parts of Palestine.

Two weeks later, the king already had a name for his plan to absorb the Arab sectors of Palestine into his kingdom. He called it "the Program for Division and Connection," separating the two sectors of Palestine, and connecting the Arab portions to Transjordan. Sassoon attempted to conduct a negotiation on the borders of the territory to be annexed by Abdullah, but he said this was premature. The king did promise that his officials would discuss the issue later with the Jewish Agency. He also asked for £40,000 and said that he needed it to bribe Syrian and Palestinian politicians, "You don't have any realist Arab leader like me in the entire Arab world." The king settled for £5,000 from Sassoon.[16]

Both sides emerged from the summer of 1946 with the feeling that agreement had been reached, in principle, for Palestine to be divided. When intensive contacts were renewed around one year later, Abdullah reaffirmed his belief in the plan, even though it remained unwritten.

He also made clear to other nations in the Arab League that he would not tolerate formation of a Palestinian government. The king wrote to a friend in October 1947, "The Mufti and [Syrian President] Kuwatly want to set up an independent Arab state in Palestine with the Mufti at its head. If that were to happen, I would be encircled on almost all sides by enemies."[17]

The following month, Abdullah fortified his secret alliance with the Jews of Palestine. At the Jewish electricity plant he had permitted to be built at Naharayim the king met a powerhouse in the Jewish Agency, Golda Meyerson, known later in life as Mrs. Meir, the prime minister of Israel. She was accompanied by Sassoon and Ezra Danin, two experts on Arab affairs, and their talks on November 17, 1947, began with a review by Abdullah of his most recent contacts with Arab leaders.

The king portrayed himself as occupying a position of strength in the region, but he emphasized that the goal should be the avoidance of bloodshed by way of an agreement between himself and the Jews. Abdullah said, "Originally, we spoke of partition. I agree to partition, but only on condition that it is not one which would cause me shame."

Danin kept up with the conversation, producing a transcript in his own handwriting. Both sides quickly agreed that the Mufti el-Husseini was their common enemy. According to Danin's account, Abdullah proposed that part of Palestine become an independent Arab republic within an enlarged Kingdom of Jordan. The Arab entity on both banks of the river would have a joint economy, army, and legislature. The king declared, however, that such a republic would not be under direct Transjordanian rule, but simply part of the Jordanian monarchy.

The details appeared somewhat complicated, but Abdullah asked how the Jews of Palestine would react if he were to seize the Arab sector. Golda Meyerson replied, "We would look positively upon it, especially if it did not interfere with our establishment of our state and did not clash with us."

Toward the end of the power station meeting, the Zionist delegation asked Abdullah if he would be willing to sign a written agreement. He answered in the affirmative, "and asked that we draw up a draft," according to the official report. The king also advised the Jews not to pay attention to radical or hostile statements he might make in public, "since these are out of compulsion rather than desire."[18]

Two weeks after the meeting, the UN General Assembly approved its partition plan for Palestine. Despite London's wishes to the contrary, the UN resolution of November 29, 1947, formally put an end to the British mandate within six months and replaced it with two states: one Jewish and one Arab.

The Jews were to have most of the Mediterranean coast of Palestine, and the Negev Desert, the two sectors barely connected at their extremities. The Arabs would have the cities where they enjoyed numerical superiority, but the UN plan also included a third, international zone taking in Jerusalem and its environs, as far south as Bethlehem.

The Zionist leadership in Palestine welcomed the vote, as broadcast to an excited Jewish populace from UN Headquarters in Lake Success, New York. Palestinian and other Arab leaders, however, angrily rejected the decision.

The battle for Palestine, to determine its future once the British would leave, was obviously reaching its decisive stages. The Zionists and Abdullah, however, kept in touch frequently. David Ben-Gurion himself never met the Jordanian king, mainly because the future first prime minister of Israel could never spare the time to disappear for a period to conduct secret diplomacy in the midst of the dramatic birth of his nation. The policy line was clear, however, through Ben-Gurion's envoys, and they and Abdullah knew they shared a supreme interest: preventing establishment of a Palestinian Arab state.

Hoping to reduce the military threat to what would soon be a new Jewish state, Ben-Gurion attempted to draw from Abdullah a pledge that the Arab Legion of Transjordan would not cross the river into Palestine. The envoy seeking that commitment was again Golda Meyerson, but this time she traveled, dressed as an Arab peasant, to Amman on May 11, 1948, accompanied by Danin.

Unlike their previous, genial conversation on the river, this meeting in Abdullah's palace was tense. The British mandate over Palestine would by ending in a matter of days, a joint Arab attack on the Jewish state seemed a certainty, and everyone attending the secret talks had to be seen as risking their own lives. It was a chance worth taking, for it was no doubt the last possible opportunity to avoid war between the Jews and a reluctant Transjordan.

The king's only proposal, however, seemed more an ultimatum than a helpful suggestion. The Jews, he said, must avoid any provocative step and thus must not declare their independence. Abdullah told them to accept autonomy under his sovereignty in Palestine. The only alternative would be war.

Mrs. Meyerson shook her head and replied, "We could not even contemplate discussion of such a proposal."

The king said that he had been honest when he originally pledged not to attack Jewish territory in Palestine, but now "I am one among five. I have no alternative, and I cannot act otherwise." There would be a joint attack by the Arab nations.

Mrs. Meyerson reminded Abdullah that he had no true friends in the region except the Jews. The king said, "I know it, and I have no illusions on that. I know [the other Arabs] and their 'good intentions.' I firmly believe that Allah has restored you, a Semitic people who were banished to Europe and have benefited by its progress, to the Semitic East which needs your knowledge and initiative."

The Jewish envoy said a declaration of independence would not be delayed. Abdullah responded, "I am sorry. I deplore the coming bloodshed and destruction. Let us hope we shall meet again and will not sever our relations."

Before her sad departure, Mrs. Meyerson said, "So we shall meet after the war."[19]

The meeting in mid-May was a fatalistic affair. As in a Greek tragedy, it was clear that both sides did not want the war that was to follow, but they did not have the strength to stand against superior outside forces, and armed conflict became inevitable.

Abdullah seemed, to the Jewish delegation that visited him, quite a different man from the monarch they had come to know in previous contacts. He was depressed, nervous, and sensitive to every small unpleasantness in a situation full of large ones.

The king, for his part, recalled later that Mrs. Meyerson was more stubborn than ever and obviously failed to understand his position. Abdullah shared these impressions with another team of Israelis, in fact, around a year after the Amman talks, and when they told him that Golda had been sent to Moscow to serve as the first Israeli ambassador there, he commented, "Very nice, keep her there, keep her there."

It is difficult to agree with Abdullah's assessment. Mrs. Meyerson absorbed fully the king's message. She understood that he had no desire to invade the Jewish state that was about to be born, and that he was joining his Arab allies in the attack out of lack of any alternative.[20]

Four days after the meeting, when David Ben-Gurion declared Israel's independence and statehood, seven Arab states declared war and invaded Palestine. Among the invaders was the Arab Legion of King Abdullah. The outbreak of hostilities, the bloodshed and the temporary break in political contacts did not, however, injure the identity of interests between Israel and Transjordan.

Abdullah and Mrs. Meyerson, at their meeting in November 1947, had reached a tacit understanding, which later guided the progress of the continuing war on the Israel-Transjordan front. The two sides pursued their military campaigns in parallel but coordinated paths.

The understanding between them was so great that Ben-Gurion did not hesitate to "cede" the front alongside the seaside town Netanya. He transferred some of the Israeli forces from the central front protecting the Mediterranean coast, to help the southern district commander, Yigal Allon, in his clashes with the Egyptian army. The prime minister made that decision against the advice of his other generals, including Yigael Yadin. Ben-Gurion, however, was confident that he well understood King Abdullah's intentions and that the Arab Legion would not press its potential advantage in the thinnest, most vulnerable part of the young Jewish state.[21]

Even without ever meeting, Ben-Gurion, the Zionist social democrat, and Abdullah, the Arabian emir, found a common language, and each understood that while Israel was fighting a war for sheer survival, the ambitions of both sides on the Jordan front were safely limited. In fact, Abdullah's decision to join the other Arab armies in the war—while leading to terrible casualties that the Jewish forces would rather have avoided—brought with it the desired effect, for the Zionists, of preventing the appearance of an independent Arab state in Palestine.

There are some in the Middle East who attempt forty years later to dismiss the conflict that the Israelis call their War of Independence as irrelevant to today's crisis in the region. It would be better, they claim, to ignore the divergent explanations of how so many thousands of Palestinian Arabs became refugees: Were they expelled by the Jews? Were they instructed to leave their villages and farms by Arab leaders who promised a safe return home after liquidating the Zionist state?

The truth, as in most Middle East issues, is a little bit of both versions and somewhere in between. A review of 1948 and 1949, however, does serve to question seriously the matter of sovereignty over the West Bank and Gaza: parts of Palestine seized, respectively, by the Jordanians and the Egyptians by the time the fighting ended.

It may be argued, of course, that after the tragedies and hardened enmities of four decades, the old questions of sovereignty are truly irrelevant because finally there is a chance to allow the Arabs of Palestine to have their own state. That chance is variously described as an opportunity, a moral responsibility or a mortal danger, depending on who is the author of the assessment.

Both sides, Arab and Zionist, have built myths and legends around the 1948–1949 war and its results, at times without much connection to the facts. Israeli historiography compares the war with the biblical victory of tiny David over mighty Goliath, a triumph of the few over the many. Arab historians refer to it as "the calamity of 1948," generally blaming the outcome on poor planning and even worse coordination by the Arab leaders of the time.

The war was not a typical military campaign. It was not a simple clash of armed forces, exchanging blows until one army or the other was proved superior. It took place on several fronts, and the conflict was interrupted and punctuated by cease-fires arranged by outsiders. Officially, the war lasted eight months, from the Arab invasion of the newborn State of Israel until the Israelis and Egyptians began their armistice talks on the island of Rhodes in January 1949. The fighting, however, took up barely one-quarter of that time, in four separate stages.

The Arab armies, with a combined population of some forty million people behind them, had an obvious numerical advantage, and they were much better armed than the Israelis. The Zionist forces, representing only six hundred thousand Jews in all, had the advantages of unity and what could be called modern sophistication. The Israeli commanders were more inventive, as when Yigal Allon found an ancient Roman road in an archaeological guide and used it to bring his men around to smash an Egyptian offensive from the rear. They were much better at deploying the limited resources available to them.

A broad view, in fact, could lead an analyst to the conclusion that the Israelis held the most important advantages in 1948, often not of the type that could be seen in individual battles.

Resupply is a strategic element in any war, and the Israelis had much better connections than did the Arabs for resupply from overseas during the cease-fire periods. Try as they did, the Arab forces did not harm Israel's ports and airports, and the Soviet Union and its Eastern European allies made major efforts to mobilize military supplies for the young, socialist, anti-imperialist Jewish state, which the communist world hoped to woo.

The Israelis were fortunate, also, to have only one military command, and an excellent one at that, which grew into the army so respected around the globe. The Arabs, on the other hand, were divided into various national forces under the commands of jealous and suspicious generals who shared a common language but not an agreed strategy.

Israel's strategists immediately learned the knack of taking advantage of Arab disunity, and they knew they owed a debt of gratitude on this score to King Abdullah. He exercised self-restraint at every turn in the 1948–1949 war, directing his Arab Legion to pursue only limited tactical goals and, in fact, had them keep the level of violence to a necessary minimum.

The king's British advisers went along with Abdullah's strategy, although there is some doubt as to whether Alec Kirkbride and General Sir John Glubb initiated the restraint against Israel. Personal memoirs often tend to cloud rather than clarify history, and Kirkbride's[22] make no mention even of Abdullah's secret meetings with Jewish leaders even though the British must have known about them.

It was clear to the Zionist leadership that "Abdullah was nothing but a British puppet," according to Yehoshua Palmon, a senior official in the Jewish Agency and later in Israel's foreign ministry, responsible for contacts with the Arab world. "He was not able to move a soldier from here to there, or to buy a bag of flour without getting permission from Kirkbride and Glubb. On several occasions, Abdullah said to Israeli officials: 'Fine, but what will Kirkbride say about it?' And so, the importance of the meetings with the king and the contacts with Jordan was more in their very existence rather than their contents."[23]

Just as Abdullah did, Glubb and other British officers in the Arab Legion labored clandestinely to reach as wide an understanding as possible with Israel's military commanders, especially in the Jerusalem region. In fact, along most of the front the Legion adopted purely defensive tactics. It should be noted that Glubb later insisted, "I had no official connection with the British government at all, nor did the latter ever attempt to interfere or give orders.''[24] Military plans had to be limited, in any event, because Britain was giving Transjordan no additional military aid, despite what might be expected from an ally at wartime.

Under Glubb's command, the Legion fought fiercely, gaining the respect of Israel's soldiers for all time, but the Jewish forces managed to capture Lydda and Ramla, two towns that, according to the UN Partition Plan, should have been in the Arab sector of Palestine. Most of the battles took place in ostensibly Arab territory, rather than within the borders of the newborn Jewish state.

Ben-Gurion did his part for the king by making no effort to capture the West Bank of the Jordan for Israel. That is not to say that the Israelis could have managed that feat in 1949, but Ben-Gurion was offered the opportunity to try by his generals. He resisted the possibility of fulfilling what some Jewish nationalists saw as their rightful destiny to regain the historic Land of Israel, for the sake of protecting his relationship with the Hashemite ally whom he never met.

Only in the area of Jerusalem did true warfare break out between the two armies. The king hurried to send reinforcements, to prevent the loss of the Arab-dominated Old City. Perhaps ironically, it was on the Jerusalem front that the opposing commanders, Colonel Abdullah al-Tel and Lieutenant Colonel Moshe Dayan, established a close relationship.

The king himself visited Jerusalem and conferred with al-Tel at the beginning of the war. He was so taken by the young officer that he immediately promoted him from major to colonel and made him a royal confidant. Abdullah eventually paid for that decision with his life.

Colonel al-Tel agreed to Dayan's suggestion that a direct telephone link be established between their two warring headquarters. The connection was extremely useful during official cease-fire periods when violations were quickly explained, and in fact the first cease-fire was arranged over this telephone line at the end of November 1948. It was also used to schedule secret meetings at a higher, political level.

With the final battles and the UN Security Council's calls for a permanent armistice in late December, the contacts between the Israeli leadership and King Abdullah were renewed. As the fighting was not quite over, Golda Meyerson did not make the trip this time. The first round took place in January 1949, in the king's winter palace at Shuneh, near the Dead Sea, and the Israelis included military men such as Dayan, Yadin, and Yehoshofat Harkabi and personages we might now call diplomat spies such as Eliyahu Sassoon, Walter Eytan, and Reuven Shiloah, the first director of the secret Mossad intelligence agency.

During World War II, Eytan had been part of the British team that broke the vital German military cipher known as the Enigma Code, and much later he served as director general of Israel's foreign ministry.

Shiloah enjoyed immediate access to Ben-Gurion and to the first foreign minister of Israel, Moshe Sharett. Shiloah had great influence, but preferred to operate behind closed doors and rarely cooperated with the press. A native

Jerusalemite, son of a rabbi, a believer in the value of strategic silence, he is credited decades later with having established a modern intelligence network more quickly than could reasonably be expected.

The passage of the Israeli delegates, dressed in Arab *keffiyeh* headdresses, into Transjordan was arranged by Colonel al-Tel, whose own automobile brought them through a series of checkpoints. Dayan was afraid, at one point, that he had been recognized by jumpy Arab Legionnaires.[25] The Israeli agenda had two items: an exchange of prisoners, and rapid progress toward a permanent, political settlement even as formal armistice negotiations under UN mediator Ralph Bunche of the United States were getting underway on the island of Rhodes.

Dr. Bunche would eventually win the Nobel Peace Prize for his efforts, but at least between Israel anad Transjordan the armistice was agreed some distance away in the secret meetings near the cease-fire lines.

The king personally greeted the Israelis to Shuneh and delivered a long speech, which claimed he had been forced by his aides, along with the Egyptians, to join the war against the new Jewish state. This caused obvious embarrassment to Prime Minister Abdul Oda[26] and the rest of the Jordanian delegation. Abdullah went on to praise Ben-Gurion, Chaim Weizmann, and Sharett in their absence. The king did not hide his grudge, however, toward Mrs. Meyerson, who obviously had deeply disappointed him on the eve of war—as though concessions from her could have prevented the conflict.

Keeping the atmosphere surprisingly light, Abdullah also arranged a performance of Arabic music for his secret guests and challenged them to several games of chess. The Israelis played, but diplomatically lost and feigned bedazzlement at the king's clever chess moves.

A further round of talks in Jerusalem, without the presence of the king himself, led to a complete agreement on an armistice but not the wider peace treaty that the Israelis said they would prefer. In part because the Jewish army remained obviously prepared to press on toward the Jordan River, the armistice lines were drawn in Israel's favor, slightly east of the actual positions of the armies. Dayan and an Arab official named Jundi hammered out their accord on April 1, 1949, and flew to Rhodes, where the formal signatures were applied on April 3.[27]

The agreement with Transjordan was one of four armistice agreements that put an end to Israel's War of Independence. Egypt, Syria, and Lebanon signed their accords at Rhodes, but the Iraqis who had sent troops through Transjordan to fight refused to reach any formal pact with the Jewish state.

The Israelis continued to hope that the armistice accords would lead to full peace treaties. The political situation was not quite synchronous, however, with the military facts on the ground. The harsh combat of 1948–1949 redrew the borders of the region, so that the UN Partition Plan of 1947 lost all meaning.

The territory that had been designed for an Arab state in Palestine was now held by three armies. The Egyptians seized the Gaza Strip, Transjordan showed no intention of withdrawing from the West Bank and East Jerusalem, and Israel held the nominally Arab sectors in Galilee and along the Mediterranean coast.

The armistice agreements only confirmed what was an accomplished fact. Israel had captured the lion's share of Arab Palestine, 2,400 square miles, in addition to the 5,600 square miles accorded the Jews in the UN partition. King Abdullah's forces gained some 2,150 square miles on the western side of the river. Basing his mandate on a conference of his own citizens and handpicked Palestinian Arabs in Jericho the previous December, the king annexed the West Bank and changed Transjordan's name to the Hashemite Kingdom of Jordan.

The recognition of the military realities dictated, more than any other factor, the course of continuing diplomacy. Britain endorsed Abdullah's retention of the West Bank and East Jerusalem. The Israelis tacked West Jerusalem onto their own sovereign territory. The UN plan would have made Jerusalem a special case, undivided but multinational. Israel and Jordan cooperated with each other by means of local arrangements, such as allowing the Israelis limited access to the Hadassah Hospital and Mount Scopus, which were in East Jerusalem.

Israel and Jordan pursued their secret diplomacy in new venues, sending envoys to meet in various European capitals between November 1949, and February 1951. There were also five meetings at the Shuneh winter palace on the Jordanian side of the river. Israel's representatives were Dayan, Shiloah, Sassoon, and Eytan.

The chief Jordanian delegate was Minister of the Royal Court Samir el-Rifai, a veteran diplomat who was previously prime minister of Transjordan and father of the future Prime Minister Zeid el-Rifai who was to become King Hussein's closest aide. Prime Minister Oda refused to take part in the talks. Much more dangerously, Colonel al-Tel was to flee to Egypt, where he supplied the mufti of Jerusalem with documentary evidence of the king's clandestine deals with the Zionists. The mufti, Amin el-Husseini, had been deposed by Abdullah and would later arrange the king's assassination.

The secret talks, however, were bearing fruit. If all the agreements in principle could be tied together, a formal peace treaty was clearly within reach. Israel agreed to grant the Jordanians access to a sea port in Egypt's Gaza Strip, and to set up a free port area in Haifa that Jordan could use. The areas of discussion and agreement included commercial ties, protection of holy places in Jerusalem, permission for Palestinian Arabs who fled to return to claim their property, and the firm outline of a five-year nonaggression pact.

King Abdullah saw the proposed pact, based on freezing the existing military lines, as an important stage on the road to mutual trust. A gradual transition from war to peace could be effected in five years, through good neighborliness and economic cooperation. The king did not want an immediate peace treaty, however.

At a meeting on February 24, 1950, Abdullah authorized newly appointed Prime Minister Rifai and Defense Minister Fawzi el-Mulki to initial an agreement in principle for the nonaggression pact. The king told his aides: "You sign, and I shall be a witness." The Israeli initials on the document are those of Reuven Shiloah and Moshe Dayan.[28]

Four days later, however, the king felt compelled to withdraw his assent and to cancel the agreement in principle. His senior aides, including Rifai, suddenly were opposed to negotiations with Israel. They feared the messages of hatred they were already receiving from the Arab world and the clear undercurrent of danger to their very lives. Egypt, Syria, and Saudi Arabia were publicly labeling Abdullah "a traitor" and a tool of Zionism and British imperialism. The documents brought to Cairo by Colonel al-Tel served as raw material for the propagandists.

In a move opposed by Arab leaders and most of the world, with the exception of Britain and Israel, Abdullah officially announced his annexation of the West Bank in April 1950. In a defiant mood, the king was also planning to renew his diplomatic contacts with the Israelis. That step was averted by his grandnephew, King Faisal of Iraq, and Faisal's Prime Minister Nuri es-Said, who persuaded the Arab world to accept and endorse Jordan's territorial expansion. Making the West Bank and East Jerusalem part of Jordan would officially be a temporary step, pending a permanent solution to the Palestinian problem. In exchange, Abdullah promised to cease his separate peacemaking with Israel.

The formal rapprochement within the Arab world, however, came too late to save Abdullah's life. On February 13, 1951, there was a final meeting between the king and an Israeli team. Shiloah felt he was meeting a lonely and worried old man. Five months later, Abdullah was assassinated in Jerusalem.

The conspiracy had taken shape in Cairo, where the traitor Colonel al-Tel plotted with Musa el-Husseini, a relative of the mufti, beginning around September 1950. Husseini, then forty-two years old, was a graduate of the University of London and a respected doctor from Jerusalem. He found a kindred spirit in al-Tel, and both men felt they had to act in the face of Abdullah's secret friendship with the Zionists.

In May 1951, Husseini paid two Palestinian brothers, Muhammad and Zakariya Ukka, to obtain a revolver and advise on the king's movements. Husseini then hired a vegetable merchant to find an assassin, and a young trainee tailor named Shukri Ashu took the job in exchange for a little cash and a talisman guaranteeing him a place in heaven.

Jordan was rapidly becoming a dangerous country. Lebanon's prime minister was shot dead by unknown assassins on July 16, while on his way to Amman's airport after a meeting with King Abdullah. Sir Alec Kirkbride warned the king not to visit Jerusalem, but Abdullah insisted he would pray in the silver-domed Al-Aqsa Mosque, saying, "Until my day comes, no one can harm me; when my day comes, no one can guard me."[29]

It was on July 20 that the king was shot in the head by the unknown Shukri Ashu.

Abdullah's contacts with the Zionists were the central reason for his violent death at the age of seventy-one. His simple plea fifteen years earlier to Sharett, then known as Moshe Shertok, had been, "My situation is always difficult, and you Jews must remember it." Now they would never forget it. A peace treaty was instantly unattainable for the Israelis.

Those who had met with Abdullah would not forget the complicated monarch and all his conflicting qualities: an experienced ruler, something of an adventurer, a self-described Arab patriot, but also an opportunist and at times frustratingly hesitant when a quick decision was needed. Perhaps, Israeli diplomats thought, Abdullah would never have signed a formal peace treaty with them anyway.

After the assassination, Jordan's new government hurriedly signaled the Israelis that there would be no more negotiations. The same pledge was given to other Arab regimes, now that the shot fired through King Abdullah's eye had warned all Arab leaders not to consider pursuing separate peace agreements with Israel.

The lesson was certainly clear to a sixteen-year-old prince named Hussein ibn-Talal, the grandson of Abdullah, who was walking only a few paces behind the king at the entrance to the Al-Aqsa Mosque when the old man was cut down. Hussein saw the blood, the body, and the fate that he himself might suffer unless he learned to be extremely clever and cautious.

Chapter 4

Hussein the Heir

Hussein had been very excited, he later recalled, to accompany his grandfather the king to the West Bank and Jerusalem on July 19, 1951.[1] For safety's sake, while Abdullah flew from Amman's airport that Thursday afternoon, Hussein traveled by road. It was one of the first times that the teenage prince wore an army uniform, and he was proud that the king had recently named him an honorary captain.

They drove to Nāblus the next morning for sightseeing and coffee with the mayor, who invited the royal duo to attend Friday prayers there. Abdullah, however, was intent on praying in Jerusalem that fateful day.

Back in East Jerusalem by midday, Hussein noticed that security was remarkably tight. He learned later that General Glubb had ordered the Arab Legion to flood the streets with troops under Colonel Abbas Majali, to hold back the crowds heading for Friday prayers on the holy elevated courtyard of the *Haram esh-Sharif*. But on arriving at the Al-Aqsa Mosque, the king turned to the colonel, acting as chief bodyguard, and said, "Don't imprison me, Abbas." The security forces eased up a bit, and Abdullah stopped to talk to some of the people massed outside the mosque's entrance.[2]

The old sheikh who served as caretaker of Al-Aqsa waited just inside the entrance to greet the king by kissing his hand, but suddenly he saw instead a young man sneak up from behind holding a revolver. Shukri Ashu lunged at the king, brought the weapon close to Abdullah's right ear, and literally blew his brains out.

After a moment of shock, Hussein tried to grab the assassin who then raised his revolver and pointed it at the prince. Ashu pulled the trigger, and Hussein was lucky to survive the first of many close calls in his life. The bullet ricocheted off a medal on his chest. The royal bodyguards finally opened fire, and Ashu was dead.

Glubb and the Jordanian government, not knowing if an outright coup d'état was underway, insisted that Hussein return quickly to Amman. His father, Prince

Talal, was abroad for medical treatment, and the British did not trust Abdullah's younger son, Naif.

Prince Hussein saw the bloody body of his grandfather loaded into one airplane at Jerusalem's airport, and he was then flown to the capital aboard another aircraft piloted by a British squadron leader, Jock Dalgleish, whose lifelong friendship with Hussein began at that moment and led to memorable experiences and adventures.[3] When he became king a few years later, Hussein appointed Dalgleish the commander of Jordan's air force. He learned to fly jets from Dalgleish, and the king enjoyed taking British-style afternoon tea with the commander and his wife, Davina. One of the adventures was launched from a simple chat Dalgleish and Hussein had about the excellent steaks at the Ledra Palace Hotel in Nicosia, Cyprus. In the middle of the conversation, they suddenly headed for the airport, flew to Cyprus, enjoyed their steaks, and returned home without anyone noticing. Kirkbride and Glubb, ever mindful of security, were furious.[4]

Before he became an eyewitness to murder, Hussein's days were almost all happy and untroubled. He was born on November 14, 1935, to Talal and Princess Zein who were Hashemite cousins. Talal, gentle and reluctant to make decisions, was in many ways the complete opposite of his father. Zein, on the other hand, demonstrated an appetite for power and became a central figure in the family— eventually as the influential Queen Mother when Hussein became king. She was also a successful mother, in the traditional measure of bearing children. She had three sons, Hussein, Muhammad, and Hassan, and one daughter, Basama.

Amman of the 1930s, where Hussein was born as the all-important eldest boy, was a small desert town. The prince had free run of this diminutive capital. He enjoyed horseback riding and reading Arabic poetry, but did poorly in school at arithmetic. When he was seven years old, he scored an A in English but a D in English dictation. His favorite school chum was his future prime minister Zeid el-Rifai.[5]

Hussein was close to his father and would go hunting with Prince Talal, at times accompanied by Britain's Ambassador Kirkbride. Tragedy struck when Talal began to act strangely without warning, suffering seizures, which could be tolerated for a few years, but which later grew into uncontrollably violent fits.

An early conflict of loyalty presented itself to Hussein, because his beloved grandfather the king was openly contemptuous of Talal. Hussein could not help but think that Abdullah was being painfully insensitive. Abdullah, on the other hand, had clearly decided that his successor would not be his unstable son but his most-promising grandson, Hussein.[6]

The British, who in many senses were the true rulers of Jordan, shared Abdullah's assessment of Talal and Hussein. After the king was assassinated, Kirkbride planned the ascent of Hussein, who was then fifteen, to the Hashemite throne.

Talal, at age forty-two, was the elder of Abdullah's two sons and the natural heir. Hussein could be the new crown prince, but to maintain stability the British gave the go-ahead for Talal's coronation on September 6, 1951.[7]

Hussein, meanwhile, was to complete his education. In part because Talal wanted his son to concentrate on his Arabic whereas King Abdullah placed emphasis on English and Islam, Hussein's schooling had been disjointed, with frequent changes of curricula and tutors. He had a good two years at a British boarding school in Alexandria, Egypt, but this was unsafe for a Hashemite crown prince in days of Middle East instability.

For reasons of safety and prestige, Hussein was packed off to Harrow, one of England's most famous private schools, where he enjoyed sports cars, met his future wife, Dina Abdul Hamed, and never knew about the visit to his housemaster by a British Foreign Office man, Geoffrey Furlong. The shadowy visitor, who was head of the Eastern Department, asked the Harrow master, "Have you ever witnessed yourself, or heard tell of any occurrence that leads you to believe that Hussein is mentally unstable in any way at all?"

The housemaster, a Mr. Stevenson, replied without hesitation, "Certainly not."[8]

Israeli leaders, however, have been among those who have often wondered about Hussein's mental health. They do not believe that he inherited his father's illness, but note that Hussein is a moody man who appears to suffer melancholy periods, makes inconsistent declarations, and changes his opinion with alarming speed.[9]

Talal's behavior intolerably worsened in May 1952, and he took to disappearing, wandering the city streets for hours. After Talal returned from a long visit to Europe, where he reportedly attacked Hussein with a knife, Kirkbride and Glubb joined Jordan's Prime Minister Oda in deciding that the king would have to step down on grounds of mental incapacity.

A doctor's report diagnosing insanity was presented to Parliament in Amman on August 11, and after some debate an abdication order was prepared and sent to King Talal in his palace. His calm reaction was, "I had expected this."[10]

Talal signed the decree and retired abroad, to be out of the new monarch's way, first to Egypt and then to a Turkish island off Istanbul. He died in 1972, barely able to recognize his son and heir when Hussein came to visit.

Hussein was not even seventeen years old when he became king. He was on vacation in Switzerland with his mother, brothers, and sister when the news came in a message from Prime Minister Oda.

Hussein flew into Amman, assumed power, and shortly thereafter decided that he could benefit from several months of tough military training at the Sandhurst Academy in Britain. Hussein was abroad again, demonstrating the habit he would maintain all his life of preferring foreign attractions to the dry and dusty horizons of his native Jordan.

In London, at age seventeen, briefly escaping from his responsibilities as the new monarch, Hussein acquired his taste for nightclubs, dancing, parties, and automobiles even faster than the fast cars of his Harrow days.[11]

He returned to Amman for his coronation ceremony in the spring of 1953, and those who worked with Hussein recall that he did not seem to know what he wanted to do. He appointed as the new prime minister, Fawzi el-Mulki, a political liberal who had been ambassador to London during Hussein's happy days there. But Hussein himself was a natural conservative, based on his education and his close ties to the British upper classes. Glubb said later that the young king would change his mind constantly, depending on who had last spoken to him.[12]

Jordan's military attaché in Paris, Ali Abu Nuwar, whom Glubb despised, became one of Hussein's favorites, reportedly because of some wild nights on the town the two Jordanians enjoyed together in the French capital.[13] It seemed an odd way to choose a monarch's closest aides, and Nuwar not unexpectedly began to plot Glubb's downfall as chief of Jordan's Arab Legion.

Nuwar was also extremely hostile toward Israel, suggesting to Hussein that the British—Glubb and Kirkbride—were keeping Jordan away from its natural, anti-Zionist alliance with the Arab world. There were border clashes along the West Bank in 1953 and 1954; Israel retaliated forcefully against Jordanian villages after occasional crossings by armed Palestinians who were angry that the armistice lines divided them from their fields.

Glubb, with the reluctant assent of the young king, sent Jordanian soldiers to stop the border incursions, but the move seemed much more aimed at controlling the West Bank Arabs. For Palestinians, this was an early and infuriating example of Hussein apparently doing Israel favors.

Hussein did not want to anger the refugees, for whom he felt great sympathy, but he accepted Glubb's advice that the Jordanian government's survival depended on keeping the border with Israel quiet.[14]

A particularly ugly retaliatory raid by the Israelis, after a mother and her two children were killed in their home by Arab terrorists, was against the Jordanian village of Qibya. United Nations truce observers reported sixty-six persons, mainly women and children, were killed and forty-two houses blown up, many with their occupants inside.

Glubb called for an immediate report from the Arab Legion, which said, "Several of the police detachment at Qibya and national guardsmen were, at the time of the raid, on frontier patrol duties trying to stop infiltrators going into Israel."[15]

Someone had to pay for the embarrassment. Left-wingers were protesting in the streets of Amman for the first time, and firing one local commander in the Legion, a Briton, Brigadier Teal Ashton, did not satisfy the crowds. By early 1956, Glubb would have to leave his beloved Jordan. He had arrived thirty-two years earlier, riding a camel from Iraq.[16]

Hussein's rude dismissal of Glubb was, indirectly, a blow at the British and a declaration of Jordan's ever-increasing independence. Concerned that Palestinians who had no natural allegiance to the Hashemites were becoming too powerful, because most of the 30,000 men of the national guard were from West

Bank origins, the king appointed his uncle Sharif Nasser to form a private army of Beduin Arabs whose main duty would be the protection of the royal palaces. The Arab Legion's 25,000 soldiers were already mostly Beduin and seemed to be reliable.[17]

Hussein could now feel sufficiently secure to take a serious look at his position in the Arab world. Egypt's President Gamal Abdel Nasser, one of the military officers who overthrew King Farouk in 1952, noted Hussein's coup against Glubb and gained new respect for Jordan's king. Egypt, Syria, and Saudi Arabia together renewed their offer to Hussein of an Arab subsidy to replace the millions in economic aid that he received annually from Britain. At the very least, Hussein said, an Arab alliance would have to include his cousin King Faisal of Iraq.[18]

The summer of 1956 saw tension growing in the region. Palestinian guerrilla attacks into Israel were followed by more reprisals. The people of the West Bank were calling for war against the Zionists, while Hussein set a parliamentary election for October 21 to get an honest picture of public sentiment.

Left-wingers did better than he wanted, and the king later wrote of the politicians who emerged, thanks to his liberalization, "I take full responsibility for the period of experiment. . . . I realized that many were very leftist, but I felt that even so most of them must genuinely believe in the future of their country, and I wanted to see how they would react to responsibility."[19]

More proud than afraid of the winds of freedom that he set free, Hussein signed a military treaty with Egypt and Syria, agreed to install Suleiman Nabulsi as the only opposition leader ever to serve as Jordan's prime minister, and then watched helplessly as Israeli forces swept into Egypt's Sinai Desert on October 29.

Hussein was furious, and even more so when he learned that Britain and France were acting in league with the Israelis to seize the Suez Canal from Nasser. The king informed Egypt that the Arab Legion would attack Israel from the East.

Nabulsi said, years later, that Hussein had ordered him to send the army to war but he had refused. "The idea was ridiculous," Nabulsi told British journalist Peter Snow. "We were no match for the Israelis, particularly with the British and the French involved on their side."[20]

Nasser also advised Jordan not to attack, because Egypt was emphatically losing, and the only benefit the Arabs could reap from the situation would be diplomatic rather than military.

Hussein felt himself more suited to fighting than talking, and after all he had little personal commitment to diplomacy. His only contact with the Israelis had been indirect and fleeting. When he was a boy, and his grandfather was meeting the mysterious guests from the West, Hussein was occasionally in the palaces of Shuneh or Amman at the time. "Eliahu Sassoon and Reuven Shiloah would sometimes stumble into Hussein the youth, in the palace, and they would pat him on the head and exchange a few polite words, but that was all and nothing more," clandestine diplomat Yehoshua Palmon recalls.[21]

The murder of King Abdullah strengthened Hussein's instinctive feeling that direct contacts with Israel should not be renewed. The only forum for any exchange of messages at all, and these were formal and even hostile, was the armistice commission in which Israel and Jordan took part. Military officers from both sides attended these meetings, with the UN Truce Supervision Organization setting the agenda every few days or weeks.

Administering the cease-fires agreed in 1949 on Rhodes was the main business, but other matters of hostile neighborliness did come up at the meetings. These included thefts of farm animals from Israeli settlements and other cross-border infiltrations and gunfire, whether accidental or intentional. Border incidents and Israeli retaliations only increased tensions, which tended to lead to more misunderstandings and attacks.

The armistice commission's talks did little good along the lengthy border, except in the Jerusalem area where both sides indeed desired quiet. It seemed that neither Israel nor Jordan wanted any revival of the proposal that the city have a special international status.

The Jordanians agreed, in 1954, to establish a secret telephone connection between the military headquarters in the two sides of the divided city. This was, for all practical purposes, a revival of the link between Colonel al-Tel and Moshe Dayan six years earlier.

Israel's commander in Jerusalem was Brigadier Chaim Herzog, who years later as president of Israel recalled, "The telephone line was connected to my office and to my home. From time to time, when needed, contact was established between me and the Jordanian commanders. I especially remember a telephone call I received at home in the middle of the night. The Jordanian commander sounded shocked. He told me that one of his soldiers at the Jaffa Gate accidentally fired a fews shots toward the Israeli lines. The gunshots heightened tension in the city, and if not for the telephone call they could have led to a major border incident.

"On another occasion, I met the Jordanian commander face-to-face, without UN representatives, just over the border at the Mandelbaum Gate. We sat around a lone table set up in the no-man's-land, and around us as guards were both their soldiers and ours. It was quite a strange picture, almost surrealistic.

"We talked and talked on the subjects with which we were concerned, and we did not notice that a photographer focusing from a distance managed to snap some pictures of us through a telescopic lens. One photograph appeared in an Israeli newspaper, and afterward in the international press, and the Jordanians were very angry about it. For a while, they even cut off the contacts, declined to meet with us or talk by telephone, until their anger was forgotten and reality forced them again to renew contact."[22]

The Israelis were simply not satisfied by having links with the Jordanians through the armistice commission alone. The principal effort, furthermore, was to establish contact with King Hussein himself.

Despite the absolute break in communications after the murder of Abdullah and during the brief reign of Talal, Israeli policy planners held on to their chief aim on the eastern front: to reach the Jordanian royal palace again. They tried every possible channel, signaling in various ways that the armistice commission was not the suitable forum for issues of substance. These included discussions aimed at a permanent peace agreement, economic cooperation, political coordination, and the exchange of military and intelligence information.

The two governments did make some use of the traditional tools used in years gone by: clandestine go-betweens from other friendly nations and secret meetings of Jordanian and Israeli diplomats and military men.

There were two distinct levels of contact in the years from 1949 to 1967, between Israel and not only Jordan but other Arab states as well. The first was the official and open channel of the armistice commissions: one for Israel and Jordan, another for Israel and Egypt, and so on. These permitted the Arab governments to maintain publicly their refusal to recognize the existence of the Jewish state, while managing to limit the dangers caused by border clashes to manageable proportions.

The second level involved secret channels of communication. These brought the important, added benefit of permitting the pursuit of deeper political agreements. Compared with the other warring pairs of nations, Israel and Jordan had many more shared interests to pursue. Since the Six Day War of 1967, which marked the end of the armistice commissions, the secret channels provided the only continuous exchange of opinions and information.

The Israelis felt they had to get through to Hussein himself if they wanted to have an effective secret channel for communication. As a first step they had to get to know him better. This task, perhaps naturally, was assigned to Israel's intelligence community.

In pursuit of its Hashemite quarry, the Mossad foreign intelligence agency worked in its usual way: searching for the man's weaknesses, his ''soft spots.'' In Hussein's case, these were judged to be fast cars, airplanes, and women. At his palace, he had set up a stable of cars, quite separate from an impressive collection of horses. There was even a gold-plated Lincoln Continental, a gift from the rulers of Saudi Arabia who had so despised Hussein's great-grandfather.

As for flying, the young king's love affair with the air began in late 1952 and paralleled his stubborn determination that Jordan should have a modern air force. Hussein had to overcome the vociferous objections of his nervous mother, Queen Zein, simply to take flying lessons with Jock Dalgleish.[23] The king never took part in any aerial combat, however.

According to information that reached Israel, Zein did not try to suppress her son's interest in beautiful women, but instead encouraged his hobby of the flesh. His first marriage to his Hashemite cousin Dina was clearly, early on, an almost loveless failure.

The Israeli intelligence dutifully recorded all these personal details about their eastern neighbor. Yoel Ben-Porat, a senior military intelligence officer at the time, recently recalled, ''Even though I never met King Hussein, thanks to the intelligence reports I feel like an old friend of his. It became clear to us that several of the ministers in his court and a few of his prime ministers who wanted to please their king would introduce him to young ladies. We learned that he was especially partial to women of Circassian origin."[24]

Through the 1950s, Israeli agents tried several times to approach the king through his hobbies. There were proposals in Israel to send him, as a gift, the latest sports car, or to introduce him to an outstanding Israeli pilot or a beautiful young woman. None of these plans was executed, and the direct connection to the royal palace that the Israelis wanted was not established.

More conventional efforts were conducted by the Israelis, in parallel with the unusual ideas, to make contact with Jordan. Israeli diplomat Yehoshua Palmon looked back at the period, "In Europe all sorts of Jordanians were going around, some of them exiled from home, including military officers and businessmen, and we tried to get close to them. We thought that using these people as go-betweens, we could approach—perhaps not the king himself—but at least his inner circle. There were occasions on which they initiated contacts with us, saying that they had good connections with the king."[25]

The Israeli diplomats referred to these Jordanian intermediaries by code names such as "the curly one" or "the doctor." One of them was Abdul Gani el-Karmi, who was chief of Abdullah's staff and participated in the late monarch's secret meetings with Israeli envoys. In August 1950, Karmi crossed into Israel's western sector of Jerusalem to deliver a letter from Abdullah. In order to impress Moshe Dayan, Karmi once boasted that his wife was Jewish.[26]

Even before Abdullah was killed, Karmi ceased to be one of the king's favorites and was sent abroad as Jordan's ambassador to Spain. He formally went into exile in 1956, taking up residence in London where he worked for the Arabic-language service of the British Broadcasting Corporation (BBC). Palmon said, "I made contact with el-Karmi, and from time to time we would meet over a mug of beer in a London pub. He claimed he still had good contacts with the royal court in Amman. But I'm not at all sure whether he had an entrée into the royal circle at all."[27]

Israeli diplomats in Rome and Paris pursued other Jordanian contacts but similarly failed to achieve any breakthroughs.

The king continued to stick to his decision not to have any contact, direct or indirect, with Israel. At the same time, the situation along the border deteriorated. Hussein, however, had inherited enough of his grandfather's political realism not to stir up armed conflict with the Israelis when it seemed unnecessary. Although with his self-image as a bold Arab fighter, he was often tempted.

Hussein's relations with his British sponsors were intertwined with his confused feelings toward Israel. He, of course, wished the Jewish state had never been created, but as he grew older so did the wisdom of his recognition that Israel was a reality that would not simply disappear. The British, in the spring of 1956, had stepped up their pressure on Jordan to reach a set of stabilizing agreements with Israel. Border tensions became so severe in 1956 that the British government seriously considered the need, should Israel invade Jordan, to send British troops to fight the Israelis.[28]

By the end of 1956, however, the defense pact between Britain and Jordan was dead. Hussein was disgusted by the three-pronged attack on Egypt by Israel, Britain, and France. The Anglo-Jordan Treaty was terminated by an announcement from Amman in late November. As a further insult to the British, Jordan established diplomatic relations with the Soviet Union and Communist China.

On January 19, 1957, Jordan set up its new defense arrangements in the form of an Arab Solidarity Agreement signed with Egypt, Syria, and Saudi Arabia.[29]

Israel and Jordan, as neighbors, were confronted by dilemmas in the late 1950s. The Jordanians found themselves in an unusual situation: forced by Arab solidarity to act against Israel, or at least to permit others to attack Israel from Jordanian territory without these bands of guerrillas asking for Amman's permission. Hussein's agents even found evidence that the Egyptian Embassy was paying individual Jordanians to cross the border to plant explosives in Israel. A cabinet minister in Amman reportedly was found to have received a £7,000 bribe from the Egyptians to supply them with inside information.[30]

Jordan, therefore, to protect its Arab political flank, remaining loyal to nominal friends such as Egypt, had to open itself up to potentially fatal dangers from within. The guerrillas attacking Israel, after all, could be revolutionaries who would eventually show antiroyalist colors.

Israel, too, was striding gently on political eggshells, aware that extreme responses to the fitful guerrilla activity could be counterproductive. The Israelis were intent on punishing the guilty, but without risking the downfall of the generally tolerable Hashemite monarchy.

The guerrilla incursions were not harmless, however, and there were decisionmakers in Israel who questioned the policy of favoring Hussein's survival on the throne. After all, they said, he was proving his Arab patriotism at the expense of the peace and prosperity of Israeli border settlements. The man at the top, David Ben-Gurion, said, ''Jordan has no right to exist and should be partitioned. Eastern Transjordan should be ceded to Iraq, which would offer to accept and re-settle the Arab refugees. The territory to the West of the Jordan should be made an autonomous region of Israel.'' Israel's first prime minister was speaking in October 1956, during a secret meeting in Sevres, near Paris, with French and British officials to plan the joint assault on Egypt and the Suez Canal.[31]

Hussein was indirectly informed of some of these verbal disputes in Israel, and reports he received from within his kingdom also made him question the free hand he had given to the guerrillas and to left-wingers in Jordan's evolving political system. Encouraged by his relatives in the security forces, Sharif Nasser and Major General Zeid ibn-Shaker, the king decided to change his direction again.

In April 1957, Hussein forced the Nabulsi government to resign after only half a year in office. A week later, the king fired military adviser Ali Abu Nuwar, who had been instrumental in the ousting of Glubb and the diminution of British influence. It was not a simple sacking, however; the dismissal of the prime minister and his cabinet had led to unrest in parts of Amman and the main West Bank towns, stirred up by left-wing leaflets demanding that "pan-Arab policies" be maintained.[32] Military units of questionable loyalty were setting up roadblocks around Amman, and the king had to act before his opponents launched a full-scale coup. After considering the death penalty for Abu Nuwar, Hussein allowed him to leave for Syria and then exile in Egypt.[33]

It was a typical performance. Hussein was lucky, once again, to survive on the throne. He had not come down hard enough against the antiroyalists in his kingdom, he had hesitated far too long, but he did finally act soon enough—just barely in time.

The danger was not immediately eliminated. Palestinians continued to demonstrate in the West Bank, and Egypt's President Nasser continued to employ agents to destabilize Hussein. The king ordered that a revolutionary radio station broadcasting to the entire Middle East from Egypt be jammed. In less than a year, he had shifted abruptly from being Nasser's sympathizer to viewing him as a deadly enemy.

The extreme test came in July 1958. Nasser was truly ascendant in the region, having formed the United Arab Republic in February by merging Egypt with Syria as, officially, a single nation. Hussein's cousin, King Faisal of Iraq, persuaded him to respond by forming a Union of Iraq and Jordan, with Jordan the junior partner because of its smaller size and population. The move came too late to save the Iraqi monarchy, as a Nasser-style military coup erupted in Baghdad in July.

Faisal and his prime minister, Nuri es-Said, were killed by the rebellious army officers, and the Hashemites—with shocking speed and surgical precision—were removed from Iraq. The accounts reaching Hussein in Amman, telling of his cousin being cut down by machine-gun fire with his family, even after surrendering to the military rebels, must have prompted nightmares rivaling the ones caused by seeing his grandfather slaughtered in Jerusalem. Hussein and Faisal had studied together at Harrow; furthermore, they were around the same age—the Jordanian was twenty-four years old and the Iraqi king, twenty-three.

Hussein was shaken, and his first orders were to his uncle Sharif Nasser (unrelated to Egypt's president) to lead an expeditionary force eastward into Iraq to restore Hashemite rule.

It was time, however, for another typical performance by Hussein. He had his immediate, emotional reaction to events, but as usual he quickly recovered his sense of reality and decided that his most loyal army units should stay close to Amman to protect him. Jordan's independence was in peril, even as the outside world heard more about a similar Nasserite threat to Lebanon. The dangers to

Hussein from within his kingdom were matched, and even exceeded, by extraordinary pressures from without.

The time had also come for help to be summoned from abroad. Britain had angered Hussein with the invasion of Suez two years earlier, but now London would be called on for aid. Hussein asked the United States for direct assistance, too. Indeed, a new era in the Middle East had begun the previous year with the first U.S. arms shipments to Jordan. President Dwight D. Eisenhower had also sent U.S. marines to Lebanon to preserve the government in Beirut.

The king knew the political price of receiving western aid. He would again be accused, in the Arab world, of being a tool of imperialism in the region. With or without knowing the facts, Nasser's broadcasts would brand Hussein as a Zionist agent. Hussein, however, saw no other choice.

There would also be hidden help from the Israelis, who may have had mixed feelings about Hussein, but with utter certainty did not want a pro-Nasser regime on their eastern border. This represented a 180-degree political turnabout for Ben-Gurion, who in 1956 had advocated dismantling Jordan. At that time, of course, the Israelis had expected the Suez campaign to cripple Nasser's power and influence. In 1958, Ben-Gurion wrote in his diary, "For us, the best thing would be to preserve the status quo."[34]

Under American and British supervision, the notion of cooperation between Israel and Jordan was being secretly revived. Israel's hopes of restoring the relationship with Amman were bearing fruit, although not due to Israeli efforts.

The United States and Britain, having lost an ally in Baghdad, were stubbornly committed to protecting western interests in Beirut and Amman. The Saudis, frightened of offending Nasser the rising star, refused to help the west in any way, and the American airlift avoided the airspace of Saudi Arabia entirely. Instead, the U.S. transport aircraft flew over Israel, with Ben-Gurion's full assent, to bring fuel supplies to Jordan.

The British also used air corridors over Israel, in a coordinated move, to station paratroops from Akrotiri, Cyprus, on Jordanian soil. The Israelis, not by mere coincidence, received some military aid from Britain around the same time.

The secret relationship, only on the verge of renewal, was immediately strengthened when Israeli intelligence agencies learned of an Egyptian plot to murder Hussein. The information was relayed through the military attaché at the Israeli Embassy in London. "I received an urgent telephone call from the embassy," Colonel Yuval Ne'eman recalls. "I was, by chance, in the Palace of Westminster at the time to watch a parliamentary debate when I was asked to return at once to my office. I got to my room on the run, and waiting for me there was a coded message. It said that Jordanian agents, who receive orders from Egypt, are preparing to kill King Hussein and to seize power. I was asked to pass the information, without delay, to the British Foreign Office, and that is what I did."[35]

The British immediately transmitted a warning to Hussein, who took the necessary steps to smash the conspiracy. The king knew the source of the information was Israel, and the event greatly speeded the development of confidence between Jordan and Israel.

Nasser's United Arab Republic (UAR) did not give up the sport of trying to assassinate Hussein. Two MiG–17 jets flown by Syrian air force pilots attempted to shoot the king down, when he himself was piloting a small jet over Syrian territory on his way to a vacation in Switzerland in November 1958. Hussein handed control of the airplane, a Dove, to his friend Jock Dalgleish, whose flying skills saved them both. The Syrians were outmaneuvered in the air, but on the ground they and Nasser denied that anyone had tried to kill the king.

In Amman, soon after landing safely, Hussein was hailed as a returning hero, and his growing band of admirers at home openly demanded war against the UAR.[36]

On another occasion, the king was astonished to find over a dozen dead cats in the courtyard of his palace. It did not take Hussein's rapidly improving intelligence service much time to discover that a palace cook had been bribed by the Syrians to poison the king. Unsure about the correct dose, the cook had been experimenting on the cats. In 1960, Hussein blamed the UAR Embassy in Amman for replacing the medicine in his nose drops with lethal acid.[37]

Each attempt on his life, which he uncovered or escaped by some good fortune, simply strengthened Hussein's impression that of all factors in the complicated Middle East equation, he could probably count most reliably on the Israelis. They might not be his friends, but they did not appear to be trying to kill him.

The most important test came after the huge bomb explosion that killed Prime Minister Haza el-Magalli in his office in Amman in 1960. It was probably an attempt to assassinate King Hussein, who had been scheduled to confer with Magalli at that precise hour but, luckily, was late. Two young Syrian agents, identified as the bombers, escaped to Damascus.[38]

Hussein was boiling with rage and spoke of taking revenge on Syria by launching a northward invasion. His mother, Queen Zein, encouraged him to do so. In late September, he sent the Arab Legion to the Syrian border.

Israel's General Chaim Herzog, who had left his Jerusalem command to become chief of the army's intelligence branch, received a message from the east: "A senior commander in the Jordanian army urgently requests a meeting with you." The message had come through the Israeli representative to the armistice commission. Herzog, as president of his nation, recalls, "I was told that the head of Jordanian military intelligence was asking to see me. I went to Ben-Gurion and received his approval for a meeting. I came to the meeting, crossing the border at the Mandelbaum Gate in Jerusalem again, but instead of the intelligence chief I was met by a lieutenant colonel from the royal palace who was King Hussein's confidant.

"He revealed to me that the Jordanian army had massed three brigades on their border with Syria. He said, 'We are about to invade Damascus.'

" 'So what do you want from us?' I asked him.

"He told me, 'We shall have to thin out our forces on the border with Israel, and we are asking that you not take advantage of the situation by moving against us.' I promised to give him an answer as soon as possible, and I immediately drove from Jerusalem to Sde Boker to report to the prime minister at his home. David Ben-Gurion authorized me to give Jordan a positive reply, and that is what I did."[39]

The message from West Jerusalem to Amman said, "You may rest assured. You have our pledge."

As could be expected from Hussein, however, his emotional sense of hurry to inflict vengeance on Syria gave way to a realistic assessment that invading the junior partner of the UAR would do little good.

Jordan did not invade Syria. But Hussein had received precisely the signal he had sought from the Israelis, and their relationship—while still at a cautious arm's length—was distinctly developing into a sense of mutual understanding. A high-level meeting to discuss the general, strategic aspects of the Middle East situation would seem to be a natural step. Perhaps even a summit conference would be possible.

There was at least one attempt to bring Hussein and Ben-Gurion together, and it was through the efforts of the shah of Iran in 1962. Shimon Peres, who was a senior aide to Ben-Gurion for a decade and later became prime minister in his own right, recalls, "The Shah very much wanted to arrange such a meeting. During the 1948 war, B. -G. did not feel he could permit himself to leave the country, and so he sent Golda and Dayan to the meetings with Abdullah."[40]

The Iranian ruler in Tehran did not quite manage to arrange a meeting in 1962. Efforts continued behind the scenes, but Israel's Labor party was busy tearing itself apart in internal dissension, which exhausted Ben-Gurion's patience. Israel's white-haired founding father, known nationwide simply as "the Old Man," surprised his countrymen in June 1963, by resigning.

The convergence of Israel and Jordan by now had impressive momentum, impelled by a keen sense of shared interests. Turning political physics into the reality of face-to-face meetings was left to the government formed by Ben-Gurion's successor, Levi Eshkol.

Hussein's physician in London would be the key player in this delicate game.

Chapter 5

The Devonshire Place Doctor

The letter that he had just opened brought a broad smile to Dr. Emanuel Herbert's face. He felt proud that the king of Sweden, Adolf Gustav himself, had written a letter of thanks along with notification that Dr. Herbert was now a knight in the Royal Order of the Polar Star.

The physician, a successful general practitioner for decades in London, had never heard of Sweden's Polar Star, but he was to learn later that the order was founded in 1748 with the Swedish monarch as its grand master. Membership was a considerable honor accorded to Swedes who had performed some notable public service or scored a scientific achievement. Dr. Herbert was elevated to this elite group on April 11, 1961, for his successful performance of a minor operation on Prince Bertil.

Sweden's was not the only royal family treated by the doctor. Quite a few princes and other titled personages visited his private office at 21 Devonshire Place in the heart of London, a few blocks from Harley Street, famous throughout the world for its exclusive clinics.

King Hussein naturally wished to receive his medical care in this most illustrious of medical neighborhoods. He was frequently in London for entertainment, seeing friends he made in his youth, and to tighten his political connections with the British government. Hussein sent his children to British schools, purchased several houses in London, and made the entire island nation his second home, far away from the tensions and troubles in Jordan.

Even in the early 1950s, shortly after becoming king, Hussein asked British diplomats and officials to recommend a personal physician in London. After consulting with Foreign Office advisers in London, the ambassador in Amman suggested that Emanuel Herbert would be suitable, as he was already recognized as a doctor with a specialty in heart disease and the sense of discretion to treat many British and foreign dignitaries without saying a word in public. His experience with the need to protect privacy made Dr. Herbert a natural choice, but the British officials may have had their own secret reasons for selecting him.

The doctor's personal history was a fairly typical odyssey of a Jewish refugee from Eastern Europe. His name was Emanuel Herzberg when he was born on February 11, 1898, in Riga, Latvia, then under the Russian tsar and later to become part of the Soviet Union. His parents struggled to provide their son with a good education, and they managed to send him to the University of Moscow and then to the University of Heidelberg, where he graduated in 1923 *magna cum laude,* with his medical degree.

A year later, the Herzberg family moved to London and in 1925, Manny Herzberg, as his friends called him, became a fully qualified physician. He was soon working at the London Jewish Hospital in the British capital's east end. He remained firmly in the company of Jews for fifteen years, at the hospital and at his home in the predominantly Jewish neighborhood of Hendon, in north London.

It was in 1940 that the doctor changed his name from Herzberg to Herbert, choosing an English name to make his ethnic origin less obvious, and he opened his own clinic on Devonshire Place. He worked at Number 5 for twenty years and then moved up the road to 21 Devonshire Place. Private fees made him a somewhat wealthy man, and he moved, with his wife and two sons, from Hendon to the luxury neighborhood of St. John's Wood, just northwest of London's huge Regent's Park.

Manny Herbert retained many of his Jewish patients from his early days in Britain, but his financial success was built on the rich and famous whom he treated thanks to word-of-mouth referrals. A host of foreigners, many of them exiled from their native lands, took up residence in London during World War II, and those who could afford luxury often lived in Claridge's Hotel. Dr. Herbert treated most of them, because he had the good fortune to be "house physician" at Claridge's.

He knew how to be charming, but not pushy, to prime ministers, princes, and movie stars, and they told their friends about the doctor with whom they could feel comfortable. Aristotle Onassis, Elizabeth Taylor, and Richard Burton were said to be among his postwar patients.

Part of Dr. Herbert's charm was his knack for languages. He spoke a dozen or more. One day, his nurse heard him speaking on the telephone in a tongue she could not recognize. "What language was that?" she asked, and the doctor surprised her with his answer: "Finnish." He built a relationship of trust with patients in French, Russian, German, and Yiddish among others.[1]

Dr. Herbert was also medical adviser to the London office of the American company Trans World Airlines (TWA), to one of the Hilton hotels and to several well-known department stores including Simpson's of Piccadilly and the Marks and Spencer (M & S) chain. He worked as a consultant to M & S for forty-seven years, until his death in July 1980, and became friendly with company directors including Lord Marcus Sieff. The Sieffs are a prominent Jewish family in Britain, and their chain of clothing and food stores is known for its business links with Israel.

The celebrity clinic he ran on Devonshire Place and his role as a corporate physician constituted only one side of Herbert's life as a successful doctor. A more hidden aspect can be glimpsed through the career of a friend of his, Dr. Simon Andrew Whitehouse.

Dr. Whitehouse shared a clinic with Dr. Herbert for several years, and among Whitehouse's prominent patients was Sir Anthony Blunt, professor of art history at Cambridge University and then curator of Queen Elizabeth's royal collection. Blunt joined Britain's counterintelligence agency, MI5, in World War II, but in 1964 was discovered to have been a spy for the Soviet Union. Only in 1979 did Prime Minister Margaret Thatcher confirm that fact, telling Parliament that Blunt had confessed, had provided evidence, and had been allowed to continue working for the queen without public scandal. Once the scandal was public, he was stripped of his knighthood. Sullying his good name was Blunt's only punishment.

He had been "the fourth man" in a spy ring, recruited by the Soviets at Cambridge in the early 1930s. He had worked with Guy Burgess, Donald MacLean, and Harold "Kim" Philby, all British secret agents who betrayed their country and caused immense damage to the west.

The security services, MI5 and MI6, had every reason to be deeply embarrassed. Word spread that the United States felt it could not trust the British with secrets, because everything would leak to Moscow.

A source close to the Whitehouse-Herbert clinic said Blunt was not the only MI5 man receiving treatment and checkups there. Whitehouse was an "agency doctor" for the secret services, said the source, who suggested that Dr. Herbert shared the clandestine clientele.

There were uncomfortable divisions within MI5, with some of the "young Turks" in the counterintelligence agency suspecting their boss, Sir Roger Hollis, was a Soviet agent. Embarrassment over the KGB's penetration of British intelligence had become paranoia. Retired MI5 official Peter Wright has revealed that right-wingers in the agency even discussed toppling Prime Minister Harold Wilson of the Labor party, believing he might be working for the Russians.

The anti-Wilson clique was especially suspicious of the Jewish businessmen, many of Eastern European stock, who were advisers to the prime minister. The conspirators called them "the Bar Mitzvah club."[2] They included publisher George Weidenfeld and clothing manufacturer Joseph Kagan, both elevated to the status of titled lords. MI5 agents were suspiciously watching them, as some of their business contacts were in Russia and the communist bloc, and it was also noted that they had financial and emotional interests in Israel.

Dr. Herbert apparently shared the interest in and affection for Israel, but MI5 would see other positive qualities in the Jewish physician. The KGB and the Soviet military intelligence agency GRU were known to be recruiting agents and gathering information up and down Harley Street, because a person's private medical history could be of considerable value to any espionage activity. To block the Soviet penetration of the world's top medical clinics, British counter-intelligence had to have its own spies there.

The British came to trust Dr. Herbert, and so it was in consultation with MI5 that the Foreign Office recommended him to King Hussein to be his physician in London.

Hussein raised no objections, even when informed that Herbert was not only Jewish but a sympathizer of Israel. The British, after all, had assured the king that one of this doctor's specialties was discretion. He was never quoted in the press and never revealed the identity of his patients, although such gossip would be priceless among the newspapers of Fleet Street.

Hidden by his own cloak of mystery, Dr. Herbert would be able to serve his adopted homeland, Great Britain, his Hashemite patient, and the country with which he felt a connection as a Jew, Israel.

Britain wished to protect its interests in the Middle East by establishing alliances with pro-western states in the region. London's aim was to minimize the strength of radical Arab nationalism as personified by Egypt's President Gamal Abdel Nasser, whom they saw as an agent of Soviet influence.

The British attempted, in 1955, to drag Jordan, Iraq, and Turkey into the "Baghdad Pact." The spies of MI6 were later developing plans to assassinate Nasser, and Britain finally joined France and Israel in seizing Egypt's Suez Canal and Sinai Peninsula.[3]

It seemed only natural for non-Arab states in the Middle East, including Turkey as well as Israel and Iran, to take Britain's side against Nasser. The British had long-standing ties with Jordan and Sudan, two Arab nations that had their own reasons to fear the fiery Egyptian leader. It is no surprise, then, that Britain encouraged secret contacts between these states and Israel, despite official conditions of hostility.

For their part, the Israelis were more than willing to have such clandestine links out of a sense of self-interest, not to do London any favors. The decision-makers, in this regard, were Prime Minister David Ben-Gurion, Moshe Dayan, Golda Meir, Walter Eytan, Reuven Shiloah, and Eliyahu Sassoon. The exclusive group—spies, diplomats, some of them Arabic speakers—worked for years to keep up with political developments in the Arab world around them. They acted whenever possible to build a network of secret understandings with their neighbors, and Shiloah and his closest aides established Israel's own intelligence network. They were the founders of the Mossad in its modern form. *Mossad* means "Institute," a shortened term for the Central Institute for Intelligence and Special Tasks, an espionage agency as famous as it is shadowy.

It is certainly noteworthy that Shiloah's name is remembered in two contexts: political contacts with Arab countries, before and after the birth of the State of

Israel, and his leadership of the Mossad, created by Ben-Gurion on September 1, 1951. Pursuing links with the Arabs was, after all, a matter of both diplomacy and intelligence.

For several years, responsibility for the secret dialogue with Arab leaders was shared between the Mossad and the Foreign Ministry. In 1957, despite protests by the official diplomats, the Mossad under Shiloah's successor Isser Harel was given exclusive authority over the hidden diplomacy. Ironically, Shiloah had officially joined the Foreign Ministry, although still serving as an intelligence officer; he was posted in Washington to help establish strong cooperation with America's Central Intelligence Agency (CIA) and then back to Jerusalem as a special adviser.

The Mossad has, as one of its primary missions, the objective of collecting political, social, and military information in foreign countries. The agency is interested in all aspects of internal Arab politics, the personal relationships between Arab leaders and the activities of Arab diplomats. Gaining access to any Arab country is a huge advantage for Israel's spies.

Shiloah and his colleagues laid the cornerstone for the two main aims of Israel's intelligence and diplomacy in the Middle East. First, Israel must take advantage of every dispute or argument within the Arab world and should even try to worsen the conflicts. Second, relations should be established and deepened with non-Arab nations or ethnic minorities in the region, to break the circle of hostility surrounding Israel.

The Mossad-driven strategy can be described as one built on "peripheral alliances." The term was first used in connection with American and British efforts to increase their influence in the Middle East. The two western powers delineated two rings in the area: "the heart" of the Arab world, meaning the most powerful states such as Egypt, Syria, and Iraq; and the secondary "periphery" states, which include Muslim, but non-Arab, nations such as Iran, Turkey, and Ethiopia.[4]

The principle at the core of this strategy was simple: The enemy of my enemy is my friend. Thus, for instance, Shiloah established relations on behalf of the Jewish Agency with the Kurdish minority in Iraq as early as the 1930s, when he worked as a journalist to provide "cover" in Baghdad.[5]

Some thirty years later, the Kurds would be treated as genuine allies when Israeli military officers were secretly sent to the hills along Iraq's border with Iran to advise the rebels. Guerrilla leader Mustafa Barzani received Israeli help for his rebellion against the Iraqi government, with Jerusalem hoping a civil war would keep the radical Ba'ath Arab Socialist regime too busy to bother Israel. The Kurds are the enemy of Israel's enemies the Iraqis, and so the Kurds are Israel's friends.

A similar attitude has dominated policy with regard to the Druze minority in Syria, the Christians of southern Sudan and the Maronite Christians of Lebanon. From 1974 to June of 1982, when the Israelis sent their own army into Lebanon, they delivered military equipment to the Christian militia leaders as surrogates there in the fight against Palestinian guerrilla groups. Responsibility for the secret relationship was in the Mossad's hands.

The espionage agency has taken on the functions of an alternative foreign ministry for Israel. The Political Action and Liaison Department of the Mossad maintains ties, often close and strategically vital, with dozens of African and Asian states that refuse to have formal diplomatic relations with Israel. Several Arab countries, despite an official state of war, are included in this clandestine list, and Morocco's King Hassan has had particularly close contacts with the Israelis. The network of alternative diplomacy was established by roving Mossad men during Isser Harel's long reign at the secret agency in the 1950s and early 1960s.[6] The links proved to be more durable over time than many of the formal diplomatic relationships in the Middle East.

A CIA report on Israel's intelligence community, never declassified but found and published by the Iranian militants who seized the U.S. Embassy in Tehran in 1979, said the Israelis consistently tried "to break the Arab ring surrounding Israel" by establishing ties with "non-Arab Moslem states." In late 1958, it said, the Mossad set up a cooperation arrangement called "Trident" with Turkey's secret police, known as TNSS, and the shah of Iran's SAVAK secret service. They would exchange intelligence data, mainly on attempts by Soviet agents to penetrate their nations, and the three agency chiefs held meetings twice a year.[7]

When Sudan was winning its full independence from British and Egyptian administration in 1954, Israelis working from their embassy in London established close ties with senior members of the Sudanese delegation at the negotiations with Britain. Israel found other Sudanese could also be valuable contacts, even friends, in northeast Africa, on the southern border of then-hostile Egypt. The height of the secret relationship came in August 1957, when Foreign Minister Golda Meir met Sudan's Prime Minister Abdullah Khalil at the Plaza Athenée Hotel in Paris. The Sudanese, with a similar need to that of Jordan a few years later, were hoping that Israel could put in a good word to win an increase in U.S. aid for Sudan. The clandestine ties were cut in 1958, when Khalil was deposed in a military coup.

The Mossad turned to old friends in Sudan and made a few new ones in the 1980s, as part of "Operation Moses," the huge, secret operation to fly over ten thousand Ethiopian Jews to Israel, most of them by way of desert airstrips in Sudan. When President Gaafar el-Numeiri was overthrown in 1985, he was tried in absentia for crimes including contacts with Israel and the receipt of huge bribes from foreign agents.

When Jerusalem's classified connection with Sudan was broken in 1958, British diplomats and secret agents stepped up their efforts to bring Israel and Jordan together. London and Jerusalem were as close as they had ever been in Israel's first decade of independence, after the coordinated attack on Egypt in 1956. Outside pressure did not succeed, however, in breaking the wall of hostility between Israel and Jordan. Only King Hussein's own decision could do that.

Nasser's prestige had been damaged in the Suez invasion by Israel, Britain, and France. The Egyptian threat was no longer so great against the Hashemite kingdom. Hussein's political perils at home also diminished, as he settled more comfortably into the power of his throne, and the monarch's growing self-confidence eased the proper organization of his nation's economy.

The king's personal life also improved, inevitably making him a more stable man. His second marriage, to a young British woman named Toni Gardiner who became Princess Muna, was a happy one. They were married in 1960. He had one daughter, Alia, by his first union with his cousin Dina, but that ended in divorce only eighteen months after the April 1955, royal wedding in Amman. Much more important for a Muslim, however, were the two sons born to Muna: Abdullah, born in 1962, and Faisal, in 1963. She also gave birth to twin daughters, Aisha and Zein.

Family life was relaxed in the 1960s because Muna had no interest in government issues, unlike the university-educated Dina who regularly intervened in affairs of state. Evenings were spent watching movies, listening to pop music, or conversing with close friends, including Muna's parents and the Rifai family.[8]

Besides his appetite for fast cars and aircraft, King Hussein is a man of simple tastes. He divides his time between two palaces, Hummar in Amman and Shuneh in the Jordan Valley, and a residence he built on the Red Sea at 'Aqaba, traveling at high speed between them by helicopter.

Hussein was comfortable as king as he consolidated his political strength. He finally felt sufficiently powerful to take the step that he had consistently refused to consider: direct contact with his Israeli enemies to the west.

The Nasser-inspired challenge to Hussein's throne in 1958, repulsed with the open help of Britain and the hidden hand of Israel, led the king to conclude that the Zionists could serve as the greatest guarantee of his continued authority in Jordan.

It was certainly difficult for the king to sympathize with the Palestinians in their claim that Israel is the ultimate enemy for having driven them from their homeland. Hussein tended to believe that the Palestinians, when led in the pre-Israel years by the mufti of Jerusalem, repeatedly made bad decisions and practically gave away much of Palestine.

His lack of sympathy for them was further driven home in April 1963, when Palestinian activists again turned to Nasserism and rioted in East Jerusalem and in other towns of the West Bank. They were celebrating a new political union of Egypt, Syria, and Iraq, and in effect demonstrating their defiance of Jordan's king.

Hussein hesitated only a few days but then dissolved Parliament, appointed an uncle as prime minister and put the entire country under military control. He sent loyal units of the Arab Legion to quell the unrest, and they imposed curfews in the West Bank and opened fire on crowds of Palestinian demonstrators.[9]

The king's immediate aim when he finally decided to initiate contact with Israel, was to win support for his request to the United States for military and financial aid. If Israeli backing could not be obtained, perhaps at least the Israelis would not attempt to block U.S. aid to Jordan.

The Americans had been opposed to the Anglo-French-Israeli invasion of the Suez and Sinai regions, and the United States was at the forefront of international pressure on the invaders to withdraw their forces. Just after the Suez affair, however, there was a paradoxical shift in Washington's Middle East policy: perceiving the threat posed by Nasser's radical Arab nationalism, there was a new "Eisenhower Doctrine."

Speaking to the U.S. Congress in March 1957, President Dwight D. Eisenhower said that Soviet expansionism constituted a challenge in the Middle East. He declared that instability in the region had worsened because of Russian intervention, and he added that American involvement in the Middle East would increase. It was clear that military might would be part of the U.S. response to the perceived challenge.[10]

The new doctrine was first exercised in the crisis of July 1958. American marines landed on the shores of Lebanon and rescued the administration of Camille Chamoun from an attempted coup by Nasserites.

As the British carried out a similar operation to prop up Hussein, the United States assisted as it could and ensured that fuel deliveries to Jordan were increased.

The growing American involvement in the Middle East was not, however, only military in nature. The strongest tool at Washington's disposal was economic assistance. The United States began, from the late 1950s, to take Britain's place as the chief financial backer of the Hashemite Kingdom of Jordan. By 1960, the Americans were pouring financial aid amounting to nearly $100 million (£18 million) per year into Jordan, six times the economic assistance from Britain.[11]

Hussein and his top officials began to concern themselves with major development projects, of the kind that they could never before afford. The king needed ever-more funding for his ambitious plans to equip his army and air force with modern armaments from the United States.

The Eisenhower Doctrine also laid the groundwork for the close cooperation, which was to grow, blossom, and bear fruit between the United States and Israel. Prime Minister Ben-Gurion, by 1961 an elderly hero of American Jewry, flew to Washington to meet the young President John F. Kennedy, who had begun to speak of "the special relations" between the two nations.

The United States, under Kennedy, began for the first time to sell weapons directly to Israel, instead of through various indirect routes. Well before the end of the 1960s, the Americans were the chief arms suppliers to the Israelis. The president had at first rejected Ben-Gurion's request for Hawk antiaircraft missiles, but by 1962 the United States was sending them to Israel. The relationship widened to include tanks in 1964, Skyhawk jet bombers in 1966, and Phantom jet fighters in 1968.[12]

The greatly improved relations between the United States and Israel did not, of course, escape the attention of the king of Jordan. He understood that Israel's influence was now great in Washington, and he decided to try and use it for his own interests.

International, inter-Arab, and intrafamily factors all combined, then, to lead Hussein to his first meeting with an Israeli official.[13] Jerusalem's chosen representative was Yaakov Herzog, deputy director general of the foreign ministry and brother of the military strategist Chaim Herzog who would later become president of Israel. Their meeting was in September 1963, in London.

The chosen venue for the historic, but secret, occasion was a wide, six-story, redbrick building containing both residential apartments and doctors' clinics. It is only a few blocks from the famous Harley Street and stands at a busy corner with one of the main east-west arteries through the British capital, Marylebone Road, affording easy access to the large Euston and King's Cross railway stations, to the east, and to Heathrow Airport, to the west.

London was an excellent choice for these meetings, thanks to British cooperation, reasonable proximity to the Middle East, and a regular flow of international diplomats that made the arrival and departure of dignitaries anything but unusual. The Mossad had the chief responsibility for selecting a specific site for the sensitive talks, and Dr. Herbert's "surgery" on Devonshire Place fulfilled all requirements handsomely.

Chapter 6

This Time in Paris

The arrangements for the first meeting between the King of Jordan and an Israeli official were relatively simple, both in terms of venue and the choice of participants. It seemed in 1963 that once there was the will, there was no problem finding a way. Hussein himself would represent Jordan, because there is no one a king can trust so profoundly as himself. And London was a natural choice, because Hussein knew no foreign city better. The Israelis could choose whomever they liked, although the king naturally wished to conduct talks at the highest level.

He had been at Dr. Emanuel Herbert's clinic on Devonshire Place many times, and nearly every time the medical checkup was accompanied by a discussion of the Middle East situation. The doctor had a keen mind, but above all he was an excellent listener.

Dr. Herbert told his patient about his friend, Marcus Sieff, and Sieff's political and business contacts in Israel. The Marks and Spencer stores chief was an ardent Zionist whose family had known the founding fathers of the Jewish state. The Sieffs helped establish the world-famous Weizmann Institute of Science in Rehovot, Israel, named for the nation's first president Chaim Weizmann. Marcus Sieff was especially close to David Ben-Gurion, having served as an adviser to the prime minister during Israel's War of Independence in 1948.

Hussein's signal that he was willing, even curious and determined, to meet a senior Israeli was transmitted through his physician. Dr. Herbert told the British Foreign Office, which had originally sent him his illustrious patient. The British immediately lauded and encouraged the king, who was apparently accepting a suggestion that Whitehall's senior ministers had made to him.

Israel immediately replied positively, although the ruling Mapai party was in the midst of a bitter internal rivalry, and Levi Eshkol had only replaced Ben-Gurion in June 1963.[1] The senior ministers of the newly formed cabinet quickly determined that Hussein's somewhat unexpected proposal did not signal the likelihood of negotiations for a peace treaty, but rather a limited discussion of the king's chosen agenda. Accordingly, it was decided in Jerusalem to send a high-ranking official, but not Prime Minister Eshkol or even another cabinet member.

The Israeli decision was more than satisfactory to Hussein, who preferred to discourage high expectations for the proposed meeting and wished to make it a cordial, businesslike event. He did make it emphatically clear that the encounter must remain a strictly held secret. The perfect Israeli official for the mission was Yaakov Herzog. The head of the Mossad, Meir Amit, might have seemed to be another logical candidate, because he extended the secret agency's activities into new diplomatic spheres, but he was having a hard time reorganizing the espionage agency after replacing the legendary Isser Harel.

Herzog and Dr. Herbert, once they met, got along extremely well. Herzog, too, had a warm, European Jewish personality, and both men were enlightened lovers of books. Above all, they were both men who could keep secrets.

Dr. Herbert never told a soul about his involvement in the secret meetings between Israel and Jordan. Even his two sons were left only to guess. Peter Herbert, one of the sons who is also a physician, recalls, "I knew that my father had contacts with both Israel and Jordan, but I never knew the details." The elder Dr. Herbert took the secret to his grave. Only his wife, who died in an automobile accident in 1986, knew of the distinguished visitors to their home.

Herzog was born to a family of Jewish clergymen in Belfast, where his father was chief rabbi of Northern Ireland. From his early years at school, Yaakov concentrated on two fields: The Biblical law of the Torah and the study of history and international relations.[2] He and his brother, the future president of Israel, were proud young Zionists. Yaakov earned a law degree at Hebrew University in Jerusalem and then received his doctorate at the University of Ottawa in Canada. He also took the time to study and be ordained as a rabbi. He was an observant Jew but also very much a rational man who adored logic, order, and western culture.

Before Israel's War of Independence, Herzog joined the intelligence corps of the Hagana underground army. After independence in 1948, he was Ben-Gurion's special adviser on Jerusalem and religious affairs and then moved to the Foreign Ministry for an assortment of jobs including minister in the Israeli Embassy in Washington and then ambassador to Canada.

During his diplomatic service in Ottawa, Herzog's intellectual strengths attracted international admiration. He took part in a public debate at Canada's McGill University in January 1961, distributed worldwide as a recording and a book. Herzog challenged British historian Arnold Toynbee, who had made harsh comments questioning the validity of Zionism as a Jewish liberation movement. The debate was a sparkling duel of intellects, reminiscent of the theological and philosophical arguments of the Middle Ages.

As a diplomat, Herzog specialized in sensitive tasks. Years later, Lord Marcus Sieff of Brimpton recalled, ''Yaakov was involved in complicated webs involving many issues, and so we called him 'the Spider' because he stood at the center of it all.''[3]

Herzog had a taste for secret missions. He enjoyed concealing two facts for every one that he revealed openly. Even in the political diary he kept, itself confidential until after his death in 1972, he often wrote code names rather than identify people in a straightforward manner. Emanuel Herbert was written about, but only as "the Doctor."

Herzog liked to use somewhat shadowy code names in the course of his work, too, never referring specifically to Hussein. In any event, only a handful of people in Jerusalem—some cabinet ministers, senior military chiefs, and a very few intelligence and Foreign Ministry officials—knew about the contacts with Jordan. Fewer, still, knew the full details.

Mordecai Gazit, then a senior diplomat in the Israeli Embassy in Washington, remembers, "Very few people were in the picture. We heard that an English doctor was connected with the subject, but we did not know his name. Our nickname for him, in fact, was 'the Engineer.' "

Herzog's official reports on his meetings with the king were written in a relaxed, unsensational style always going directly to the main point. An Israeli researcher who has had access to the papers says, "His words are written clearly but in the dry style you would expect from a Foreign Ministry man. He leaves one with the impression of a man of mystery."[4]

Gideon Rafael, another leading Israeli diplomat of the 1960s, recalls, "Herzog always leaned toward caution and tended to be hazy in what he said."[5]

When the historic day quietly came in the latter half of 1963, Yaakov Herzog was waiting in Dr. Herbert's reception room in London when King Hussein arrived. Herzog and Dr. Herbert rose and respectfully bowed their heads slightly for a second. The king walked over to the Israeli and shook his hand warmly. After some brief, polite chitchat, the doctor excused himself and left the two interlocutors to explore each other's positions alone.

Hussein quickly came to the point, telling Herzog that Jordan hoped to receive Israel's help in winning financial aid from the United States.

Herzog agreed, in principle, to the request, adding that he would, of course, have to consult with Jerusalem before making a final commitment.

The king then made another, surprising request. He explained that he had deep doubts as to whether he would ever finally be rid of the external threat of Nasserism and the internal challenge of Palestinian nationalism. And that, he said, is why Jordan needs the latest, modern weaponry—the kind that he could only receive from the Americans. Hussein wanted the Israelis to understand the request he would lodge with the United States, and he even wanted their backing.

"What kind of weapons?" Herzog asked.

"Tanks."

It was a request that no Israeli official could support. A tank is a highly portable and powerful instrument of firepower. The Jordanians might say that tanks are needed to confront X, but they could just as easily be turned against Y, and Y would be Israel.

When Herzog began shaking his head in disagreement, Hussein hastened to say that his defense against Egypt and its allies, Syria and Iraq, would have to include the very latest tanks.

Herzog was frank. Not only was he unauthorized to endorse any Jordanian plea to upgrade his armored divisions, he said, but Israel would never be convinced that the tanks could not be aimed at it.

The two men moved on to other issues. Hussein said he objected to Israeli plans to draw water from the Sea of Galilee for a long pipeline to irrigate the Negev Desert, saying that the water levels in the Jordan River would inevitably suffer. The king said he had his own plans for agricultural development along his side of the Jordan Valley. Herzog responded that to the best of his knowledge, the existing balance of water between Israel and Jordan would not be significantly affected. Hussein was not satisfied.[6]

The conversation, conducted entirely in English without any difficulty, lasted two hours but did not reach agreement on the two main issues: rearmament and water. Hussein and Herzog, however, were clearly satisfied that they had met and taken the opportunity to exchange views. They agreed that contact should be maintained in the future, and they arranged an exchange of messages through Dr. Herbert.

The king and the senior Israeli official left London, confident that there would be another meeting but not knowing that as long as two years would pass before the next conversation. The delay was caused by a new set of storm clouds sweeping over the diplomatic skies of the Middle East.

The challenge of Nasserism was ever-more potent, as Egypt's president successfully convened, in Cairo, the first Arab summit. It was January 1964, and Nasser was encouraged to believe that he was the unrivaled leader of the Arab world by the failure of Syria and Iraq to set up their own binational union. Iraq's government had tried to steal some of Nasser's thunder by proposing publicly that a "Republic of Palestine" be established in the West Bank. Needless to say, King Hussein was even angrier over the proposal.

Hussein was not to be left out of any broadly based Arab political event, and so he attended the Cairo summit, greeted at the airport by Nasser with hugs and kisses on both cheeks. The two men met four times that year.[7]

The summit agreed to form a united Arab command under an Egyptian general, to plan a future confrontation with Israel. In the short term, the national leaders agreed that Israel's irrigation plans were dangerous, and they commissioned a study of ways to divert some of the Jordan River's waters away from the Sea of Galilee, also known as Lake Tiberias. It was also at this summit that the PLO was formed with Nasser's ally Ahmed Shukairy as its leader. The three principal results of the Cairo conference led, within three and a half years, to war with Israel.

Hussein was managing to quell unrest at home, led mainly by West Bank

Palestinians, but the founding of the Palestine Liberation Organization and the emergence of the el-Fatah guerrillas in 1965 put the Hashemite king to the test: Was he on Fatah's side or Israel's?

The first time Jordan's army shot and killed a Palestinian guerrilla, a commando named Ahmed Musa who was on his way back from a raid on an Israeli pipeline, in January 1965.[8] Hussein failed the test—as far as Arab unity was concerned.

Jordanian policy, subtly and inevitably, changed. Pan-Arabism was the fashion and—who could tell?—perhaps the future. Hussein wanted, as was his habit, to protect all his fronts at once. While he had taken a secret step toward greater understanding with Israel, a higher priority was to sidestep any dangerous moves against him by Nasser at a time when the Egyptian leader's power and influence were growing.

In the words of one Israeli analyst, reaching for a cliché to explain Hussein's attitude toward Nasser and his friends, "If you can't beat them, join them."

The policy dictated that the king smile politely at the PLO, and he permitted Shukairy's group to hold its founding conference in East Jerusalem. Shukairy was one of a handful of Palestinian politicians who emerged after the "disaster" of 1948. Representing his people at Arab League conferences, he was known as pro-Egyptian but was working to form a recognizable Palestinian nation. Shukairy was watching his step around Hussein, because the Palestinians in Jordan were a key part of the early PLO's concept, and the king's consent would be needed for any political activity.

The Jerusalem conference ratified the famous PLO National Charter, which called for the replacement of the State of Israel by a secular, democratic state in which Jews who had arrived in Palestine before 1917 could reside, but Zionists who arrived afterward would have to leave.

Shukairy, in his keynote address, said the organization's aim was "to liberate our greater homeland to the West of the West Bank." There was no threat to undermine Jordan or even to seize control of Jordan's West Bank. The king knew, however, that the PLO would inevitably compete with him for the hearts and minds of the West Bank's Palestinians.[9] He had little choice, however, but to appear cooperative.

Hussein also took part in the Arab plan to divert water from the Jordan River's source away from Israel. Water rights were among the most bitter issues in a region where prosperity and productivity depend on irrigation, and there was a volatile point at which the borders of three nations met.

Two important tributaries that feed into the Jordan, the Banias and the Hazbani, are in Syria. The Yarmuk runs from Syria into Jordanian territory. The tiny Dan River is within Israel's borders. The product of these and other tributaries, the Jordan River, is vital to both Jordan and Israel.

In the early 1950s, Syria, Jordan, and Israel bitterly debated, through the United Nations, the division of water resources. President Dwight D. Eisenhower sent a special American envoy, Eric Johnston, to the Middle East. After five trips to and through the region in thirty months of negotiations, Johnston hammered out the Jordan Valley Plan for equitably sharing water. The Arab states considered the plan in 1955, but after an Israeli reprisal raid on Gaza early that year any thoughts of cooperation were dismissed. Johnston's plan, complete with complex maps, gather dust on a shelf with all the other Middle East peace plans that have failed.

The Arab nations kept up the pressure on the water front in 1964. They set up a fund of $30 million at their second summit in Alexandria, Egypt, in September to divert water from the Yarmuk so that Israel would have none of it.[10]

Indeed, Israel would tolerate none of it. Syrian and Lebanese engineers began to build diversion canals, and Israeli tanks, artillery, and later the air force flattened the bulldozers several times.[11]

So long as Hussein was marching on the path of Arab unity, he saw no need to maintain direct contact with Israel. The king did note, however, that the Israelis had kept their promise by lobbying in Washington—even with the American Jewish community—against any plan to fight Jordan's request for U.S. economic assistance.

When relations among the Arab states deteriorated, returning to their pre-summit bitterness, Jordan again found reasons to pursue its own foreign policy. Hussein found himself forced to carve out a "nice place in the middle" of Arab politics.

The expected clashes between Hussein's army and the PLO's guerrillas became more frequent. A new radical Ba'ath party government in Syria sponsored the commandos of Fatah, and they were attacking Israel from both Syrian and Jordanian territory. But Hussein was not being asked for permission. He would have objected, in any event, so as not to incite Israeli retaliation.

The king brought back his old friend Wasfi el-Tell to serve as prime minister in February 1965. Tell was considered anti-Egyptian, and the appointment signaled the end of Hussein's adherence to pan-Arabism.[12]

Hussein also rejected requests by Nasser's deputy, the ostensible commander of the united Arab forces Lieutenant General Abdul Hakim Amar, to station Iraqi and Saudi troops in Jordan to confront Israel.

In the autumn of 1965, King Hussein said to Dr. Herbert in London, "I would like to see Yaakov Herzog. There have been interesting developments, and we have much to talk about."

Through contacts in Britain, Dr. Herbert immediately sent the message to Jerusalem. Herzog flew to London and made all the necessary arrangements there. He was to become accustomed to synchronizing schedules, checking on the arrivals and departures of airplanes, and inventing excuses for sudden trips abroad for any officials who took part in the secret diplomacy.

There was indeed more to arrange than there had been for the first meeting two years earlier, because this time Hussein would meet a high-level Israeli. The subjects he wished to discuss demanded more-senior representation.

The king did not disguise his pleasure when told that Israel's foreign minister herself would confer with him. Hussein knew that Golda Meir had met with his grandfather King Abdullah, and he liked the sense of historical continuity.

He told Herzog, "On the day we are proposing, I shall be in France, so let us meet in Paris this time." The Israeli agreed.

Israel's then-ambassador in France, Walter Eytan, recalls, "I was asked to locate an apartment which would be vacant for several hours." Eytan asked the Weill family, French Jews whom he knew, and without asking why, they loaned him an apartment on Rue de Raynouard in the sixteenth arrondissement.[13]

Hussein's previously scheduled visit to Paris was his cover, so his presence would not arouse suspicions. Mrs. Meir, however, flew to Paris especially for the meeting with the king. As for Eytan, who also had taken part in talks with Abdullah fifteen years earlier, there was no suggestion that he attend the meeting with Hussein. The ambassador may have felt offended, but Hussein felt safer when a smaller number of people knew his secrets. Even in Amman, only Prime Minister Tell and the king's uncle Sharif Nasser knew of the London and Paris meetings.

Hussein had learned in 1963 to trust Herzog. The king simply liked the man, and they shared an interest in British culture and traditions. The monarch with his Arabian desert roots established a rapport with the Jewish scholar. Their cordial, even friendly, relationship was to last nine years, until Herzog's death in 1972.

Herzog, in that period, accompanied every Israeli official who met the king. He was the only Israeli from whom the king would willingly receive telephone calls. Herzog was welcome in Hussein's London and Paris hotel rooms. The relationship was so good that Herzog even dared to introduce several of his British friends to the king. One of them was Marcus Sieff, of Marks and Spencer, who was brought by Herzog to meet Hussein at Dr. Herbert's home.

In Paris, in 1965, the only participants were Hussein, Golda Meir, and Yaakov Herzog.

When Hussein entered the Paris apartment, which the Israelis had found, he warmly shook hands with Mrs. Meir, and they both reminisced about the late Abdullah. The foreign minister recalled how she had dressed as an Arab woman to cross into Amman for one meeting. Hussein spoke of the love he had had, as a youth, for his grandfather.

Nostalgia was not, however, the main purpose of their meeting, and the conversation quickly turned to Middle East politics. Hussein spoke of worrying changes in the Arab world, and he expressed concern that Egypt's Nasser, the Ba'athists of Syria, and the PLO would unite in efforts to topple the Hashemite throne in Amman. The king said his Arab enemies would try to incite the Palestinians of the West Bank to rise up against him.

Hussein surprised the Israelis by returning, as though two years had not gone by, to his discussion of tanks and how Jordan needed the latest American models.

He again asked that Israel help him purchase the tanks from the United States. "They will never be used against you," the king pledged.

"We cannot rely merely on promises," Mrs. Meir replied. "We need some real guarantees."

"I am even willing," the king said, "to give my crown as a guarantee that I shall not use these tanks against you." The Israelis were surprised that he was so vehement on this point, and Hussein later offered to give his pledge in writing to the United States.

The other familiar problem discussed in Paris had to do with water rights. Mrs. Meir said Israel would continue to respect the principles of the defunct Johnston Plan, which limited the amount of water taken from the Jordan River for Israel's Negev Desert pipeline, and she added that Jordan has nothing to fear from the pipeline.

Hussein gave a fairly detailed presentation of his kingdom's plans for economic development based on water, including a canal to the east of the river and a construction project on the border with Syria. He said Israel's water usage would not be adversely affected.

The conversation was most useful, because a tacit understanding emerged that both Israel and Jordan would respect the general outlines of the United States-sponsored Johnston Plan, acting independently but taking care not to harm each other's water interests.

Near the end of the meeting, Hussein emphasized that he was doing all he could to preserve peace along his border and that his army was preventing Palestinian guerrilla incursions into Israel. He blamed Syria for the hostile commando activity.

The king asked Israel to exercise restraint and not to launch retaliatory attacks against Jordan, which he said only weakened his position within the kingdom.

Mrs. Meir and Herzog agreed to the request. At another meeting in mid–1966 in Dr. Herbert's London clinic, Herzog reaffirmed the commitment of the Israelis, at least as far as they could influence events along the border. The violence, however, grew out of control in the next two years.

Three Israeli soldiers were killed on November 11, 1966, when their "command car" was blown up by a land mine as they drove near Arad, barely a dozen miles from the Dead Sea border with Jordan. Military commanders in Tel Aviv could not be restrained from retaliating, and two days later, the Israeli army made a massive stab into Jordan. The air force and artillery provided cover for a large number of tanks, infantry, and engineers whose task was to blow up houses. The target: the West Bank town of Samu, which the Israelis called a Palestinian guerrilla base. It was Israel's biggest military move since the Sinai invasion in 1956.

Samu was flattened, and when Jordan's army attempted to intervene, twenty-one of the Arab Legionnaires were killed. The strategy was most likely aimed at giving Hussein an excuse to crack down on Palestinian guerrillas, on the grounds that they were jeopardizing peace along the border.[14] The Israeli commander of the southern region, General Yeshiyahu Gavish, said the incursion should "prompt Jordan to close the Hebron area to Fatah activities."

The Israelis had made a mistake. The Palestinians were enraged at Hussein, and incited by broadcasts from Egypt and Syria they launched a series of huge demonstrations in the West Bank. They accused the king of being unable or unwilling to protect them against Israel.[15]

Foreign diplomats began to doubt that Hussein could hold on to power in Amman. PLO leader Shukairy publicly called for a Palestinian Republic, and his supporters organized commercial strikes and riots in all the major West Bank towns including East Jerusalem.

It took two weeks for the king to restore order, by sending in the Arab Legion and giving his troops the go-ahead to open fire on rioters and impose curfews in towns and refugee camps.

The Samu attack left Hussein in a political state of shock. He had, until then, believed he could get along with the radical Arabs of Egypt, Syria, and the PLO. A visiting British correspondent had written in May, "Jordan has enjoyed a remarkable spell of political tranquility since the serious rioting and demonstrations three years ago. The benefit can be seen in the tourist boom, the well-stocked shops, the high rate of building and the newly planted fields and orchards."[16]

Samu had put an end to the relatively calm and successful period, and Hussein would never forgive the Israelis for spoiling his splendor.

"Why doesn't anyone confer and coordinate?" shouted Mordecai Gazit, deputy director general for Middle East affairs in Israel's Foreign Ministry.

"Look," replied Yehoshua Raviv, bureau chief for the new Foreign Minister Abba Eban, showing Gazit a telegram. "This is a message which we have sent to King Hussein."

Gazit quickly scanned the single page, and his hair practically stood on end. "I hope you did not send this message yet."

"I'm sorry," said Raviv, "but the telegram has already been transmitted."

Gazit recalls, "I was at a total loss for words. All I could do was shout even more angrily: 'Why doesn't anyone confer?'"

In Gazit's view, the message sent to Hussein was merely a harsh conclusion to an incident which in its entirety was inexcusable. In the five weeks before the retaliation against Samu, there had been six attacks on Israel from Jordanian territory, four from Syria, and one from Lebanon. It was clear to all that the Syrians were the initiators.

It was also fairly clear that Hussein and his government were doing what they could to prevent the guerrilla attacks. The Israelis knew that Jordan's intelligence service was infiltrating, breaking, and imprisoning Palestinian commando cells. The Jordanians even used a brilliant tactic of sending false instructions to PLO guerrillas in Syria to move south to specific locations in Jordan. They were then arrested, weapons and all.[17]

All in all, the telegram designed to soothe Hussein's anger and wounded spirit could have made matters worse. It was an insensitive message, which began with the positive words, "Israel expresses regret for the operation." It went on to say, however, that the retaliation had been launched "in an area over which Your Majesty does not exercise control."[18]

The statement would have caused great offense to Hussein, and Israel was lucky that the U.S. State Department, which had been asked to transmit the message to Amman, had read it, deemed it unhelpful, and refused to pass the telegram onward.

The damage had been done and was left unrepaired. Hussein considered the Israelis to have been treacherous, considering the pledge he had received from Golda Meir in Paris the previous year.

The king then felt freed from his own obligations. He had repeatedly promised the Israelis that if he received modern tanks, he would never station them in the West Bank. American envoys, including the veteran diplomat Averill Harriman, even showed the Israelis a written commitment to this effect from Hussein. They persuaded the Israelis, as arranged, to drop their opposition to the sale of U.S. tanks.[19]

The sale was completed, but the secret agreement was violated when war erupted on three of Israel's borders several months later. The Jordanians rolled their new M–48 Patton tanks across the bridges into the West Bank.

Why did Hussein join in the war against Israel? Why was he so willing to link his fate to the Arab nations with whom he had continually quarreled? The Israelis even attempted on June 5, 1967, after their preemptive attack wiped out Egypt's air force, to persuade Hussein to sit idly by. Prime Minister Eshkol sent a message to the king through the United Nations forces in Jerusalem that said, "We shall not initiate any action whatsoever against Jordan. However, should Jordan open hostilities, we shall resist with all our might."[20]

The Israelis sent a second telegram, warning Hussein to keep out, which was delivered by the U.S. ambassador in Amman.

The king's reply to U.N. General Odd Bull was, "They started the battle, and now they are receiving our reply by air." Jordan's air force bombed several targets in Israel on June 5, and the Arab Legion's artillery shelled West Jerusalem. Still, the Israeli political leadership hoped that Hussein was merely demonstrating solidarity with Nasser and would leave it at that.[21]

He did not stop there. He believed Nasser's unremittingly optimistic version of events in the first hours of the war and did not know about the crippling Israeli air strikes.[22] In several conversations after the war, Hussein indicated that the Egyptian General Abdul Monim Riad had practically dragged Jordan into armed combat. The general had been sent from Cairo, only on June 1, to be supreme commander of Jordan's forces. It was Riad who had Jordan open fire on Israel four days after his arrival, while Hussein remained at his palace.[23]

The king's uncle Sharif Nasser, serving as deputy commander of the armed forces, tried to keep them out of the war and advised Hussein to wait at least twelve hours to hear news from the Egyptian front. The king refused to wait.

Some analysts consider that Hussein's actions were motivated by his basic weakness. They, of course, believe that standing up against Egypt would take great courage, as though going to war against Israel did not.

The king had concluded that it was too late to avoid a war, in light of developments in the previous half a year and certainly after Egypt's Nasser ordered the UN peacekeeping troops to leave the Sinai in mid-May. The Arab world was going to war against Israel, and that left Hussein with a dilemma: either join the conflict and risk the loss of the West Bank, or refuse to join and lose the confidence and support of his people on both riverbanks—leading to the loss of his entire kingdom.

Failing to fight would expose Hussein to charges of being a traitor and a puppet of Zionism and imperialism. The rumors that he was in league with the Israelis would be seen as proved.

Hussein truly believed, with the confidence that an Arab of any social class, born in a tent or a palace, might have, that fate had taken over. And so, he sincerely told the U.S. ambassador in Amman, "The die is cast. We are at war!"[24]

His military intelligence, his army commanders, his weapons and equipment, and his battle plan were all far from prepared. Israel had a fairly easy time sweeping into East Jerusalem and then the entire West Bank. The king lost nearly half his subjects, as he had feared, but he did keep his throne.

Chapter 7

A Phone Call to the Palace

Hussein was deeply shaken by the Arab Legion's setbacks, and the look on his face spoke louder than his words ever could. The king seemed on the verge of tears all the time, in those first days after joining the attack on Israel.

The Six Day War, in fact, lasted only three days for the Jordanians. The Israelis swept the well-trained Legion out of the West Bank and East Jerusalem, and Hussein lost most of his productive, fertile soil as well as the holy places of Islam.

The chief of Jordan's military staff, General Amar Hamash, watched the king closely and was amazed to find that His Majesty did not catch even a moment's sleep. He hardly ate anything and survived those few days on herbal tea and a chain of cigarettes. He was unshaven and appeared feeble, except when he lost his ferocious temper. General Hamash had to report to Hussein almost by the minute, and he hated doing so.

The disaster, after all, was without doubt the king's fault.

On the final day of combat, Hussein conferred with his senior officers at the Damiya bridge where they watched the Legion flee across the Jordan River. Hussein came under severe pressure from General Zeid ibn-Shaker to order the remaining units to keep on fighting, to defend the West Bank.

Suddenly, above the armored vehicles and the royal escorts, two Israeli jet fighters tore through the sky and began to dive in attack formation. One of the Jordanian generals moved quickly to shield his king, and as he pushed Hussein into a ditch the officer shouted, "We have lost the battle, but we do not want to lose you, too."[1]

The king's advisers and foreign diplomats recall his striking exhaustion and pessimism on June 5, 6, and 7. Hussein had poured so much of his time and energy into building an army of which he was proud, and now it had been smashed within seventy-two hours. The gloomy truth slowly sank in: the loss of half the kingdom, the odd reality of Jordan without Jerusalem, Bethlehem, Nablus, Hebron, and Jenin.

Hussein's deeply felt sense of history left him ashamed to have lost the plaza of prayer called Haram el-Sharif, with the gold-domed mosque of Omar and the silver-domed Al-Aqsa mosque atop Jerusalem's ancient walls. He knew that his great-grandfather, the Sharif Hussein, early in the century had lost the two other sacred sites of Islam, Mecca and Medina, to his rivals in the Wahhabi sect, later known as the House of Saud. Now the present-day Hussein had allowed the Jews to capture Al-Quds, as the Arabs call Jerusalem. The name means ''The Holy.''

Hussein's defeat was somehow typical of his career. If he had only refused to join Nasser's war or at least had delayed the Arab Legion's shelling of Israeli positions until the course of the conflict was clear, Jordan might still have its West Bank. The king's natural valor, however, even in times of crisis, made it inevitable that he would join this war. He was not so weak and new to the throne as in 1956, when he sidestepped the war against Israel, and Hussein truly believed the Zionists could be taught a lesson.

Instead, the king learned the lesson of his life about his fellow Arabs. He did not attempt to hide his bitterness toward Nasser and the Syrians, whom he accused of betraying Jordan by doing nothing to help his army. Hussein would remain grateful only to Iraq, which sent troops westward across the desert to try and help the Jordanians despite Israeli air raids.

Hussein met the Egyptian leader several times in the next three years, however, and never bothered to demand an explanation for the calamity of 1967. He did not even ask why Nasser had led him astray for thirty-six hours, from the outbreak of hostilities until the admission that Egypt's air force had been destroyed by Israel's swift, preemptive air strikes.

The king knew it was his own fault for having swallowed Nasser's pan-Arab line. It was a mistake he was determined never to repeat.

Broadcasting to his nation on June 7, Hussein said, ''We have fought with heroism and honor. One day the Arabs will recognize the role Jordan played in this war. Our soldiers have defended every inch of our earth with their precious blood. It is not yet dry, but our country honors the stain. They were not afraid in the face of the total superiority of the enemy's air power, which surprised and destroyed the Egyptian air force, on which we were relying. What is done is done. My heart breaks when I think of the loss of all our fallen soldiers.

''My brothers, I seem to belong to a family which, according to the will of Allah, must suffer and make sacrifices for its country without end. Our calamity is greater than anyone could have imagined.''

Many politicians in the world, and even in Israel, felt sympathy for the young king. Others, however, felt he was developing into a hard luck case who brought misfortune on himself and then blamed everyone but himself. For weeks, after the war, Hussein continued to claim that Israel had benefited from American and British air cover.

Israeli intelligence intercepted a telephone conversation between Hussein and Nasser on the second day of the war, in which the Egyptian president allegedly said, "Shall we say the U.S. and England? Or just the U.S.?"

Hussein: "The U.S. and England."

Nasser: "Does Britain have aircraft carriers?"

Hussein's reply was not heard clearly, but he probably reminded the Egyptian that the British have small carriers and bases on Cyprus.

Nasser: "Good. King Hussein will announce it, and I will declare it, too."

The king, years later, confirmed this account.[2]

Israel's radio monitors also leaked the transcript of a conversation on the first day of the war, in which Nasser fed false information to a seemingly naive Hussein to draw Jordan into the conflict.[3]

The reports on the Hashemite ruler and his failures were reaching Prime Minister Levi Eshkol in Jerusalem, who felt he had made an honest effort to dissuade Hussein from entering the war. Now the Israeli leader saw the king as little more than "paralyzed and in a state of shock," according to his widow Mrs. Miriam Eshkol.[4]

The Israeli first lady's diary, based on what her husband was telling her at the time, shows how the official assessment that the king was incapable of action made it impossible to advance toward a peace settlement in the immediate aftermath of the war, on the so-called seventh day. Eshkol and his top ministers were ignoring, however, their own contribution to the political paralysis in Amman. The Israeli people and their leaders were in an unprecedented state of euphoria, based in part on the sheer relief of having survived an onslaught from the united Arab nations but even more on the astoundingly quick victory scored by the Israel Defense Forces (IDF).

"*Kol ha-Kavod le-Zahal*" became a popular slogan for many years. Literally meaning "All Respect to the IDF," this Hebrew expression of praise also signaled the general belief at the time that only military solutions could be found in the Middle East.

The mood in Israel was the opposite of what it had been before the war. Fear was abolished, and Israelis began to believe that time was on their side. The Arabs would now have to beg for peace.

The new Defense Minister Moshe Dayan, with his black eye patch, was a worldwide symbol of Israel's triumph, and he signaled the new attitude by saying he was now waiting for "a telephone call from Hussein." But the telephone on his desk, in the defense ministry building in the fortified Tel Aviv compound called the *Kirya* (the Town Center), did not ring.

It took Hussein several weeks to recover and accept that he had to wipe away the past and confront his truncated kingdom's problems. First, he had to consider Jordan's economy, badly damaged by the war's expenditures and the loss of productive land. While Britain and the United States rejected his appeals for financial aid, Saudi Arabia and Kuwait agreed to help.

The second and third aspects of Jordan's crisis were intertwined: how to live with Israel's occupation of the West Bank and how to preserve the Hashemite throne when the Palestinian population on the East Bank had grown and would swell further.

The victorious Israelis went on the record with an offer—or perhaps a demand—to negotiate face-to-face with their Arab neighbors. In principle, this should not have been a problem for Hussein, who had decided from his early days on the throne that the Arab world would have to reconcile itself to the existence of a Jewish state in its midst. After the most disastrous six days of his life, the king was even more convinced that the solution to the problem of Israel could not be found through warfare.

The king began to speak with American and British diplomats about the need for a peace settlement—"a just peace," as he called it—which would return to the Arabs their lost territories. Hussein also called for an Arab summit to discuss possible solutions to the conflict with Israel. It was quickly clear, however, that the Hashemite king would not negotiate and would not sign a peace treaty without the support of other Arab states.

Hussein also learned from the western diplomats about a secret decision made by the Israeli cabinet in the wake of the war. The cabinet was an odd national unity coalition, in which the traditional Labor party leaders had brought the nationalist Herut party and its leader Menachem Begin into the government for the sake of wartime morale. A four-day debate, in which Eshkol presided but could scarcely be said to have dominated, was marked by sharp differences.

Begin lost no time in proposing that the West Bank and Gaza be annexed as part of the ancient lands of biblical Israel.

Defense Minister Dayan did not jump to that conclusion, but he did declare privately that the West Bank should not be returned to Hussein.

Deputy Prime Minister Yigal Allon also spoke about Hussein in negative terms, indicating that the views of the tiny Hashemite dynasty need not be considered paramount in a regional solution. "We should stop any nostalgia we may have for the Hashemites," Allon said to his cabinet colleagues. "Abdullah screwed us. Let's stop being Hussein's guardian."[5]

The Allon Plan, which is well known to Middle East historians and analysts, called for the Jordan Valley and the strategic heights of the West Bank to be retained by Israel while the densely populated cities and villages could be returned to Arab jurisdiction.

What is less well known is that in 1967 Allon proposed to the cabinet that Palestinian refugees be persuaded or somehow transferred without bloodshed out of the West Bank and Gaza, preferably to foreign countries.

Finance Minister Pinhas Sapir suggested that efforts be made to resettle the Palestinians in Syria and Iraq.

Long before the word became fashionable in the 1978 Camp David Accords, the notion of "autonomy" can be found in secret cabinet minutes. A Swiss-style system of "cantons" was also proposed, to allow Arabs to run some of their own affairs in an area still under Israeli military occupation. Eshkol gave his powerful endorsement to Tourism Minister Moshe Kol's vision of Arab autonomy in Samaria, roughly the northern half of the West Bank, but the prime minister did not rule out the possibility of returning the entire territory to Jordan. Only Jerusalem was an exception: the eastern sector, comprising the Old City, had been "liberated" by Israel and annexed a few days after the war by Knesset legislation.

Behind closed doors, Dayan, Allon, and even Prime Minister Eshkol considered the possibility of ignoring Hussein while negotiating directly with Palestinians. Eshkol assigned a working committee of the Mossad intelligence agency to explore the mood among Arab leaders in the newly conquered West Bank and Gaza. The committee's chairman was David Kimche, a young and talented operative who would rise in the next decade to the number-two post in the Mossad.

Kimche and his team met with mayors, wealthy merchants, and intellectuals in the occupied territories, in the weeks following the Six Day War. Their report to Eshkol suggested that Israel could take advantage of "the shock of the humiliation" among the Arabs and their new, close "encounter with the Israelis," by engaging in discussions with prominent Palestinians.[6]

Dayan was hearing similar views from the military administrators he had appointed in the territories. The Israelis took special interest in two local Arabs: Sheikh Jaabri, the mayor of Hebron, and Hamadi Kenaan, mayor of the West Bank's largest town, Nablus. It was the first serious thought the Israelis gave to pursuing a "Palestinian option" rather than the "Jordanian option" for a peace settlement on their eastern front.

Another study team in the prime minister's office, under economics Professor Michael Bruno, recommended that Israel put together an international fund to rehouse the Palestinians who were living in squalid camps. This, the team argued, would help heal the damage that had been done on a human level. This could clear the way for a dialogue between Israelis and Palestinians.

Even the moderates, such as Foreign Minister Abba Eban, while stressing the need to renew dialogue with King Hussein, were unwilling to return all his land to him. A seemingly unbridgeable difference of views was inevitable between the Israelis and the Arab states, but here were differences of concept and ideology, which emerged in the first weeks after the 1967 war and continue to haunt Israel more than two decades later.

The secret resolutions passed by the cabinet, on June 15 and 19, 1967, said, "Israel insists on the signing of a peace treaty." At this early stage, the ministers agreed that peace treaties with Egypt and Syria could be signed "on the basis of the international border" when "the Sinai and the Golan Heights are demilitarized," but "the Gaza Strip will be made part of Israel."

Because of the cabinet's disagreements over the future of the West Bank, notably the refusal of Dayan and Begin to consider ceding the territory, the future of the West Bank and potential negotiations with Jordan were not mentioned at all in the resolutions.[7]

Hussein learned of Israel's stubbornness on the eastern front—his side of the Middle East conflict—and was further enraged by the official annexation of East Jerusalem. He was, therefore, in no rush to pursue an immediate settlement with the Israelis.

Prime Minister Eshkol did, however, try to send the king several messages through Yaakov Herzog and Dr. Emanuel Herbert in London. These were oral hints that it could be worth Jordan's while to negotiate with Israel, because the West Bank might well be on the bargaining table. There was even a brief meeting between Hussein and Herzog in early July 1967.[8] Seduction is often a slow process, and it could be said that Hussein had reason to believe that the Israeli leaders' hearts were not in it anyway—not in any mood to compromise, that is.

The Arab summit went ahead, however, convening in the Sudanese capital, Khartoum, on August 29, 1967. The Arab world appeared to be united in defeat and in anger, but even that unity was incomplete because both Syria and Algeria refused to attend the meeting.

Still, diplomats recall that Hussein was optimistic, that he was breaking out of his postwar depression. The king had been promised by Egypt's Nasser that he would support a call to regain the captured territory from Israel through diplomatic means.

Once Nasser felt the mood of the conference, however, he chose instead to join the Arab radicals in hopes of controlling them. The final resolutions of the Khartoum summit were quite definite, but they did not resemble Hussein's hopes. The declaration emphasized "the rights of the Palestinians in their own land," insisted that "the results of aggression be wiped away" and that Israel's forces withdraw from every inch of captured territory."

Khartoum is truly remembered, however, for "the three noes: 'no' to peace with Israel, 'no' to recognition of Israel and 'no' to negotiations with Israel." All hope of a quick and peaceful resolution to the Middle East dispute, after the Six Day War, thus seemed to disappear.

Israel's leaders felt they would have to stand firm, holding on to the territories for the indefinite future while the radical Arab world left no room for diplomatic maneuvers.

Hussein, however, felt he had a little bit of space to pursue a negotiated solution. Visiting London after the Arab summit, he tried to persuade his British friends that all was not lost for Middle East moderates. Prime Minister Harold Wilson reviewed the Khartoum declaration with despair.

The king said it was merely a matter of translation and interpretation. Negating the possibility of diplomatic recognition did not mean there could be no "recognition in principle." As for refusing to consider "peace," the king pointed out to the British that Khartoum had said "no" to the Arabic word *sulha*, which would suggest a complete settlement and reconciliation, but did not reject *salaam*, which would be an official state of peace—that is, the absence of war. He said there was still no choice but to pursue the narrower *salaam* with Israel, and insisted that saying no to peace was not the final word. Wilson, still unconvinced, suggested sarcastically that the Arabs might mean peace with "no kissing."[9]

Hussein could not hide his disappointment at the Arab summit's outcome, but he continued to tell the west that the resolutions should not be considered too seriously. He was extremely grateful when, in November 1967, the British drew up United Nations Security Council Resolution 242 and secured its passage.

The resolution survived as the centerpiece of superpower policy in the Middle East, calling for all states to live in peace within secure and recognized boundaries but controversially referring to the Palestinians only as "refugees." Here, too, there was an ambiguity linked to translation: the French text of 242 suggested Israel should withdraw from "the territories" it had captured, but the English language does not require the word "the" and thus the Israelis said they were only required to return part of the captured land in exchange for a lasting peace.

In any event, King Hussein welcomed the worldwide acceptance of the notion of exchanging peace for territories, and it was against this background that he agreed to renew his secret contacts with Israel.

Hussein had two more good reasons to do so. The American administration of President Lyndon B. Johnson, which was stepping up its interest in the Middle East, passed a top-secret document to the king. In it, the U.S. ambassador to the United Nations, Arthur Goldberg, pledged that the United States would wield its influence on behalf of a reasonable settlement in the region. Goldberg said he could not promise that Jordan would regain all its land, but he said the United States would do its best to arrange a fair solution.[10]

Hussein also learned that Israel's attempts to negotiate with local Palestinians had led nowhere. Mayors Jaabri and Kenaan were not willing to discuss any settlement that would be based on the continued presence of Israeli troops in the captured territories. Even the Israeli politicians who opposed pursuing a Jordanian option had to admit that there was no realistic Palestinian option for negotiations. The king felt that the Israelis would most likely approach him. And they did.

In Jerusalem, Moshe Dayan and the other Israeli leaders realized that the telephone call from Hussein they publicly claimed to be awaiting was not likely to come. After consulting his senior ministers, Prime Minister Eshkol decided that Israel would make the first contact. Passing messages through Dr. Herbert, Yaakov Herzog arranged a meeting with Hussein for May 3, 1968.

Herzog prepared an unsigned, secret memorandum for the prime minister, which set out Israel's goals:

- to assess the possibilities of coexistence with Jordan, using the existing cease-fire agreement as the basis for an open and separate peace;
- to establish whether Hussein is willing and able to conduct separate negotiations with Israel, and whether he would sign a peace treaty even without the support of other Arab states;
- to clarify whether the king would agree to the demilitarization of the West Bank;
- to see whether Hussein would agree to minor border rectifications;
- to test the king's attitude toward Jerusalem remaining united and under Israeli sovereignty;
- to explore ways of housing the Palestinian refugees through cooperation among Israel, Jordan, and international bodies;
- to begin setting up, even before a formal peace treaty, temporary systems for preventing terrorism, quick communications in case of border tension, and economic cooperation;
- to agree that Israel, without Hussein's agreement, would not change the status of the West Bank's residents;
- to help improve the international and regional standing of the king; and
- to encourage the Palestinians to work for an agreement between Israel and Jordan.

London, again, was chosen as the venue for the secret meeting in May, but there was one difference: instead of meeting the king at the Devonshire Place clinic of his personal physician, the talks would take place in Dr. Herbert's private home on Langford Place in the St. John's Wood neighborhood. It is only a ten- or fifteen-minute drive from the clinic to the house.

St. John's Wood is a wealthy section of northwest London, which was known in the nineteenth century as the "Love Nests' Quarter," because the great and powerful tended to find accommodation for their mistresses in the houses and apartments there. The residents in the twentieth century, however, tended to be diplomats, highly successful merchants, bankers, and doctors.

Number 1 Langford Place was home to the Herberts, only a few blocks north of the huge Regent's Park and just down the block from Abbey Road, made famous by the recording studio used by the Beatles among other musicians. The redbrick house is an elegant corner property, surrounded by small lawns and fronted by a crescent-shaped driveway of pebbles.

The Israelis sent Foreign Minister Eban and Herzog, who two years before had left his foreign ministry post to become the director general of the prime minister's office in Jerusalem. Eshkol himself could not attend, because his right-wing coalition partner Menachem Begin threatened to resign if a summit at the highest levels was held. Begin was willing to allow Eban to represent Israel, on condition that the foreign minister not be empowered to reach any agreements with Hussein. Begin was supported by Dayan, who was not a Herut member but agreed with the party's refusal to consider returning the West Bank to Jordan.

Organizing the meeting in May was more difficult than before the Six Day War, because tight security on Middle East dignitaries was imposed with the increase in the threat of Palestinian terrorism. Israeli officials simply had many more bodyguards than they used to have, and Hussein also began to feel the Palestinian guerrilla threat. The king was known to carry a pistol, even on his foreign journeys.

Hussein's personal guards were credited with preventing several attempts on his life, and their number was also increased after the war. The king was constantly surrounded by a ring of armed and trustworthy men. Most of them were recruited from the Beduin Arab village of Shubaq, south of Amman, outstanding for its loyalty to the Hashemite throne.

In addition, rapid developments had been made in the area of wiretapping and electronic eavesdropping. The telephone became an instrument of suspicion, and keeping clandestine plans secret was far from assured. Despite advice from security experts on both sides to avoid using the telephone, Herzog developed an almost amusing reputation for not being cautious in his long-distance calls.

While making an overseas call from London, Paris, or Washington to one or another official in Israel to report on the arrangements for a meeting, Herzog used a few simple code phrases; he seemed to believe that was all the security needed in such conversations. At times he would refer to Hussein as the *Yanuka*, the "little boy." He was also known to say down the line to Israel, "There was a contact with the boy king—you know the little one, the one whose grandfather was murdered." Herzog never supposed, it is said, that foreign intelligence services were listening and easily figured out what was occurring.

The British secret service, MI5, certainly knew about the clandestine meetings. Eavesdropping on the telephone calls of foreign officials is known to have been a regular MI5 habit, and the agency's contacts with Dr. Herbert are likely to have kept Britain's government in the picture, too. It was again Prime Minister Wilson who exercised his wit, when he once winked his eye and remarked to Abba Eban, "It certainly is interesting that you and King Hussein have the same physician!"[11]

The king also had to make excuses to the British for his brief disappearances, as Scotland Yard would always assign Special Branch officers to protect the visiting monarch. Two British bodyguards accompanied the Jordanian security team, but Hussein kept his personal schedule in London from all of them. They would enter their cars, and only then would he say, "I am not feeling well." His driver would naturally take him to Dr. Herbert, where Hussein would ask the British detectives to wait outside. "The doctor is treating me for some sensitive problems," the king would say, and the policemen would obey.

Hussein knew that the mere fact that he was meeting Israelis was an invitation to murder at the hands of radical Arabs, and so he took extraordinary precautions. He kept to a minimum the number of people who knew about the secret encounters or who might suspect the truth. Having received so many threats and after actual assassination attempts, Hussein himself was highly suspicious. He confined even the daily affairs of running his kingdom to a very few ministers, aides, and military officers. Hussein formed some unusually strong friendships with those whom he truly trusted, but only a select elite were told of the contacts with Israelis.

An Israeli analyst assessed Hussein's top team.

People originating from the East Bank generally held the key positions in the Jordanian Establishment. The political leadership which actively makes decisions, with the king at the pinnacle, is extremely limited. It includes only a minority of the cabinet, such as the prime minister, the interior minister with his responsibility for domestic security, and the information minister. It is important to underline that the defense and foreign ministers are not in this group.

Unlike most Western countries, the foreign minister in Jordan limits himself to standard diplomacy as directed by the king. The defense minister's responsibilities are also limited mainly to administrative functions and do not involve policy-making. The political leadership also includes a so-called "Friends of the King" group, the members of which occasionally hold official posts but not necessarily.

The Jordanian élite was and remains thin in the number of leaders of stature who can take part with the king in the permanent burden of running an administration in conditions of continuous pressure and crisis.[12]

Members of the Rifai family are notable in the limited group of trusted royal aides. Abdul Mon'im el-Rifai was one of Hussein's prime ministers. The elder Samir el-Rifai, despite his Palestinian origins, was a top aide to both Abdullah and Hussein. Samir crossed the river into the East Bank only in the 1920s but gained Abdullah's full confidence and became an expert in picking up any whispers of civil unrest among the population.

Zeid el-Rifai, Samir's son, inherited absolute loyalty to the throne and was suckled on the difficult facts of Jordanian political life. He was born in Amman on November 27, 1936. Because his father was so involved in royal affairs, Zeid became known to the young Prince Hussein at an early age. The prince was only a year older, and the two men studied at the same primary school before going to Victoria College together in Alexandria, Egypt.

Their paths diverged for a few years, when Hussein became king and Zeid went to the United States to complete his education. Rifai earned a bachelor's degree in government at Harvard in 1957 and then a master's degree in law and international relations at Columbia University. The result of his early years is that, like King Hussein, Zeid el-Rifai is a pro-western opponent of socialism and radical movements of any kind.

Returning home in the late 1950s, Rifai joined the Jordanian foreign service but within a year was assigned to the prime minister's office in Amman. He quickly displayed another quality that brought him close to the young king: courage. On Monday, August 29, 1960, Prime Minister Haza el-Magalli asked Rifai to bring him a packet of documents from the adjoining room. Rifai barely managed to close the door behind him when a huge explosion destroyed the office. The prime minister and ten of his aides were killed. Rifai was saved by a miracle—not the last time in his life—and his calm and measured behavior impressed Hussein, who rushed to the scene of the terrorist blast.

A return to the diplomatic service included postings to London, Beirut, Cairo, and the United Nations for Rifai. In 1964, he was appointed the chief aide to the director of the royal court in Amman, and within two years Rifai became chief of protocol.

After the Six Day War, Rifai was chosen by Hussein to be his personal aide. Rifai had become the king's confidant through the years, and the position was now official. Through the Palestinian uprising of September 1970, Rifai was at Hussein's side, along with Prime Minister Wasfi el-Tell.

Rifai's courage continued to encourage the king and strengthened their friendship. They were almost blood brothers, as they together survived not only the civil war but other attempts on their lives.

While serving as ambassador to Britain in the summer of 1971, Rifai's Daimler with its diplomatic license plates came under fire in London from a Palestinian "Black September" gunman. Rifai was wounded in one hand, but he lay on the floor and calmly told his driver to hurry up and get away. Israelis who have met him have noticed his dislocated left hand.

Rifai returned to Amman in 1973, and after holding several cabinet jobs served twice as prime minister. But he is in that informal "Friends of the King" club, meaning that whether he is holding a formal post or not Rifai is among the first to be consulted by King Hussein on all subjects.

As early as 1968, the king did not go alone to the meeting with Eban and Herzog at Dr. Herbert's London home. Zeid el-Rifai was there, too.

The two Israelis were already waiting in the wood-paneled dining room, just to the left after entering the doctor's residence. Abba Eban could barely conceal his excitement and immediately greeted Hussein as "Your Majesty." The king responded, "Mr. Minister." The graciousness persisted through the three hours of conversation that evening, and every few sentences Eban would remember to say "Your Majesty." He recalls that Hussein was polite, but also very regal, taking himself very seriously. After the first hour, the king relaxed slightly and permitted himself a few smiles.

The aides, Rifai and Herzog, barely interfered in the conversation of the principals. They said little and acted only as notetakers.

Eban presented Israel's concept of the possible outlines of a peace settlement. He said that even after an agreement, while the Israelis would return most of the West Bank to Jordan they would insist on retaining certain strategic positions that were practically devoid of population.

The king had done his homework, however, based on what he had learned from western diplomats about the disagreements within Israel's cabinet. Hussein asked whether Eban was authorized to deal on behalf of the entire government.

The foreign minister knew his limitations and answered, "We do not have a cabinet decision on this subject, but the prime minister will be able to pass a resolution of this kind.''

Eban's suggestion was basically for minor changes in the pre–1967 border and Hussein said he would not rule this out so long as the principle of ''mutuality'' applied. Perhaps land could be exchanged. Israel might keep parts of the West Bank, but would then have to cede small sections of Israeli territory to Jordan. The king insisted on ''mutuality,'' even if it was ''swapping a mouse for an elephant.''[13]

The king also showed interest in acquiring part of the Gaza Strip, which Israel had captured from Egypt. This could provide a Mediterranean seaport for Jordan.

The two sides agreed to meet again soon, so that the king could receive Israel's replies. Eban flew home and immediately tried to persuade the cabinet to approve some of the principles suggested at the London talks. But the ministers who are remembered as ''hawks,'' including Menachem Begin and Moshe Dayan, attacked the very first principle that Eban had suggested to Hussein: that Israel would return most of the West Bank to Jordan.

The general feeling in postwar Israel, with the added territorial buffers captured in 1967, was that time was on Israel's side. Yaacov Herzog, in his personal diary, noted that the cabinet was in no rush to reach a settlement and was not crushed by the Arab summit resolutions in Khartoum. Herzog wrote, ''In any event, there is no feeling here of disappointment or frustration that the Arabs rejected all notions of negotiations for peace. The recognition is growing that the current situation, as long as it continues, is good for us.''[14]

Eban, urging his cabinet colleagues to give up territories in exchange for peace, was in a small minority. Trying to stand against the prevailing political winds, the foreign minister warned that a wider hurricane could follow. Just before Prime Minister Eshkol left on a trip to Washington, Eban said that if Hussein asked for negotiations but Israel refused, ''The Americans will know about it.''[15]

The euphoria of victory grew, meanwhile, with increasing celebrations of ''the return of the Israelites'' to biblical sites that happened to be in the West Bank. Few paid attention to Eban's warnings, and in international forums the foreign minister was achieving unprecedented success in explaining Israel's policies to the outside world. He could not be seen to be a dissident at home.

The Israeli political scene was changing, too. A dream of the Zionist Labor movement came true with the establishment, in January 1968, of a united Labor party. The Rafi faction, including Moshe Dayan and Shimon Peres, and the Ahdut Ha'avoda (Labor Federation) of Yigal Allon and others, merged with the mainstream Mapai.

Mapai leaders Levi Eshkol, Golda Meir, and Pinhas Sapir were relative moderates who were interested in making a deal with Jordan. They were now under pressure from within their expanded party, however. Dayan and his Rafi people put Israel's security first, above all other interests.

The cost of the historic unity of Israeli workers' representatives was high: diplomatic paralysis. Prime Minister Eshkol was asked, at the time, why Israel did not make a new peace initiative. He replied, "I cannot initiate any plan of that kind when the Labor Federation is on my left and Rafi on my right."[16]

The influence of domestic politics on Israel's foreign policy could also be seen in smaller, trivial matters. Before the second postwar meeting with Hussein, when the king was to hear Israel's answers, the Labor Federation ministers in the nominally united Labor party insisted that one of their own join the clandestine delegation. The Allon people said they could not put their total confidence in Eban. Eshkol reluctantly nodded and said Deputy Prime Minister Allon would take part in the next secret meeting.

Dayan, on the other hand, refused to take part in the talks with Jordan. "Hussein cannot make peace," the one-eyed war hero said to Eshkol and Eban. "If I go, you'll be sorry, because I would just blow up the talks. I wouldn't maneuver around like Eban. I don't know how to play those games."[17] In the end, the one who really would not play the game, however, was Hussein.

And so, around the end of September 1968, a three-man delegation set out from Israel without any public announcement: Eban, Allon, and Herzog. Hussein was waiting for them at Dr. Herbert's house in St. John's Wood, accompanied only by Zeid el-Rifai. Allon knew Arabic from his early days living among Arabs in Galilee, and immediately monopolized the conversation—which was much to the king's liking. Allon had also studied at Oxford and so possessed an impressive grasp of British culture, which also appealed to Hussein. Their first handshake in London was the beginning of a ten-year relationship, which can even be called a friendship.

Allon's view of Jordan, as a result, almost immediately softened. It was he, ironically, who had proposed to Prime Minister Ben-Gurion in 1949 that the Israelis conquer the West Bank and seize it from Abdullah. Allon had said the Palestinian Arab residents would almost all leave of their own accord. In private conversations, he was known for phrases such as "I vote no-confidence in the Hashemites." Even after the Six Day War, he wanted the government to find ways to encourage "the departure of the refugees."[18] Allon decided later that the road to Israeli security should be paved by way of a compromise with Amman.

The famous Allon Plan for peace and security through compromise was formally submitted to Israel's cabinet on July 27, 1967, but surprisingly it was never officially endorsed. It was, however, an acknowledged offer from Israel should Jordan ever care to accept it.

The deputy prime minister declared, "I propose to set the River Jordan and the line cutting midway through the Dead Sea as the borderline between Israel and the Kingdom of Jordan." This was not a simple call for annexation, however. "So that the border will be practical and not mere theory," Allon continued, "I believe a strip of land between 10 and 15 kilometers wide, the length of the Jordan Valley up to the Dead Sea, should be connected to Israel itself. North of the Dead Sea, the border should run toward the West, so as to avoid Jericho and extend to the northern boundary of Jerusalem so as to include the highway from Jerusalem to the Dead Sea within Israel."[19]

By judiciously drawing his proposed border, Allon estimated that the expanded territory of Israel would take in only around 15,000 additional Palestinian Arabs, not including the tens of thousands in the already annexed East Jerusalem.

Allon was a respected military strategist, and he knew that on security grounds alone his was not the best possible solution for Israel's interests. Defense Minister Dayan's ideas for commanding the West Bank's heights by building fortresses in the Samarian hills were more attractive on military considerations, but Allon believed they would stand in the way of a peace agreement.

Perhaps he was deluding himself, but Allon felt that his own plan—the inclusion of a strip along the river in Israel's sovereign territory—would give his nation at least some new security, would preserve the vital Jewish majority in Israel, and would not close the door to peace.

Even though Hussein seemed positively taken with Allon's personality, the king "did not very much like" the deputy prime minister's proposals. Allon had brought a map of the area to the doctor's house in London. He immediately treated Hussein to a personal presentation of the Allon Plan. The geographical exposition did not help.

To put it mildly, the king poured cold water on the plan and its author. Hussein, in fact, could barely contain his anger. He said he had returned to London to hear Israel's replies to the ideas previously discussed with Abba Eban, including mutual exchanges of territory to modify the pre–1967 border, and now he was forced to listen to the details of an entirely different plan.

Hussein was off on a tirade, the kind that the Israelis had read about in intelligence reports, and his temper flared even more as he glared at Allon, still standing and holding his pointer over the map he had brought from Jerusalem.

The monarch's objections centered on the conversion of the "algebraic" proposals of a land exchange into pointers and zones on a map that added up as follows: the vital valley along the river remaining in Israel's hands, along with all the important hilltops, totaling some 30 percent of the West Bank. Israel offered none of its own sovereign territory. Hussein seemed to like arithmetic, but he did not like this equation at all.

Allon hastened to say that his proposals were not on a "take it or leave it" basis, and he attempted to persuade Hussein to examine the Israeli map more closely. Hussein was not interested.

Rifai, at this point, voiced his reaction. Also reflecting a mathematical view of history, he said angrily that 30 percent was the precise proportion of Finland absorbed by the Soviet Union in World War II. "His Majesty will not be able to accept any part of such a proposal," the royal minister said.

Hussein and Rifai behaved as "good-guy bad-guy" interrogators often do, as the king spoke only in positive terms when stating Jordan's requirements while Rifai came forward with the negative statements.

Thus it was Rifai who told the Israelis that it was totally unacceptable that they had publicly offered to return all captured lands to Egypt and Syria in exchange for peace but would retain part—a large section—of Jordanian territory.

The king, in turn, demanded not 70 percent of his lost land but the entire West Bank and East Jerusalem, giving no regard to Israel's annexation of the Old City. Unlike Allon, however, Hussein did not state that his views were only an opening position.

On a brighter note, the king emphasized the risk he was taking merely by meeting with Israeli officials. Hussein even seemed on the verge of tears as he said, "I always remember in my eyes and my spirit the sight of my grandfather falling in his own blood and rolling down the steps of the mosque." He said he needed to regain East Jerusalem, the site of Abdullah's murder.

"I am an Arab nationalist," the king stressed. "I would prefer a Middle East without Israel. But because I see no chance of that, and because we have to deal with reality as it is, we must reach an agreement. I am ready to do so, but not at any price."

The Israelis, especially Allon, were surprised by Hussein's honesty. Recalling what Dayan had said back in Jerusalem, they realized that the king also preferred to speak frankly rather than playing games.

Allon tried to rescue the meeting from apparent failure. He reminded the monarch that Israel was not issuing an ultimatum. "Perhaps you have other proposals?" Allon asked, still gesturing at the map with his pointer.

"No, we will not enter into a detailed discussion of your totally unacceptable ideas," Rifai said.

The conversation went on for hours, but the tension lifted when Mrs. Herbert served some refreshments in her dining room to the guests of whom she would never speak. Just before the two delegations parted, Hussein reminded the Israelis that he felt himself too weak in the Arab world to be the first to make peace with Israel. His Arab brethren would be angry, and he specifically mentioned Egypt's Nasser, "who might send his killers."

The king advised Allon and Eban to try and reach a settlement, first, with Egypt, the largest and most influential of the Arab states.

Hussein and Rifai returned, disappointed, to Amman. They could already feel that their main aim, the recovery of the entire West Bank and East Jerusalem, was gradually slipping from their grasp. The Palestinians, in the meantime, were building their own power centers—angry guerrilla groups with no loyalty to the Hashemite throne. The PLO, formally founded in East Jerusalem in 1964, was growing like a dark shadow over Hussein and his authority.

After the war, the Israelis were busy constructing what they came to call "facts in the field": new neighborhoods in East Jerusalem, the Jewish city of Kiryat Arba alongside Hebron, and new settlements in the Jordan Valley.

Allon, Eban, and Herzog duly reported to the cabinet in Jerusalem that Hussein had said no to the Allon Plan and the very principle of territorial compromise, but they did not suggest that the king's rejection was final and immutable. The glimmer of hope they saw was based simply on the fact that he had not slammed the door on future contacts with Israel.

The exchange of views did continue, through the ever-useful Dr. Herbert. Eban was never ill when he visited London, but he frequently visited the doctor to receive news from Amman. He once even left a gift with the doctor for Hussein: Eban's own book, *My People*. On the advice of the secret intelligence agency Mossad, the foreign minister was careful enough not to autograph the tome, knowing that the king might be too embarrassed to place it on the bookshelves of his library. At their next meeting, Hussein told Eban that he had enjoyed the book, which was about the history of the Jews, very much.

The encouraging etiquette and grace could not change one basic fact: the immediate aftermath of the Six Day War was not, in any way, progress toward a lasting peace. The two meetings in London in 1968, from a historical perspective, are especially important because they reflected all that continued to be typical of the secret relationship between Jordan and Israel. In the minds of Israeli officials, they certainly set the pattern for Hussein's behavior—his willingness to talk in private, yet his fear of an open agreement; his demand for the return of all captured territories; the keenly felt threat to his life from radicals in the Arab world; and the recognition that the key to Middle East peace lay in Cairo.

The 1968 meetings also demonstrated to Hussein that the Israelis were strong and feeling confident after their victory. A better word for what he saw, perhaps, was arrogance. The king was also gaining an instinctive feel, from afar, for Israel's internal political struggles and learning how they limited any flexibility in foreign policy. He quickly learned that territorial compromise was not easy for the Israelis to offer, but without wider Arab backing Hussein had to demand every inch of his territory.

The September talks in the doctor's house were the final, serious attempt for at least twenty years to reach an overall settlement between Israel and Jordan. The Israelis accepted Hussein's advice, after putting it aside for a decade, that a peace treaty would first be possible with Egypt. They could only cling to their assumption that Jordan would be the second Arab state to sign a peace accord.

Jerusalem and Amman chose not to waste their energy on impossible goals, concentrating instead on practical questions and solutions that make life easier for everyone. Hussein, Eban, and Allon had begun a process of "regularizing" a most irregular situation: the military occupation by one nation of land ostensibly belonging to another country with which it shared many interests.

The two nations pursued the best path they could see, after the mixed record of 1968, to transform their relationship. No longer enemies, they became good neighbors. But they preferred that their other neighbors not know about it.

Chapter 8

"Operation Lift"

"My, what a nice toy you've got!" General Amar Hamash, chief of staff of the Jordanian army, liked the weight in his hand and admired what struck him as an unusual weapon.

"Go on, take it, it's yours," Israel's chief of staff General Chaim Bar-Lev replied with a smile, handing his cigar clipper to the Arab.

The two military chiefs, wearing remarkably similar business suits, sat alongside each other, in the deep, slightly squeaky easy chairs of Dr. Herbert's examination room in London's St. John's Wood. Relegated to the harder, metal chairs were Jordan's Prime Minister Rifai and Israel's Yaakov Herzog.

The generals were getting along beautifully. The small room, its one long wall lined with bookshelves, quickly filled with the well-known odor of affluence as the two men enjoyed their Cuban cigars. Each time Bar-Lev clipped the end off, thinking how this was far more elegant than biting and spitting, he could see Hamash's eyes following him.

They had agreed that there is nothing like a Havana when it comes to a good smoke, but they had agreed on nothing when turning to the subjects that brought them to London in October 1968.

This time, the Jordanians had requested the meeting, which took place only a short time after King Hussein had his talks with Allon and Eban. The monarch was worried about border tensions and the Palestinians whose guerrilla activities he could not control. The Israelis were using their own means of control, and just a few days before the chiefs of staff got together in London, Israel's artillery shelled the outskirts of Irbid, a city in northern Jordan. Bar-Lev recalls: "I ordered our artillery to fire just four shells as a warning, but this was the first time we ever shelled a city."[1]

Bar-Lev was referring to military policy on the eastern front with Jordan, because the Israelis did stage such attacks on Egyptian cities during the "war of attrition," which followed the Six Day War. President Nasser sent commandos into the Israeli-occupied Sinai, triggering an unending series of lethal artillery exchanges over the Suez Canal. The Israeli positions on the eastern bank of the canal formed the "Bar-Lev Line," and it was becoming painfully expensive, in manpower and munitions, to maintain it.

Israel's response came in the form of massive shelling and air raids on cities on the western bank, the African mainland of Egypt. Life became so unbearable that the people of Port Said, Ismailia, and Suez City fled inland. The Israelis did not want a second war of attrition, but their shelling of Irbid was intended as a warning to the Jordanians that their cities, too, could become ghost towns.

It was just as the 1967 war ended that Yasser Arafat's Fatah organization and Dr. Georges Habash's Popular Front for the Liberation of Palestine (PFLP) joined other fedayeen in declaring a guerrilla war, which the world would call "terrorism" but they would call "the popular struggle." The objective: to "liberate" the West Bank from the Zionists. Ideological support came from Arab revolutionary governments in Syria and Algeria and, more distantly, from China and even North Vietnam.

The most important faction was Fatah, founded in the late 1950s by young Palestinian professionals who had settled in Kuwait, seeking employment but becoming highly politicized. The group's founding fathers came from similar backgrounds: Yasser Arafat, Salah Khalaf, Khalil el-Wazir, Farouk Kaddoumi, and others were teenagers when their families lost their homes in the 1948 war. As the refugees became bright students, they developed a loathing of the old leadership of the Palestinian generation that lost its land.

While the war was a joint victory for Israel and Jordan, Palestinian historiography recalls it as the *Nakba*, the "Castastrophe." The creation of Fatah was fueled by the revival of the demand to "liberate" a "Palestinian entity," which gained momentum with the pan-Arabism of Egypt's President Nasser. No wonder that the name of the group, read backwards as an Arabic acronym, stands for "Palestine Liberation Organization."

In the years leading up to the 1967 war, the variety of Palestinian organizations that popped up like mushrooms after a rainstorm provoked an escalation of the conflict by repeatedly attacking Israel—drawing the Arab armies toward war. After the brief and disastrous conflict, the Palestinians realized that their hopes to liberate their land would not be achieved by others; they came to rely on themselves. The influence of the guerrilla groups, among the Palestinian community, grew markedly.

By February 1969, Fatah, together with violent groups such as the PFLP, took over the PLO and threw out the old guard. Arafat became the chairman of the entire movement, and his unshaven visage, olive-green military fatigues, and red-and-white *keffiyeh* headdress became the symbol of Palestinian nationalism. While his old colleagues were wiped out, either by the Israelis or by each other, Arafat survived to lead the movement.

The guerrilla commanders, already in 1968 with Arafat as their leading light, set up clandestine headquarters in the occupied West Bank itself. Their ideology had found great justification in the Six Day War, as it became obvious that Israel could not be eliminated through conventional warfare but rather through an uprising of the masses.

The Fatah leadership declared that one million Palestinians in the West Bank and Gaza Strip could make the theoretical "war of popular liberation" a reality. The ideologues were thrilled that a guerrilla struggle could be mounted by a united, oppressed people.[2]

The revolutionaries did not, however, count on the effectiveness of Israel's security services. No one could have expected the Shin Bet, or General Security Service, to master the unfamiliar towns, villages, and terrain of the West Bank and Gaza so quickly. Once reality triumphed over theory, the road to guerrilla victory was blocked by Shin Bet intelligence, a failure by the Palestinians to organize, the generally low capability of the underground operatives, and a lack of coordination and solidarity between the various fedayeen groups.

It rapidly became apparent that the supposedly oppressed residents of the West Bank and Gaza did not care for "armed uprisings." By the end of 1967, the guerrillas had snatched total defeat from the jaws of revolutionary zeal. Hundreds of activists were under arrest, armed cells were broken and their caches captured. Barely six months had passed since the Six Day War, and the Israelis had scored another lightning victory. It was as though the Palestinian guerrilla organizations had never existed in the occupied territories.

Arafat himself barely escaped to the eastern bank of Jordan, literally a few minutes before an Israeli snatch squad swooped on his secret base in the West Bank town of Ramallah. The Palestinian militants set up new headquarters in Jordanian territory and had to organize themselves anew.

The fedayeen, becoming better known as the PLO, resumed their campaign of violence with the help of Iraqi military units stationed on the Jordanian side of the river. As 1968 began, the Palestinians stepped up their bazooka assaults and other "hit-and-run" raids on Israeli positions. After crossing the shallow Jordan River, the guerrillas laid explosive mines on roads, opened fire on both military and civilian vehicles, and attacked Jewish settlements.

Through Dr. Emanuel Herbert, Israel sent several warnings to the Jordanians and demanded that King Hussein stop the Palestinians from attacking. The king hoped for a peaceful solution with Israel, and the fedayeen would only sabotage diplomacy. Worse still, he knew that the Palestinians, when armed, could be highly dangerous, and any revolutionary would eventually attempt to topple a king almost as a reflex action.

A more immediate consideration was that the Israelis would not long tolerate "terrorist cells" just across the river, and Jordan would find itself either the object of an invasion or a subject in a new war of attrition.

King Hussein's wish to have it both ways, a desire he displays with alarming regularity, found its perfect expression in one of General Hamash's more surprising statements: "Jordanian policy is to encourage the Palestinian fighters to cross the river, but to prevent them—by force, if necessary—from firing their weapons from our eastern bank."[3]

When the violence resumed, Israel stepped up its counterpressure. At dawn on March 21, 1968, a large force of infantry and armor, supported by air strikes, crossed into Jordan and attacked the village of Karameh. Headquarters of the various Palestinian guerrilla groups, including Arafat's offices, were flattened, but this largest of retaliatory raids is remembered as an embarrassing setback for Israel's army, which suffered 30 deaths and 80 wounded when Jordan's Arab Legion put up an impressive fight. Jordanian casualties were officially put at 61 killed and 108 wounded, and the Israelis claimed to have killed 128 "terrorists."

Arafat himself escaped shortly after hearing that the Israelis were crossing the Allenby and Damiya bridges and before paratroops landed in Karameh. (During the Palestinian uprising in early 1988, residents of the West Bank celebrated the twentieth anniversary of the PLO "victory" at Karameh.)

Guerrilla activities continued. The command bases moved yet again, this time farther into Jordan and farther from the Israelis. This did, however, make incursions into Israeli-held territory more difficult, as the Palestinian fighters took to the heights rather than the valley along the river. But the PLO's pride at having dealt the Israeli army a blow attracted many new volunteers in Jordan for Arafat's forces.

It was a gradual process, but before long the Israelis were charging that terrorist headquarters had been set up in the capital, Amman. The retaliatory raids continued, and Israeli army commandos become well acquainted with Jordanian terrain after repeated crossings onto the East Bank to strike at the PLO. They also blew up railway bridges, damaged roads, and called in the Israeli air force to bomb guerrilla camps. And this was before Irbid was shelled.

The attack on the Jordanian town prompted Prime Minister Rifai to arrange the London meeting with Herzog, and both sides quickly agreed that the military chiefs of staff would be the ideal participants. In the two-hour talk through the haze of cigar smoke, General Hamash insisted that his army was doing all it could to prevent Palestinian guerrilla activity. General Bar-Lev, however, was well prepared with intelligence reports demonstrating the opposite was true.

Sharing some of the secret reports with his Arab counterpart, Bar-Lev accused Jordan's army of aiding PLO guerrillas or, at the very least, turning a blind eye to their attacks on Israeli positions. The Israeli general said Jerusalem had no intention of harming the authority of the Hashemite throne but was acting in legitimate self-defense, having been left no options.

Bar-Lev pointed out that Israel's targets had been the guerrillas themselves, but he warned darkly that if farming settlements and border towns such as Bet She'an, within pre–1967 Israel but just across the river from Jordan, came under attack, then Jordanian villages would be singled out for retaliation.

Despite the amicable start of the meeting at Dr. Herbert's home, the conclusion was completely fruitless. Jordan had asked for the contact but failed to elicit any promise to stop Israel's cross-river raids.

Bar-Lev and Herzog returned to their hotel, preparing to return to Jerusalem the next day. They were surprised to find a message waiting for them at the reception desk. In the code that by now was quite familiar to Herzog, the message indicated that Zeid el-Rifai had telephoned and asked them to come to the doctor's house again "tomorrow." Herzog called Dr. Herbert to signal the Israelis' acceptance.

When they arrived at 1 Langford Place the next day, they were again surprised. Not only were General Hamash and Prime Minister Rifai there, but King Hussein himself. The monarch, it emerged, had not been pleased by the outcome of the first meeting.

Hamash attempted to lighten the atmosphere and steer the talks in a friendly direction. He reached into his jacket's inner pocket, pulled out a gold-plated pen and handed it to Bar-Lev, saying, "Here, this is for you." The Israeli general used his new fountain pen only a few times before misplacing it. He never found it.[4]

The king took the lead in trying to achieve progress before the two chiefs of staff parted. Israel and Jordan, after all, were on the edge of open warfare, and having lost the West Bank it was obvious to Hussein that his capital might next be at risk. Turning to Bar-Lev with an obvious sense of urgency, the king said that he was in the middle of his own clash with the Palestinian guerrillas and would take all possible steps to prevent incursions into Israel.

Bar-Lev's response was simply that if the attacks by the guerrillas would stop, then so would Israel's retaliatory raids. No binding commitments were made.

The London talks, including Hussein's unexpected intervention, reflected the new reality in relations between Israel and Jordan. There was no attempt to propose a long-term diplomatic settlement, not even a mention of the subject. The clandestine connection had become an exercise in damage control.

In part, this was a result of the failure of Hussein and Abba Eban to even talk on the same wavelength the previous month in Dr. Herbert's home. Long-term changes, more importantly, were occurring back home in both Israel and Jordan.

Prime Minister Eshkol died in Jerusalem in February 1969. Unprepared to decide between the two main contenders for the top job, Moshe Dayan and Yigal Allon, the Labor party leadership instead elected a compromise candidate: Golda Meir.

Dayan's influence in the Meir administration grew from the first day onward. The one-eyed hero of the Six Day War was at times a simple farmer and at others an aggressive archaeologist, but he was always fervently attached to the "Land of Israel," in terms of both the biblical "Eretz Yisrael" and the soil itself. One of his books was titled *Living with the Bible*, and Dayan certainly believed in Israel's right to build Jewish settlements throughout the lands captured in 1967. He also believed that the diplomatic and territorial status quo operated in Israel's favor. His personal and political motto was, "Things have never been better for us."

Dayan, in short, was an agnostic when it came to Hussein. The general, now the defense minister, did not believe a diplomatic solution based on territorial compromise would be good for Israel.

He formulated his own plan, which came to be known as "functional compromise."[5] Instead of returning the West Bank or parts of it to Jordan, in exchange for a peace treaty, Dayan felt it would be better for Israel to agree with Jordan on a division of responsibilities in the territory. Israel should remain responsible, in his view, for defense and settlements, while Hussein could take charge of the day-to-day lives of the Arab majority. From his East Bank capital, the king could once again rule over the West Bank's commerce, education, health, and legal affairs.

Allon, meanwhile, persisted with his own postwar plan for carving up the captured territory, if Hussein would take what he could get in exchange for his signature on a peace treaty. Allon supported programs that would make his plan more likely to be the chosen solution. He gave his backing, for instance, to the construction of Kiryat Arba, a large Jewish settlement on the heights alongside and over the bustling Arab town of Hebron. For fervent Zionist nationalists, the plan marked the return of Jews to a region from which they fled after Arab pogroms in 1929.

Also choosing to fortify the areas that the Allon Plan would retain in Israeli hands, Allon supported the settlement of paramilitary and civilian farmers in the Jordan Valley near the river, and the construction of new Jewish neighborhoods surrounding Arab East Jerusalem.

Officially, there were no policy changes in the transition from Levi Eshkol to Golda Meir. In practice, however, there were new points of emphasis, which perhaps did not negate the possibility of reaching a peace accord with Jordan but certainly did not encourage the prospects, either.

Deep and rapid changes could be seen in Jordan, too. The Palestinian guerrillas continued to take advantage of Hussein's hospitality and hesitancy, managing to widen their presence and their influence. Western diplomats reported as early as the autumn of 1968 that Amman itself had become a PLO stronghold. Armed Palestinians strolled the streets and set up roadblocks, a common Middle East habit of demonstrating power by security check.

The guerrilla groups were no longer simply an obstacle to calm relations between Israel and Jordan, but a danger to the very existence of the Hashemite throne. The Palestinians constituted their own army and police force. Hussein was indeed in a clash with them, as he told Bar-Lev in October 1968.

Arafat became chairman of the PLO four months later, filling the vacuum left by the removal of Ahmed Shukairy immediately after the defeat of 1967. Arafat formed a political alliance with opposition circles in Jordan, including the Communist party, the Ba'ath Socialist party, and the remnants of anti-Hashemite nationalist parties, which united in an informal and illegal "National Compact." Former Prime Minister Suleiman el-Nabulsi was leader of the group, passing messages and spreading slogans calling for the downfall of the kingdom and its replacement by a "Palestinian Republic." This was to encompass the East Bank, the original Transjordan formed by Britain, but the eventual goal was "the liberation of all Palestine."

Leaders more radical than Arafat retained the revolutionary slogans, and the leader of the Democratic Front for the Liberation of Palestine, Nayef Hawatmeh, was fond of saying that "the path to Jerusalem leads through Amman."[6]

The threat to Hussein's regime also worried his friends in the American and British governments. For two decades the Hashemite kingdom had been a reliable haven of western orientation. Decision makers in Washington and London were concerned that unrest in Jordan would likely increase Soviet influence in the Middle East.

America's active role in the Middle East had begun with the Suez campaign of 1956, when the United States pressed British, French, and Israeli troops to withdraw from Egypt's canal and the Sinai peninsula. Until then, Britain had ruled the roost when it came to influencing Jordan. For reasons largely born of sentiment and nostalgia, the British have always adored Hussein. But in 1956, angry that they had acted against the Arabs in concert with Israel, Hussein did not reciprocate London's affections.

The Americans became chief arms suppliers to Jordan. Diplomats recall that the U.S. State Department, and later even the Israelis, called Hussein, in private, "BYK," an acronymic nickname for the "Bright Young King." This was not derision but genuine approval of Hussein's actions and sympathy for his position.[7]

The west's recognition of the king's value and the worry that he might not survive formed a connecting cord through the Middle East policies of presidents Dwight D. Eisenhower, John F. Kennedy, Lyndon B. Johnson, and especially Richard M. Nixon. American diplomats and Central Intelligence Agency operatives kept a close watch on events in Jordan.

Every small sign that the power of the Palestinian guerrillas was increasing, sharpening the threat against Hussein, gave the United States even more reason to support the notion that two friends of America—Israel and Jordan—should themselves develop a mutually beneficial relationship.

The strengthening, quite separately, of Jordan's and Israel's relations with Washington led the two governments to confide in the United States. The top echelons of the American administration soon were made fully aware of the clandestine contacts between Amman and Jerusalem. The CIA and State Department had already heard rumors that Hussein frequently met with Israeli leaders. Hussein even asked Eban, in 1968, to send a report on their talks to President Johnson.

When the Israeli foreign minister next visited Washington, he made an unusual request while visiting the president in the White House. Eban asked that the president's advisers and even the Israeli ambassador, Yitzhak Rabin, leave the room. The aides were clearly unhappy, but they left for a few minutes. Only then did Eban have a frank discussion with Johnson on the lack of progress toward a peace agreement between Israel and Jordan.[8]

The use of the United States as a sounding board and, when necessary, a communications channel, led Hussein and the Israelis to stop almost completely using the British channel.

The preference for American go-betweens was convenient for all sides concerned, and all found certain advantages. The first change was that the venue of most secret meetings was changed from Europe to the Middle East itself. This provided some relief to Hussein, who was reluctant to leave Jordan because of the threat of unrest or even a coup d'état at home.

Golda Meir and Moshe Dayan were also happy with the new procedures for contacting Jordan, in part because they diminished their dependence on Eshkol's trusted aide, Yaakov Herzog. He was considered a man of the past, and his influence on foreign policy quickly faded. The Russian-born and American-educated Meir had no need, unlike Eshkol, for Herzog's command of the English language.

She had her own long-time assistants, notably Simcha Dinitz as her foreign affairs adviser and Mordecai Gazit, who was appointed to Herzog's old job as director general of the prime minister's office. Colonel Israel Lior was the new military affairs adviser. The three comprised the new team behind Prime Minister Meir when she met the king. Her personal secretary Lou Kaddar was usually present, too.

As for Dayan, he changed his mind over a two-year period and agreed to do what he had rejected in the Eshkol era: to meet Hussein. Dayan, however, was a soloist, dubbed by some observers "a lone wolf," and it was not in his nature to operate through go-betweens.

Herzog's last remaining asset on his way out, however, was his personal relationship with Hussein. For years, he was the only Israeli the king would trust. Herzog took part in one more secret conference, but the brusque manner in which he was dropped from the front line irked him for the rest of his life.[9]

The advantages to the United States were clear. All contacts between Jordan and Israel were now arranged through American intermediaries, giving them both immediate information and the extraordinary power that stems from it. The U.S. ambassadors in Amman and Tel Aviv became an important part of the process, although they never took part in any of the meetings themselves. American communications technology never failed to serve the officially hostile neighbors well.

When, in May 1975, President Gerald R. Ford met Egypt's President Anwar el-Sadat in Austria, Israel sent a secret message to be delivered to the two leaders. An official at the Israeli prime minister's office asked a U.S. Embassy contact in Tel Aviv, "How long will it take you to get this message to them?" The American happily replied, "Around a minute and a half."[10]

With the dawn of the 1970s, the United States installed a computerized communications system between Amman and Jerusalem to help America's two friends. The State Department's computers in Washington, meanwhile, chose a project name for the arrangement of contacts between Israel and Jordan. Without any particular meaning, the random choice was "Operation Lift."

A few Israeli officials who knew of the name found it symbolic, considering both the uplifting nature of the secret search for a settlement with Jordan and the thought that the United States was hitchhiking "a lift" on the coattails of the two Middle East nations, garnering political benefits by essentially being passive. There was also the notion that the venue for the talks had been "lifted" or transferred from Europe to the region itself.

The Jordanians and Israelis could now call each other with scrambled telephones and telexes, linked to encoding devices for both speech and written communications. On the Israeli side, there was, of course, limited access to the secret facilities, but on the Jordanian side there was outright paranoia that only the king and his closest aides should know of the system's existence.

The Americans found that when either side wished to arrange a meeting, it would take the U.S. ambassadors no more than two or three days to arrange. In other words, the leaders were quite willing to talk, especially when there was trouble brewing that might cause complications or even violence.

The first meeting site set up through the Americans was aboard an Israeli navy missile boat in the heart of the inlet known to the Jordanians as the Gulf of 'Aqaba and to the Israelis as the Gulf of Eilat.[11]

In March 1970, Moshe Dayan, Abba Eban, Chaim Bar-Lev, and Yaakov Herzog met King Hussein and Jordanian General Zeid ibn-Shaker. The Israeli team had been on the missile boat for some time before the Jordanians arrived aboard a small motorized launch. The king was coming from his 'Aqaba villa where he often retreats for relaxation.

The fact that Hussein was willing to have this meeting, at the height of his clash with the PLO, suggests not only his courage but his desperation to find support wherever he could.

The king was also more mindful of security than ever, knowing that a leak of the fact that he was meeting Israelis would add fuel to the Palestinian flames already burning around the royal palace in Amman. The PLO, fortified by Beduin tribal officers who had defected from Jordan's army, was particularly strong in the southern part of the kingdom, on the Jordanian side of the Arava Valley forming the border with Israel. Even in 'Aqaba, Hussein's enemies were not far away. The Israelis were hoping to persuade him that they could well be his only potential friends in the region.

Eban, Bar-Lev, and the others reported later that Hussein looked bad. His political distress showed on his face. He might be losing the war of his life, and the Israelis felt they were gaining some insight into what the king must have been like less than three years earlier when they trounced him in fewer than six days.

They learned that Hussein's health was suffering, that he had summoned Dr. Herbert from London for treatment at his palace in Amman. The king underwent surgery on his jaw in 1969 and suffered a fairly minor heart irregularity.[12]

Rumors spread that he was considering stepping down from his throne,[13] but on the other hand television news film showed that Hussein spent most of his time in military uniform as a symbol of his might and defiance against the rebel threat. There was little time for pleasure, and the royal family had missed going to their winter palace at Shuneh because it was in an insecure area.

Amateur radio operators reported that one of their favorite contacts in the Middle East, Hussein the avid "ham" who loved to talk informally with foreigners over the shortwaves, was off the air. The king postponed his usual ski trip to Austria, and the only occasion on which he went water skiing off 'Aqaba was actually to provide cover for his visit to the Israeli missile boat.

The Israelis had been under some pressure from President Nixon and National Security Adviser Henry Kissinger to be lenient toward Hussein, to consider his perilous position caught between Palestinian unrest and Israel's demands that he impose order along the border. If Dayan and his team played along with the Americans, they were on that boat to hand Hussein a small victory of some sort.

The talks at sea went on a good deal longer than expected. Israeli security men, maintaining lookout positions on deck, also had to help out as waiters bringing food and drink to the conferees. The waves were rough that day, and the missile boat rocked from side to side. Herzog, attending his last meeting with the king, was further embarrassed by suffering mild seasickness. As a result, the only easy agreement at the talks was that future sessions be held, whenever possible, on land.[14]

Dayan was the dominant figure at the talks and quickly granted Hussein the achievement he required. Israel's army, the defense minister declared, would withdraw from two villages on the eastern side of the Jordan, Al-Safi and Fifi, which were captured in retaliatory raids against guerrillas a few months earlier. The Israelis had seized the villages after the PLO, under Arafat's almost absolute control since February 1969, fired Russian-made Katyusha rockets at the nearby Israeli chemical factory known as the Dead Sea Works. Israel's army even paved a road into Jordanian territory and had not previously given any indication of any intention to withdraw.

The missile-boat talks became a discussion of military details. The king and General Shaker promised to restore order, not only in Al-Safi and Fifi but along the entire border with Israel and particularly in the Arava Valley and the zone between Eilat and 'Aqaba. Earlier in the year, there had been several attempts by PLO guerrillas to attack Eilat from the Jordanian side. The Israeli team told Hussein that if the people of the southern port were prevented from leading a normal life, enjoying the revenues of shipping and tourism, then the residents of 'Aqaba would similarly suffer.

From the boat, the lights of both cities, their low-rise homes and warehouses built right down to the Red Sea's gulf, sparkled in the cool night air as the talks continued past sundown. Two towns, side-by-side, provided a visual reminder that the security and livelihood of Israel and Jordan are unavoidably linked.

The Israelis withdrew from the Safi-Fifi corridor, but not before agreeing to allow the king to stage a fantasy for the benefit of his troops. He ordered them to "recapture" the two villages from the Israelis. The official announcement from Amman said the Al-Safi area was "conquered" by Jordan's Arab Legion in a military clash, "and the enemy suffered heavy casualties." Rumors were duly leaked in Amman that the king had personally commanded his combat forces.

Officials in Jerusalem, who knew the truth, were utterly shocked by the Jordanian declarations, but orders came from the highest level not to issue an Israeli correction.

After recovering their strip of land, the Jordanians kept their side of the bargain. Arab Legion units did, in fact, keep the peace along the entire 125-mile section of the border from the Dead Sea, running south through the Arava Valley to the Gulf of Eilat.

Guerrilla attacks on Israel and the West Bank did not, however, stop. The locations changed, and at times it seemed the severity worsened. Israeli self-restraint was tested to the limit.

Because the Americans saw a need to reduce the tension, they arranged another secret meeting. The venue this time was small Coral Island, also known by the Arabic name Jezirat Far'on, in the Gulf of Eilat just off the eastern coast of the Israeli-occupied Sinai Peninsula. An Israeli army unit put up a large tent, near the remains of a Crusader fortress, which was declared off-limits to tourists for the day.

King Hussein arrived by sea, along with two officers of his army. The Israeli side raised its level of representation to the ultimate, for the first time, as Defense Minister Dayan, Foreign Minister Eban, and the army chief of staff were joined by Prime Minister Meir herself. She had, after all, already met the king when she was merely foreign minister. The ice between them had been broken. She was willing to talk again.

Both leaders were quite excited about the meeting in the days leading up to the Coral Island rendezvous. They had not seen each other since their talks in Paris some five years earlier. If, however, Hussein expected a sense of nostalgia would lead Golda to make new concessions, he was mistaken.

The king was repeatedly asking Israel's leaders to consider his difficult position. Even before the meetings on the missile boat and on the tiny island, Hussein sent the Israelis three questions, through the U.S. Embassy in Amman. An American diplomat in Tel Aviv passed them on to Eban.

1. Will Israel decline to exploit the situation for her own advantage if Jordan finds it
   necessary to move its forces from the border to move against Palestinian groups? (As

they had through Chaim Herzog a decade earlier, the Israelis promised not to take advantage of such situations by attacking Jordan.)

2. Could Israel promise not to react to provocations from the Palestinian guerrillas? (No, Jerusalem replied. Hussein was disappointed, but the Israelis reserved the right to retaliate as they saw fit.)

3. Could Hussein depend on Israeli aid, in the event that Syria or Iraq sent their armies into Jordan to support the Palestinians? (Here, too, the king did not receive a satisfactory reply. The Israelis avoided a binding commitment, saying only that a request for help would be weighed if and when it came.)[15]

It may seem surprising that Hussein would put these matters of life and death for his regime in the form of an indirect message sent through Washington, when he could simply wait for his next encounter with the Israelis themselves. Abba Eban, however, understood the motive. Jordan did not simply want Israel's support, but U.S. attention and sympathy. The king would happily accept security guarantees from the Americans, and if not, he hoped they would exercise their influence over Israel.

Hussein continuously received strong advice from his relatives Sharif Nasser and Zeid ibn-Shaker, from his longtime personal aide Rifai, and from Rasoul Kilani, the interior minister who was in charge of the domestic security apparatus, all urging the king to wage all-out war on the Palestinian guerrillas. The advisers feared that Hashemite authority in Jordan would wither, and the army and secret police were preparing for an explosive event such as an attempted PLO insurrection.

The king hesitated, looking for alternatives to violence. He was loath to tear his country apart in what would be a gamble on all-out victory. Unfortunately for him and the Israelis, Amman was gradually becoming the Palestinians' capital city.

The guerrillas strutted around Amman and most of Jordan as though they owned the place. Even members of the royal family were inconvenienced and endangered. The king's second wife, Princess Muna, was stopped in her official car by a Palestinian roadblock in December 1969, and she was detained for an hour.

Prime Minister Wasfi el-Tell's was the strongest voice in favor of suppressing the guerrillas by force. The PLO would long remember Tell as a powerful enemy, but his viewpoint generally matched that of Hussein himself. Their temperaments, styles, and tactics were different, however. The king, even in situations that had long shed all niceties, persisted in his dedication to diplomacy and legitimacy. Tell believed in getting a job done, quickly and with surgical precision. In the struggle with Arafat that followed, the prime minister himself was seen leading military units searching for illegal arms caches.

Suspicions and uneasy feelings quickly gave way to lethal events. On the first day of September 1970, members of the Popular Front for the Liberation of Palestine attempted to assassinate the king, opening fire on the royal motorcade in an ambush similar to another in July for which no Palestinians had claimed responsibility. In both incidents, Hussein fired his own pistol to repel the attackers.[16]

Five days later, the PFLP staged an international spectacular under the command of Dr. Wadi el-Haddad, deputy to the terrorist group's founder Georges Habash. Four passenger airliners were hijacked almost simultaneously. Swiss, British, and American TWA jets were flown at gunpoint to Dawson's Field in the Jordanian desert. A Pan American jumbo was hijacked to Cairo and blown up after the passengers were set free. A fifth hijack attempt, aboard an Israeli El Al jet over Britain, failed when Israeli security men captured two Palestinians including the infamous Leila Khaled.

The PFLP demanded the release of seven "commandos" imprisoned in Israel and Western Europe, but Dr. Haddad's true aim was publicity. He wished to shock the world, and he succeeded. The week-long siege ended with the explosive destruction of all three airliners at Dawson's Field, televised around the world and deeply embarrassing King Hussein.

Elements in his own army accused him of hesitating, and some soldiers of the Arab Legion threatened suicide in emotional face-to-face meetings with their king.[17] He attempted negotiating with the PFLP and with Arafat's mainstream PLO, which officially endorsed the hijackings.

The king went into action on September 16, summoning to Hummar Palace Brigadier Muhammed Daoud, a Palestinian who had been captured by Israel while fighting for Jordan in 1967 but was released after the war. Hussein ordered Daoud to form a military government, and a state of emergency was declared encompassing the entire nation.

The civil war, which the Palestinians would later remember as "Black September," began on that day, when Hussein's legendary patience finally snapped. He was to confront the gravest challenge the Hashemite throne had ever had to face.[18]

Hussein's army attacked every known stronghold of the PLO and the other guerrilla groups. The advantage lay with the Jordanians and their 55,000 soldiers. At least half were loyal to the king without question. The Palestinians had nearly as many armed men, but their training and discipline were poor.[19]

After two days of fighting, the Arab world was silent with the exception of Damascus. The Syrians did not only protest the Jordanian crackdown. They sent some 250 tanks toward Jordan's northern border. Limited fighting broke out between Syria and Jordan, and Hussein feared that an Iraqi armored brigade based at the important Jordanian base of Mafrak might take the side of Syria and the Palestinians. What had been a civil war was threatening to become all-out war. Hussein sent messages to the world's major powers that he was facing a critical situation, that Jordan was being invaded by Syria and required urgent assistance. The western ambassadors in Amman were given to understand that air raids even by Israeli warplanes on the Syrians would be welcome.

A more explicit message from Hussein was sent to the Israelis through White

House National Security Adviser Henry Kissinger. The Americans themselves withheld comment, but told the Israelis that King Hussein would have no objection to their attacking the Syrians from the air. The Jordanian message added that Israel was not being invited to send ground forces across the river.[20]

The United States sent its own messages to Syria, demanding that the invasion force be withdrawn from Jordan, and to the Soviet Union as chief ally of the Syrians. The National Security Council, under Kissinger, held emergency meetings and promised to help Hussein, even with American troops if need be.

Israel's leaders were watching the Jordanian civil war with great interest and some concern. Still, the request for air strikes came as a surprise. It is rare for any sovereign leader to ask foreigners to bomb his own territory.

The National Unity Government, which saw the Israelis through the 1967 war, had finally been shattered a few weeks earlier, because Prime Minister Meir and her Labor party ministers agreed to a cease-fire arrangement with the Egyptians and an attached peace plan drawn up by U.S. Secretary of State William Rogers.

The departure from the government of right-wing Herut party leader Menachem Begin, without doubt the minister most opposed to any conversation or cooperation with Hussein, was not enough to ensure Israel's immediate acquiescence to the request for air strikes. Arguments broke out among politicians and military chiefs who knew of the message from Jordan. Some of the army officers made the unusual suggestion that if Israel takes any side, it should help the Palestinians topple Hussein.

The so-called Jordanian Lobby had powerful members, however, from Golda Meir at the top, to Yigal Allon, Abba Eban, and the ambassador in Washington, Yitzhak Rabin. The prime minister flew to Washington for urgent consultations, and there she reached agreement with President Nixon on a program to support King Hussein.

Backed by an American pledge to confront any threat by Soviet forces, the Israelis mounted an implied challenge to the Syrians by transferring an armored division from southern Israel to the Jordan Valley near Bet She'an in the north. The usual military secrecy was abandoned, so that Syria would know that it would face a formidable tank force if matters got out of hand.

Israeli forces in the occupied Golan Heights, barely 50 miles from Damascus, were also put openly on alert. Deputy Prime Minister Allon publicly declared that Israel's vital interests were endangered by the Syrian invasion and by indications that Iraq's army might become involved. The word "war" was finally mentioned, if only in Latin, when Allon said Israel was beginning to detect a *casus belli*.[21]

Israel's flexing of its armored muscles was sufficient to deter war and limit Syria's incursion. The invasion force in northern Jordan never grew to what it might have become, in part because the Syrians had to defend the stretch of land between the Israeli-held Golan and their capital.

Hussein's army and air force were able to turn back the Syrians without further help from abroad. Parts of Amman were devastated in the bloody civil war that continued, but the king was victorious over Arafat's men, and the Palestinian guerrillas were forced to leave Jordan in July 1971.

Hussein would never admit that the Israelis had indirectly helped him triumph, but the shared interests were apparent when the king suggested that the guerrilla groups were the enemy of the Palestinian people.

Arafat's men said the same of Hussein and his government, of course, and on November 28, 1971, Prime Minister Tell was murdered in a Cairo hotel. Egypt's President Nasser was dead and gone, but Hussein had a bitter bone to pick with his successor Anwar el-Sadat when an Egyptian court freed Tell's Palestinian assassins three months after the shooting.

It was in December that chief royal adviser Rifai escaped an assassination attempt in London with only a wound to one hand.

"Black September" was no longer just a slogan but a terrorist team organized by Arafat's Fatah core of the PLO to seek revenge against Jordan. The ruthless group's activities widened in 1972 to include the massacre of eleven Israeli athletes at the Munich Olympics.

A whole new set of diplomatic doors were suddenly open. Israel and Jordan could no longer deny to each other that their most basic interests coincided. As in 1958, Hussein had very little support from other Arab nations in the turmoil of 1970 and instead found that of all Middle East countries it was Israel that provided the king's best guarantee of survival.

Chapter 9

Why Not in Tel Aviv?

Israel's military moves in September 1970, which neutralized the combined Syrian-Palestinian threat on northern Jordan, were the product of a careful calculation in Jerusalem of security interests.

All the neighboring Arab states might seem to be Israel's enemies, but choices constantly have had to be made between the lesser of two evils. It was often a balance between Arabs who hate the Jewish state and can do something about it, and Arabs who reconcile themselves to Israel's existence. Hussein was added to the equations as an element from the latter group: not loving Israel, but accepting it. He was a factor well worth retaining, from Jerusalem's viewpoint.

It was not only a military calculation, however. Israeli diplomacy was also built on delicate balances, and the Israelis truly wished to pursue a compromise deal with Jordan for the future of the West Bank. The significant moves that forced a Syrian retreat and helped keep Hussein on the throne would leave the king with a sense of gratitude, the Israelis hoped, and would also improve the chances for a political solution.

Hussein, quickly recapturing all the self-confidence he had lost in recent years, conducted his own review of his working relationship with Israel. He was frightened by the increasing pace of Jewish settlement in the West Bank, and he spotted indications that the new Egyptian president, Anwar Sadat, might consider making peace with Israel. Doing nothing could be dangerous for Jordan.

Israel's decision to renew the dialogue with Jordan came at the height of the crisis in September. The cabinet held a special meeting in Tel Aviv to discuss developments in Jordan and to hear a report from Golda Meir on her visit to the United States. The senior ministers decided to make contact with Jordan, and the United States was asked to help with the arrangements.

Only two months later, Yigal Allon was having a two-hour meeting with King Hussein. The topics were ordinary enough, but the conversation had its emotional moments, too. They greeted each other with warm hugs, as would any Middle Eastern friends who had not met for a long time.

The Israeli minister congratulated the king on his victory over the Palestinian guerrillas. Hussein did not disguise his thanks to Israel for its support.

The meeting took place in an entirely new and different location. Hussein and Allon were talking in a tent, set up along the desert border between the two nations, to the south of the Dead Sea. Israeli soldiers pitched the tent thirteen miles north of Eilat, in the barren and uninhabited plain called the Arava. Hussein reached the location in a Jordanian military helicopter. Allon was waiting for him.

The two men reviewed the regional situation, and they established a procedure for arranging future meetings. They agreed on the desirability of reaching a political settlement between Israel and Jordan, but they also considered many secondary areas in which agreements might be reached. These included water rights, agriculture, and economic development.

Over the three years that followed, the pace of contacts between the two states was greatly increased. The circle of participants also widened on both sides. King Hussein let his brother and designated successor, Crown Prince Hassan, in on the secret diplomacy. Other officials in Amman became involved, too. On the Israeli side, Agriculture Minister Chaim Givati and other senior officials were brought into the talks.

No other participants, however, could come close to the rapport achieved between Hussein and Golda Meir, a relationship built on mutual respect.[1] Mrs. Meir considered the king a progressive and credible leader, who was both a western-oriented moderate and a true Arab patriot. She spoke of Hussein warmly, in tones that one participant describes as "motherly."

Her great interest in maintaining contact with Hussein, bordering on affection for the king, stemmed from Mrs. Meir's personal background. Although born in a little Jewish village in Russia, Golda apparently had a weakness for the flourishes of royalty. It explains why her customary coolness gave way to obvious excitement when an opportunity arose to meet a flesh-and-blood king, and an Arabian king at that.[2]

Mrs. Meir did not hide her sentiments and was able to touch Hussein's emotions by retelling tidbits of her meetings with his grandfather. Her most successful anecdote concerned Hussein himself, when he was a young child. She told him that once when she was meeting Abdullah, the little grandson tried to let the air out of the tires of her car. Hussein did not remember being so mischievous, but he exploded in laughter—one of the few times he did so in all his meetings with Israeli leaders.

Hussein even asked to hear more about it. Mrs. Meir told him that her driver, who was waiting in the courtyard of the Transjordanian palace, did not know the identity of the naughty youth. The driver walked up to the brat and slapped him on the cheek, and, she continued the tale, the child Hussein broke into tears and ran to find his grandfather the king.[3]

Hussein, for his part, recognized Golda Meir as one of the century's great leaders, and he saw his meetings with her as the closure of an historical circle. He had far more respect for her and for Moshe Dayan than he did for any other Israelis. When Hussein heard that Mrs. Meir's sister, Shana Korngold, died in August 1972, he took the opportunity to exhibit his special feelings toward her, sending Prime Minister Meir a telegram of sympathy.[4] Mrs. Meir once made a personal gesture of her own, giving Hussein a gift for his eldest daughter, Alia.

The king and Mrs. Meir never gave each other any gifts, however. In general, despite rumors that made their way through the halls of government in Jerusalem,[5] Hussein was not in the habit of showering expensive gifts on the Israelis with whom he met.

There was a pen for Chaim Bar-Lev. Abba Eban also received a gold-plated fountain pen bearing the emblem of the Hashemite crown. As far as Eban was concerned, he was going to save it for the signing of a peace treaty between the two nations.

Hussein gave Yigal Allon a German-made assault rifle, the type used by Jordan's army, but the Israeli deputy prime minister did not care for the logic behind the choice of gift. It seemed that the king saw Eban as the scholar, and Allon as the warrior.

The Israelis gave Hussein a few presents, but their generosity was far from excessive. Abba Eban recalls, "We Israelis do not excel in choosing gifts." Eban tended to give the king books—often Eban's own literary works.[6]

Hussein's meetings with Mrs. Meir were very formal, although friendly in tone. No gifts were exchanged, except the one for Alia, because the king apparently could not think of anything appropriate for a woman for whom he held such deep respect. Mrs. Meir felt it would seem too forward for her to give a present first. In their conversations, she addressed him as "Your Majesty," and he usually responded with "Madame Prime Minister."

Another strong sign of the special relationship between the two leaders was Hussein's willingness to meet Golda Meir in the heart of the State of Israel.

When the Israelis first proposed that their secret meetings with their eastern neighbor be transferred from the Arava desert plain to Israel's largest city, it seemed a madman's notion. A senior official in the prime minister's bureau advised Mrs. Meir that "The king will never agree." A second aide warned that Hussein would be offended, and a third said the dangers of organizing such an encounter and keeping it secret were too great.

When the matter was considered in greater detail, all three advisers seemed to have erred. The most convenient place, in fact, for such a secret meeting was just outside Tel Aviv. The Israelis discussed the possibility with American liaison officials, and the proposal of a new venue was passed on to the Jordanians.

To the surprise of the Israelis, Hussein did not fall off his chair in shock or anger, and without much delay he agreed to come to Tel Aviv. He was flown in his helicopter across the Jordan River and into Israeli territory. The rendezvous point, where he landed, was at the foot of Masada, the historic mountain fortress overlooking the Dead Sea where nineteen centuries earlier a revolt against the Romans by Jewish zealots reached a climax in mass suicide.

The sun was setting, its brilliant colors filling the horizon to the west as an Israel air force helicopter, which had been waiting at Masada, immediately flew Hussein into the sky toward Tel Aviv. At the king's request, the helicopter took a small detour to fly over Jerusalem.

A few years later, Hussein confided his impressions of the aerial tour to a member of U.S. President Gerald Ford's cabinet. The king's description was an emotional account of seeing the grand mosques of the Old City again, the golden Dome of the Rock and the silver-domed Al-Aqsa where his grandfather was assassinated, both bathed in the hues of sunset. The cabinet officer and other Americans who saw the report filed with the Central Intelligence Agency were impressed by Hussein's strong Islamic faith, expressed through a mystical tie with Jerusalem.

The king is said to have spoken with some pride of his visit to Golda Meir's home, where he enjoyed her hospitality. No one ever bothered to correct the king's misapprehension. Israel's prime minister did from time to time use the apartment Hussein visited, but it was not Mrs. Meir's apartment in the Ramat-Aviv neighborhood of Tel Aviv. It was an Israeli government guest house, to the north of the city.[7] The property had been in service for years for important visitors who would rather not be seen in Israel.

Several of Mrs. Meir's aides joined in her discussions with Hussein, including Lou Kaddar, Israel Lior, and Simcha Dinitz. Dinitz would be sent to Washington as Israel's ambassador in 1973, but in 1971 he was the chief of the prime minister's bureau and her adviser on foreign affairs. Dinitz was the notetaker for the Israelis in the secret talks; Mordecai Gazit took over the task after Dinitz moved to the United States.

Mrs. Meir also liked to have Moshe Dayan at the meetings, preferring his style of diplomacy to that of Yigal Allon. It was mainly a matter of personality, as the prime minister continued to support and defend the Allon Plan for returning much of the occupied West Bank while retaining the vital valley and hilltops in Israeli hands. Abba Eban also found himself pushed aside.

Dayan took an unusual view of Hussein. Unlike all the other Israeli ministers who heaped praise on the king after meeting him, Dayan was always reluctant to say anything too positive about him. The war hero with his single eye patch wrote in his Hebrew-language memoirs,

Leading Jordan is a king who, unlike his grandfather, is a man of the world, a liberal, a humanist, valiant and enlightened. He has great charisma. But with all his enlightenment, awareness and understanding of world events, he does not take a deep view or a practical one. There is no doubt that he knows the limits of his ability to act in the Arab world. It is clear that there are agreements which he would make, except he cannot because the Arab public in his nation and outside it would never accept them. Yet in spite of all this, he permits himself to paint an idealistic picture and keeps his head in the clouds whenever he proposes settlements and solutions to Israel.

Dayan continued,

He believes that Israel must withdraw to its previous borders and should trust his words, as though from this moment a new epoch begins and the Arabs will keep the peace and respect Israel's rights without exception. He excuses the past by saying that those were mistakes that will not be repeated, and the Arab world will be generous and fair toward Israel if we only withdraw to our old borders.

I am not sure whether his people, Zeid el-Rifai and others, see the world through rose colors as Hussein does. But Hussein without doubt believes sincerely in what he says. His opinions are a synthesis of someone who grew up in a royal world but has a humane and lyrical spirit.[8]

Dayan's essay on Hussein is itself the product of an individual who felt frustrated that no political settlement could be reached with the king. The anger felt by the defense minister was even worse after the Yom Kippur War of 1973, for which Dayan practically blamed Hussein. Mrs. Meir held a similar view. They were particularly angry at Jordan because it was the only Arab nation that was willing to talk, albeit secretly, after the Six Day War of 1967. But while secondary issues could be resolved, the central core of the crisis was left untouched.

One of the problems which did find its solution in the secret diplomacy was connected with the development of the Jordan River Valley. Most of the area had been ignored, while in Jordanian hands, because of the constant threat of reprisal raids by Israel. The artillery fire and attacks from the air, which were responses to Palestinian guerrilla attacks on Israel, changed the Jordan Valley from a green, cultivated area to a barren wasteland.

After the Six Day War and the defeat of the PLO in Jordan three years later, the government in Amman announced a development program aimed at encouraging farmers and other residents to return to the valley and again to be productive there—on Jordan's East Bank.

Hussein and Mrs. Meir reached a series of understandings that made it possible for the farmers to return. Precise details were arranged by lower officials of both nations, although not junior aides who might leak information to the press. The two governments quickly concluded that a long period of quiet could be expected along the river valley border, and there was thus no reason not to cultivate land right up to the very edge of the water.

Where the twists and turns of the Jordan River made it difficult to trace the precise border, there were inevitable conflicts over alleged infringements of territory. Israel and Jordan accepted, however, that their armies would have to hold the land in some agreed pattern, or else Palestinian guerrillas would find their way into the area. Security fences would have to be built, along with mine fields and suitable roads for border patrols.

After the PLO commandos were expelled from Jordan in 1971, political tensions eased greatly, and instead of two armies facing each other over the river, farmers on both sides found they were benefiting from many hundreds of additional arable acres, which the military returned for agricultural use.

When villagers and farmers in both Israel and Jordan found mosquitoes growing in the river had become an intolerable nuisance, representatives of their governments met on the riverbanks to find a solution. A massive campaign of spraying the mosquitoes and their hatching grounds was launched on both sides of the river—light aircraft spraying poison: Jordanian airplanes on the East Bank, and the pilots of Israel's Chemavir company doing their work on the West Bank. The attack on the mosquitoes had been coordinated, so the pilots had no need to fear any dangerous misunderstanding at the border would prompt one army or the other to open fire. It was an unusual degree of freedom and calm along an ostensibly hostile border.

It is not surprising, then, that one of the senior Israeli officials involved in the contacts with Jordan said the cooperation between 1970 and 1973 ranged "from anti-mosquito to anti-terrorism tactics."

Despite his victory in expelling the PLO and its radical splinter groups, the Israelis harbored some doubts as to King Hussein's ability to keep the peace along the entire border. Their worries focused on the Arava desert plain, to the south of the Dead Sea, where there was no river to demarcate an easily protected frontier.

At every one of his meetings with the Israelis, they asked Hussein to pledge again that his army would continue to stop Palestinian commandos from crossing into Israel from Jordanian territory. Because of the worldwide terrorist campaign by the Palestinian "Black September" group, Israel and Jordan found themselves on the same side of the barricades.

It was only natural that the states exchange intelligence information on Arab terrorism. Israel was selective in providing clandestinely obtained data on the intentions of the terrorist bombers and gunmen in the Middle East and Europe, so as not to endanger Israeli secret agents. But the Israelis had to give something of value to receive the information that Jordan was receiving from governments and agents in the Arab world.

The shared interest was, again, not sufficiently strong to lead to negotiations aimed at a lasting settlement between Israel and Jordan. Cooperation against terrorists was conducted at a tactical level, where peace treaties could not be discussed.

Prime Minister Meir did not simply give up on the possibility of peace, however. She naturally supposed that the vast improvement in the clandestine ties with Jordan after Hussein's triumph over the PLO could lead to an open, peaceful relationship. Mrs. Meir proposed the outlines of a permanent settlement to Hussein. It was a combination of the Allon Plan, with its notion of compromise over territory, and Moshe Dayan's concept of functional compromise.

The points of the secret proposal included the following:

- A Jordanian administration would be set up over most of the West Bank.
- Jordan would have special rights to oversee the Muslim holy places in Jerusalem's Old City, including the appointment of the Supreme Muslim Council, which is responsible for the mosques of the Temple Mount.
- A deep-water port would be built at Gaza to provide Jordan's first access to the Mediterranean, a desire harbored by King Abdullah.
- Jordan would be able to station its army and police forces in the Gaza Strip.
- Israel would raise funding worldwide to finance new housing for the Palestinians of the West Bank and Gaza.
- Gaza's Palestinians would be given Jordanian citizenship.
- All Jordanian citizens would be entitled to own property and reside in Israel.
- Jordan and Israel would enter into wide-ranging cooperation for economic development.
- The two nations would cooperate in exploiting the natural resources of the Dead Sea and would together build a railway line, for export purposes, from the Dead Sea to the twin ports of Eilat and 'Aqaba.

Jordan would benefit greatly from sweeping changes of such magnitude, and Mrs. Meir sincerely believed she could make the concessions without endangering her country, so long as Israel gained from her other proposals, which were that

- Jordan would sign a peace treaty and would establish diplomatic relations with Israel.
- Israel would have the right to station troops in the West Bank, in specified bases to be mutually agreed.
- Jewish settlements in the West Bank would remain in place.
- Israel would be permitted to build more settlements, so long as no Arab-owned land was taken.

Golda Meir and her senior ministers had learned from Israel's previous rounds of discussions with Hussein. They took care to frame their proposals on the basis of mutuality as demanded by the king when he met Eban and Allon in 1968.

The principal Israeli aim was to persuade Hussein to accept a permanent settlement that would permit Israel's military and civilians to remain in the West Bank. For some, it was a matter of a religious and biblically based connection with the land. For all Israelis, it was a matter of national security. They spoke of "defensible borders" and believed they would have to keep their army stationed at the Jordan River. Even the United Nations Security Council, in the famous Resolution 242 of November 1967, would guarantee "secure and recognized boundaries."

Mrs. Meir and her team hoped that Hussein would be satisfied, in this regard, by their proposal that Palestinians and other Jordanian citizens be allowed to purchase land in Israel. Similarly, they believed that fair compensation for the Israeli military bases in the West Bank could be found in their offer that Jordan be allowed to station troops for the first time "on the Mediterranean coast"—in Gaza, along with a port. Israel's military government chief, General Shlomo Gazit, had a conversation with King Hussein and confirmed that the Arab Legion's presence would be acceptable.

The Israelis felt they were offering unprecedented and broad concessions. Their disappointment was deep, when the responses they received from Hussein were much the same as the rejections he had issued to Eban and Allon a few years earlier.

Jordan was not willing to consider any permanent settlement that constituted less than a total return of the West Bank to Jordanian sovereignty. Hussein told the Israelis that he would include special guarantees to help them feel more secure—such as demilitarized zones and even minor adjustments to the frontier's demarcation, so long as territories were exchanged on a mutual basis.

Hussein also said he was willing to agree on arrangements for Jerusalem that would preserve its post–1967 character as an open and united city, but the king said East Jerusalem would formally remain part of Jordan's West Bank. In other words, he was prepared to discuss everything and reach all-encompassing agreements, if it were clear from the outset that the international borders would be almost exactly what they were before the Six Day War.[9] Hussein was offering peace to Israel, so long as he regained all his territory. His prestige, authority, and self-respect demanded the reunification of Jordan.

The discussions between the king and Mrs. Meir on these broad but vital questions were at their most intensive in March 1972, when Hussein went public with an entirely new proposal that had great propaganda value but little practical effect: a federal plan based on a "united Arab kingdom" in two parts. The western sector would be "Palestine," meaning the West Bank and any other part of pre-Israel Palestine that could be "liberated" and where the Arab residents chose to join the federation. The eastern sector would comprise post–1967 Jordan.

The king was demonstrating to the world his loyalty to a supposedly united Arab front. His public declarations referred to Israel only in negative terms, as "the enemy." On the front line itself, Jordan would be portrayed as the pioneer soldier in the battle against the Zionists.

Hussein gained a measure of support from Arab nationalists, but his public proposal also contained a hidden message to Israel. The plan was not a call to arms against the Jewish state, but a suggestion that negotiations toward a settlement would be possible. In keeping with the modern traditions of the Middle East, even an offer to negotiate had to be cloaked in anti-Israel rhetoric. King Abdullah's behavior was similar in the 1940s, and Hussein acted in a like vein in the 1950s.

In 1971, Hussein and his government were concerned by the possibility that Israel and Egypt would reach an interim agreement for peace in the Sinai, perhaps including a partial withdrawal of Israeli forces. The Jordanians feared that they would be pushed outside the central focus of peacemaking efforts in the region.

Hussein had also heard that the Israeli military governors in the West Bank were proposing that Jordan be ignored, that Amman be given no role in the future administration of the territory. There were voices in Israel calling for a local Palestinian leadership to be found or formed, and these would be popular leaders who might not feel allegiance toward Jordan but would be suitable partners for peace negotiations with Israel.

His federal plan was a signal to Israel, the Arabs, and the outside world that Jordan remained the dominant factor in the West Bank and had no intention of surrendering the authority to represent the Palestinians who lived there.

As always, it was Zeid el-Rifai who elegantly and succinctly explained the intentions of the king. Rifai summarized Amman's policy in a slogan, "Peace in exchange for all the territory." Israel, the Jordanian official said, would have to choose between peace and land. "The two of them you will not have," Rifai told the Israelis.

Israel did not choose either of the two supposed alternatives, preferring instead to maintain the status quo. The inevitable stalemate between Israel and the neighboring "Arab confrontation states" led to the Yom Kippur War in 1973. Jordan, despite Rifai's analysis, stood aloof from the conflict. On the other hand, several unseen episodes during the war illustrated the surrealistic quality of relations between Israel and Jordan.

Having learned the bitter lesson of military defeat in 1967, Hussein was in no hurry to make his intentions clear, even after the coordinated Egyptian and Syrian attacks led to fierce fighting in the Sinai and on the Golan Heights. Strange but pastoral calm reigned over the Jordan River Valley, however. Farmers plowed their fields and shepherds tended their flocks. Jordan's army followed the progress of the war by listening to conflicting radio reports, but simply remained on alert in their bases in the mountains of Moab and Gilad overlooking the river.

Israel's army and air force were struggling hard to beat back the Egyptians and Syrians. The attack on Yom Kippur had been a true surprise, and the Israelis were losing territory—especially in the Sinai, where Egypt's relatively new president, Anwar el-Sadat, had instructed his forces to cross the Suez Canal and recapture at all costs some part of the land lost six years earlier. The challenge to Israel, indeed the atypical military crisis, would have been much more severe if Jordan had opened fire on a third front.

Hussein, to Israel's eternal relief, decided instead to wait and watch the war unfold. So as not to be branded a traitor by the Arab world, Jordan did send one armored brigade to the Golan Heights to help the Syrians. It was his only participation in the war, and even this made Hussein feel deeply uncomfortable. He is known to have consulted with Britain's Prime Minister Edward Heath and with the U.S. Secretary of State Henry Kissinger, urging them to tell the Israelis that Jordan's tanks were mere symbols in Syria and should not serve as an excuse for an Israeli attack on Jordan. Kissinger, in his memoirs, said such a request could only be found in the strange Middle East, but Israel gave the required response.[10]

On another occasion, Israeli warplanes were about to bomb the Jordanian tanks on the Golan Heights, not because the Jordanians were special targets but because they were sitting on one of the objectives of that day's order of battle. By coincidence, one of the officers at the front was Zeev Bar-Lavie, who was head of the "Jordan Desk" at the intelligence branch of the Israel Defense Forces (IDF). Looking across at the enemy lines through binoculars, Bar-Lavie spotted an odd crowd of Arab soldiers and vehicles. Based on the unusual activity and a few clues received in the preceding hours, Bar-Lavie, who admitted having a certain fondness toward Jordan, concluded that King Hussein himself was visiting his men. The intelligence officer hurriedly consulted with the IDF intelligence chief, Eli Zeira, and with the Chief of Staff, General David Elazar, and they decided not to bomb the gathering—as easy a target as it was.[11] Once again, Israel had spared Hussein's life.

With hindsight, it may be said that King Hussein committed two grave errors in his long confrontation against Israel. The first was in 1967, when he joined in the war against Israel. The second was in 1973, when he stayed out of the war and could not share in the benefits reaped by Egypt. The first mistake cost Hussein the West Bank. The price he paid for the second mistake was no lighter: within a year, the king lost the West Bank a second time.

Chapter 10

"Must I Make War on You?"

It was really the last chance, and Israel's prime minister knew it. Golda Meir and Moshe Dayan were sitting in a large, trailer with King Hussein and his prime minister Zeid el-Rifai. The Israelis appeared calm and attentive, but in fact they were nervously hoping for a positive response. Only the word *yes* from the king could save their government.

It was late March 1974. In Israel, there were ever stronger calls for the resignation of the leaders who were blamed for the lack of preparedness that had made the Yom Kippur War such a shocking and bloody surprise half a year earlier. In the Hebrew press and angry political speeches, the intelligence failure was known as the *mechdal*, which means "the omission."

Some two months after the Sinai and Golan battles, however, as negotiations with Egypt and Syria began through the shuttling mediation of U.S. envoy Kissinger, Mrs. Meir's government was reelected. The Israeli electorate's behavior was something of a paradox. Opinion polls, letters to the editors, and the obvious consensus in the coffeehouses reflected great animosity against the prime minister and Defense Minister Dayan. Their party, known as the Labor-Mapam Alignment, had a platform that indicated a willingness to negotiate on the future of the occupied territories, and after the jolt of the October war, voters preferred a softer line rather than the hard-line stand of the right-wing Likud bloc, whose leader Menachem Begin was opposed to the return of territory.[1]

Shortly before the election, the government appointed a commission to investigate the *mechdal*, under the chairmanship of Shimon Agranat, the American-born president of Israel's supreme court. After the voting the Agranat Commission issued an interim report, which was devastatingly critical of the army and recommended the dismissal of Chief of Staff Elazar and Intelligence Chief Zeira. The two generals left the army, but not before suggesting that their political bosses deserved at least part of the blame for the lack of military preparedness the previous October. The press clamored against Dayan, saying he had been happy to take credit for the success of the Six Day War in 1967 but now refused to be linked with the failure of 1973.

As Mrs. Meir and Dayan sat in the so-called desert caravan with the leaders of Jordan, they sensed the storm to come and knew that only some startling diplomatic triumph could save the Meir government from its fate.

Hussein and Rifai had arrived by helicopter, flown to the meeting point in the barren southern desert by the king's confidant and personal pilot, Lieutenant Colonel Baader Zaza. The helicopter landed along the Arava border, and the director general of Mrs. Meir's bureau, Mordecai Gazit, was there to greet the Jordanians.

Even as Zaza shut down the engines and the rotors turned more slowly, the king and his prime minister were walking some 200 meters to the caravan entrance, which was partly covered with the dry and dusty soil of the Arava. A unit of Israeli soldiers had erected the wheeled trailer only a few hours earlier, of course not knowing who would be using it. Another unit of soldiers guarded the site from some distance away where they could not see who was inside.

For the comfort of the participants, a large air conditioner kept the temperature tolerable, even low, within the trailer. Padded chairs were provided, as were a portable toilet and a sink with cool running water. The simple kitchen was amply stocked with food, and there was a telephone in the corner.

Hussein and Rifai were surprised to see the gloomy mood of their Israeli hosts, despite the fact that the king keeps up with Israeli politics by reading *The Jerusalem Post* (a daily newspaper) and listening to Israel Radio in Arabic and English. His intelligence officers had told him not to expect Mrs. Meir and Dayan to be in office much longer. Still, Hussein had not expected their personalities to change compared with their previous meetings.

Dayan was especially sour, and even his polite smile of greeting was tinged with bitterness. The king later recalled, "This was not the same Moshe Dayan whom I had met years before. I found myself faced with a completely broken man and I felt sympathy toward him."[2]

It was the second time in three months that Hussein met Dayan. They had conferred in December 1973 in Dr. Emanuel Herbert's home in London, when Dayan was accompanied by his military secretary, Brigadier Arye Bar'on. Hussein arrived with Prime Minister Rifai. At the time, there was much talk of convening a Kissinger-inspired international conference for Middle East peace, and Israel and Jordan were ascertaining whether any substantial progress were possible. The world at large was expecting a conference, and the two governments might secretly coordinate their positions if their joint interests could thus be served.

Rifai suggested, in London, that working parties be set up to arrange a withdrawal of Israeli forces from the West Bank. Dayan rejected the proposal, and it was clear that no progress would be made on Jordan's notion that "the opposing armies" should pull back based on the pattern set by the "disengagement" agreements Israel was negotiating with Egypt and Syria.

The international conference met in Geneva, attended by foreign ministers of Israel, Jordan, Egypt, the United States, and the Soviet Union. Syria boycotted the conference, as did all Palestinians because there was no agreement on whom to invite when Israel refused to meet with the PLO. The delegates were surprised when Rifai, who also held the post of Jordan's foreign minister, proposed to the entire forum that his country negotiate a "separation of forces" pact with Israel, too.

The idea of separating forces, even in the absence of a permanent peace settlement, was introduced into the Middle East in 1971 under a different title, "partial settlement." Dayan had then suggested that Israel, in exchange for a nonaggression pledge from Egypt, withdraw to a new defensive line some 10 kilometers east of the Suez Canal.

Dayan's proposal was passed to the Egyptians by United Nations envoy Gunnar Jarring. On February 4, 1971, President Sadat told the UN that he liked the idea, but it was the Israeli government that refused to proceed with the plan. Sadat said later that the turnabout by Israel was among the factors that finally persuaded him to launch the war in 1973.

Secretary of State Kissinger adopted the idea of a partial settlement, renaming it "disengagement." Separating the hostile armies was considered a first step to reducing the possibility that fighting would again break out. The long-range aim was to bring about an atmosphere more conducive to diplomatic negotiations for a permanent peace.[3]

By March 1974, an agreement to withdraw troops from the immediate vicinity of the Suez Canal had been reached between Israel and Egypt. Israel and Syria were still negotiating through Kissinger. And Jordan, at the secret meeting in the Arava desert trailer, was insisting that its turn had now come. Hussein used the words "separation of forces," indicating that he should not be left standing at the side of the suddenly busy diplomatic road. Rifai gave these details:

- The armies of Israel and Jordan should withdraw to a distance of 8 kilometers (5 miles) from the Jordan River Valley, to be stationed in new positions in the hills.

- Jordan would establish civil authority in the area from which the Israeli forces withdraw.

- Jordan's army would not be permitted to cross the river and in any event would have to remain 8 kilometers to the east.

- Working parties would be set up, to ensure that Jordan would be the recognized negotiator on behalf of the Palestinians.

The ancient West Bank town of Jericho was not mentioned in the clandestine Arava talks, but Jordan was intending to run its civil administration of the 8-kilometer zone using Jericho as headquarters. Amman's proposal eventually became known as "the Jericho Plan."

It was not, in fact, an original Jordanian proposal. Hussein was given the idea by Henry Kissinger, during one of his many visits to the Middle East. Every time he shuttled from Jerusalem to Damascus and on to Cairo, Kissinger would stop in Amman to brief the king.

But even before Kissinger, Israel's own Yigal Allon is credited with inventing the "separation of forces" concept in the context of Jordan. Allon shared his idea with the Americans, and when it reached Washington it was backed by President Richard M. Nixon. Kissinger brought it to the Middle East, and it came back to Israel's leaders from Hussein and Rifai.[4]

When Golda Meir heard the demand for a disengagement along the Jordan River, she replied with a quizzical look on her face, "I do not understand why we need to separate our forces. After all, we didn't just have a war between us."

Hussein was clearly annoyed. "Must I make war on you in order to receive what you are already ready to give to Egypt and Syria? Do we have to fight in order to reach a separation of forces? If you agreed to separate forces in the Sinai and pulled back from the lines you reached in combat, why will you not agree to withdraw when there has been no war?"

Mrs. Meir, who obviously did not agree with the formula suggested by her own cabinet minister Allon, stood firm on her insistence that the Israeli army would hold its ground. She told the king, "In the agreement which we reached with Egypt, we agreed to pull back from several points along the Suez Canal, but not along the cease-fire line. And that was where we just had a war. We are willing to transfer to you a certain strip of land on the western side of the Jordan River, where you could rule with the help of a civil administration. The area would, of course, be de-militarized."

Prime Minister Rifai sounded interested. "The area would have to be under our sovereignty," he said. That would set the helpful precedent, from Amman's point of view, that the West Bank is Jordan's.

Moshe Dayan wondered, however, "Why is sovereignty so important?" Legal complications could also complicate Israeli politics at a delicate juncture.

Prime Minister Meir took up the point: "Your Majesty, I would of course not be able to make such a decision on my own. I would have to ask my government and call new elections to have a transfer of territory endorsed." She explained some of the problems she faced in holding together a ruling coalition in Jerusalem.

King Hussein returned to his proposal, as he saw it, "An agreement to separate our forces must be for the entire length of the line, and not only for a limited portion of it."

The talks in the Arava ended without agreement. An opportunity to make progress was wasted, perhaps a unique and historic opportunity. If only the two sides had showed a bit more flexibility, the road to a peace settlement might have begun.

As the talks ended, the mood was dark and Mrs. Meir and Dayan were gloomier than when they started. The participants shook hands with obvious sadness. It was the last time that King Hussein saw Golda Meir, and it was the closure of an historical circle that had taken some twenty-eight years to circumnavigate. Although they never again met, Hussein would occasionally send personal regards to her through trusted intermediaries such as American diplomats.

Mrs. Meir and Dayan returned to Jerusalem empty-handed, without the breakthrough that they had hoped could save their government. Two weeks later, on April 10, 1974, the prime minister and her cabinet submitted their resignations to Israel's president.

A new government was installed, with Yitzhak Rabin as the compromise prime minister chosen by a divided Labor Alignment. The Knesset, Israel's parliament, gave its formal vote of confidence on June 3. Shimon Peres was the new defense minister, replacing Dayan, and Yigal Allon became foreign minister.

Barely two weeks later, President Nixon arrived in Israel. He was on a Middle East tour as a foreign-policy distraction from the Watergate scandal, which would force his resignation two months later. Nixon was the first American president to visit the region while in office.

Nixon's set speech for the tour suggested that the "disengagement" agreements that Israel reached with Egypt and Syria were not the end of the road. To continue the peace process, he told the Israelis, they should negotiate a similar accord with Jordan. Kissinger was stronger and more precise, telling Prime Minister Rabin to make a deal with Hussein while he was still "a player," predicting that otherwise, the world would recognize the PLO leader Yasser Arafat as spokesman for the Palestinians within six months.[5]

The Israelis did not, in fact, need an American push to renew the secret dialogue with Jordan. Rabin was quite anxious to do so, and within two months the new government made its first contact with Amman. The prime minister himself met Hussein and Rifai on August 29, 1974, and they became well acquainted through over a half a dozen meetings in the three years of the Rabin administration.[6]

Israel initiated all the meetings, and they all took place on Israeli soil. The king never offered, and the Israelis never asked, to hold any sessions in Jordan. Rabin and his senior ministers assumed that Hussein would not be able to guarantee secrecy and security.

The Israeli team had to include the main factions of the Labor Alignment, and so Rabin had Peres and Allon at his side at all the clandestine encounters. Only rarely did Rabin have a chance to exchange a few words in private with Hussein, for instance when accompanying the king to a helicopter. The Jordanians could detect the divisions within the Israeli administration, but there had been similar disagreements on foreign policy in the 1960s under Prime Minister Eshkol.

All the meetings but one took place in the Arava. Only once more, after Golda

Meir's departure from office, did Hussein go to the guest house in the northern outskirts of Tel Aviv. For security reasons, the caravan trailer was erected in the Arava at a different site each time.

Hussein and Rifai arrived by helicopter, usually flown by the royal pilot Colonel Zaza. Only twice were the Israelis—Mordecai Gazit, and later Amos Eran, who replaced him in 1975 as director general of the prime minister's bureau—surprised to see the king himself piloting the aircraft. From the landing site, the Jordanians were taken by car or by helicopter to the venue of the talks.

Hussein tended to arrive in the evening, and the talks usually lasted three and a half hours, so dinner was usually served during the meetings. The king made no special culinary requests and ate what was offered. After each session of talks, Hussein and Rifai returned to their side of the border. They never spent the night in Israel. As for reports in the European press that the king wore a disguise and strolled past the sidewalk cafés of Tel Aviv's Dizengoff Street, they were simply untrue.[7] Hussein never took the risk and was not so curious about downtown Tel Aviv, not during Mrs. Meir's time and not during Rabin's three years of rule.

Knowing his concern for security, the Israelis never even asked to be photographed with Hussein, much as they would have liked to do so. Jordanian officials do assume, however, that the Israelis used hidden cameras and microphones to record the encounters.

Preparing for each meeting, officials on the Israeli side drew up agendas, intelligence reports on Hussein and events in Jordan, and position papers based on the previous rounds of talks. Psychologists, doctors, and Middle East analysts contributed to the reports, although they could only guess that their subject—Hussein—was actually in direct contact with Israel.

Basing their diagnosis on films, tapes, and intelligence data, the medical experts said that the king did not appear to have inherited any serious mental illness from his father, Talal, but that Hussein did suffer from occasional bouts of melancholia and milder depression. Intelligence analysts combined the medical views with the files on previous meetings to draw up recommendations to Israel's senior ministers on how best to behave and speak with Hussein.[8]

At the end of each meeting between the king and the Israelis and after the king left, sometimes as late as midnight, Gazit or Eran would rush to their office in Jerusalem to prepare a full report based on the notes and partial transcript they wrote during the talks. Their secretary had full security clearance and typed the report for presentation to Prime Minister Rabin in the morning.

The reports are held in Israel's government archives, classified as "secret—not to be published" for at least thirty years. It is doubtful that they will ever be published. The governments of the twenty-first century will be empowered to extend the ban should they choose to do so.

As a matter of protocol, each clandestine meeting began with a general review of the political situation in the Middle East and the world at large. These were discussed, in turn, by King Hussein and by Rabin. These introductory remarks tended to be lengthy, in part because both men spoke English very slowly. Rabin would emphasize every other word with a sharp exclamation.

Hussein would tell of his recent visits to Arab and other foreign countries, revealing parts of his conversations with foreign leaders that strengthened his call on Israel to make concessions. The king frequently complained about American foreign policy, saying the United States consistently failed to understand the problems of the Middle East.

The first meeting in this period was in late August 1974, and as the Israeli who had met the king before, Yigal Allon introduced Rabin and Peres. Hussein said that he had, of course, read and heard much about them and felt he knew them to some degree. The two sides exchanged pleasantries, including some harmless jokes at the expense of Henry Kissinger who carried his ego as an extra piece of baggage on his international diplomatic missions.

Prime Minister Rabin said that he would soon be visiting Washington. Peres added, with a smile, that Kissinger would be there, too, prompting Hussein to quip, "In Washington, for a change."

Israel's objectives during Rabin's period in office were

• to assess the possibilities of making any deal at all with Jordan;
• to overcome the tactical difficulties, such as minor border infringements and environmental problems, which inevitably crop up between neighbors;
• to find a common point of view between Israel and Jordan with regard to developments in the West Bank, especially the threat posed by Palestinian guerrilla groups; and
• to explore the possibilities for economic cooperation.

Jordan put forward two proposals at the talks with Rabin, Peres and Allon: either an interim settlement, to include a partial Israeli withdrawal from the West Bank; or a full peace treaty in exchange for the return of all captured territory, including East Jerusalem, to Jordan. Although Jerusalem's sovereignty would be divided by the pre–1967 border, this could be drawn only on maps and would not require a physical separation between the two halves of the holy city. A single municipal administration could remain.

Hussein did say that minor modifications of the border could be acceptable, and he told the Israelis that they could retain a few military and civilian outposts in the Jordan River Valley with the understanding that these would be isolated points within Jordanian territory. Hussein also asked that the Gaza Strip be made part of Jordan.

When the king, at his first meeting with Rabin, proposed an interim arrangement, Hussein stressed that the "separation of forces" pact should be effective along the entire river valley. The Israeli team felt the king was out to neutralize the Allon Plan, which would have kept the valley in Israeli hands as a defensive line against invasion.

Rabin seemed nervous at this first encounter, and he rejected Hussein's proposal out of hand, adding with an emphatic and negative shake of his head that he would not even consider it as an option for the future. Rabin said the "separation" would in fact be a unilateral retreat by Israel's army, and the former military chief of staff said it was out of the question.

Hussein's face twisted in anger, but before he could speak, Shimon Peres raised another idea he had discussed in recent years: a federal arrangement, which would have Israel and Jordan administering the West Bank together. The Jordanians listened attentively as Peres filled in some of the details. West Bank Palestinians would continue electing members to the Parliament in Amman, while Jewish settlers would vote in Israel's Knesset elections. The two populations would live peacefully, side by side, each under a different flag—Israeli and Jordanian coexistence.

Peres conceded that his plan might seem only the product of an active imagination, "but fantasy is the only way to resolve this situation."

Hussein appeared to be losing his patience and shot back, "I suggest we talk about the present," and the immediate requirement, he added, was for a "separation of forces" agreement.

Allon, who knew the king best, intervened in the hope of rescuing the meeting from failure. Allon proposed that Israel allow Jordan to set up a civilian administration in a small part of the Jordan River Valley. It was a similar idea to one put forward by Golda Meir in the past, but Allon went further with a specific offer to make Jericho the headquarters for the Jordanian administrator.

The U.S. State Department, which was deeply involved in the contacts between Israel and Jordan, informally labeled the proposal "balloon and sausages." Jericho and its outskirts resembled a round balloon. The Americans hoped that if such a plan were to become reality and Israeli troops pulled back, it would be the start of a broader process. Israel could later withdraw from heavily populated Arab villages, the outlines of which appeared on a map as sausage shapes.

When Hussein first heard the specific mention of Jericho, the possibility of regaining even a small chunk of the West Bank seemed intriguing. The meeting in the Arava was about to end, and the king simply said that he would think about Allon's proposal and would give his considered response at the next session.[9]

Hussein returned to his palace in Amman. He had to turn his attention to another matter: the approaching date of the Arab summit in Rabat, Morocco. At the top of the agenda stood the Palestinian issue.

For various and complex reasons, the PLO's prestige and influence had grown since the October 1973 war, even though the Palestinians played no role in the fighting. An Arab summit in November, in Algiers, conferred on the organization the status of "the sole representative of the Palestinian people," with all the Arab League nations except Jordan voting for the resolution.

Israeli analysts believed that the next summit would more explicitly remove from Jordan the right to represent the Palestinians in peace negotiations. The Rabin cabinet debated the issue, and then quickly split into two camps. One, led by Allon, clung stubbornly to the Jordan option and called for a more intensive push to clinch a deal, to boost Hussein's prestige before it was too late. Rabin and Peres gave their weight, however, to the second group identified as "Egypt-oriented," saying the next major diplomatic initiative should be aimed at an agreement with Cairo to build on the earlier separation of forces along the Suez Canal.

Rabin recalls, "I had strong doubts as to whether Jordan could withstand the pressures which would be applied if it signed a peace treaty with Israel. We must remember that not a single Arab state, not even Egypt, was willing to sign a peace treaty after the war. It wasn't that Jordan did not want peace. She even tried to break through toward peace, but my judgment was that she could not withstand the pressures."

A week before the Rabat Summit, on October 19, the Israelis had another meeting with Hussein and Rifai. The three Israeli ministers had expected to meet a dejected king, or so they had been advised by their intelligence analysts who saw Hussein's standing in the Arab world quickly and surely declining. The monarch, however, was in a smiling, jovial, and self-confident mood.

Allon asked him, "Your Majesty, aren't you concerned that the Rabat conference will take from you the right to represent the Palestinians?"

"No," Hussein replied, explaining that he had coordinated his position with the Egyptians.

"You have nothing to worry about," Prime Minister Rifai added. "You will see how the leaders of the Arab states stand in a queue to shake His Majesty's hand."

With no apparent haste or worry, Hussein and Rifai again campaigned for the proposal they had nurtured for ten months: a withdrawal by Israeli forces all along the Jordan River.

Rabin did not even want to hear about it again. In his first months as prime minister, he had obviously lacked confidence. His coalition was fragile, and because Labor could not muster its own majority he depended on the National Religious party to stay in power. Rabin had promised the religious ministers that if Israel were ever to consider withdrawing from the West Bank, with its biblical links, the public would have its say in a referendum.

A short time earlier, Rabin told press interviewers that his diplomatic strategy was to drive a wedge between Egypt and Syria. At the secret meeting, a full year after the October war, Hussein knew how to read Rabin's intentions because the king had read the interviews.

He listened to Rabin's long presummit analysis, which said, "If the Rabat conference gives to Jordan a mandate to negotiate with Israel, it will be good for both sides if Israel first opened a dialogue with Egypt." The precedent that would be set in talking to Cairo, the Israeli added, would ease the path to peace for Jordan.

And if not? Without a mandate from the summit, and without peace negotiations between Israel and Egypt? Where would Jordan be left? None of the participants in the clandestine conference cared to discuss such a gloomy but likely possibility.[10]

The Rabat Summit fulfilled all the worst expectations of Israel and Jordan. King Hussein delivered an emotional speech, a dramatic call to the other Arab leaders not to undercut Jordan's prestige and power. He spoke of the deep historical roots of Jordanian-Palestinian unity, and he pointed out that his grandfather King Abdullah had defended Transjordan from Jewish expansionism. It was Jordan, he said, that managed to keep the Old City of Jerusalem and the West Bank out of Zionist hands in 1948.

Hussein reaffirmed Jordan's support for the right of the Palestinians to determine their own future, and he said he backed the PLO in its struggle for a homeland. But the king said a division of labor was required. Jordan, he said, should represent the Palestinians who live under Israeli occupation and the PLO could represent the Palestinians scattered among a dozen or more countries.

The conference seemed unimpressed by Hussein's speech. He was in a minority again, perhaps a minority of one. The final declaration in Rabat said the summit decided "to confirm the right of the Palestinian people to establish a national, independent authority on any Palestinian soil which shall be liberated, under the leadership of the P.L.O., which is the sole, legal representative of the Palestinian people. The Arab states will help that authority, when it is established, in every way."[11]

The PLO's international standing reached its height a month after the summit. Yasser Arafat, a gun in his belt, delivered a speech before the UN General Assembly in New York. After its terrible defeat at the hands of the Jordanians in 1970, the PLO was cutting off their political legs.

Hussein entered one of his dark and angry periods. His temper flared at the entire world: at Israel, at the Arab states, and at the United States. The king believed that they all betrayed him. Demonstrating his frustration over the Rabat Summit declaration, Hussein issued his own: Jordan would no longer be responsible in any way for the Palestinians living under Israeli occupation.

Despite continued pleas from Jerusalem through secret communications channels, Hussein refused to meet with Israeli leaders. "I don't want to hear from them," the king told the U.S. Ambassador in Amman, Thomas Pickering.

Hussein's stubborn silence lasted half a year. On May 28, 1975, the king had his third meeting with the Israeli triumvirate led by Rabin. Jordan was concerned about another interim accord Israel was to sign with Egypt. As in the past, the Jordanians wished to be kept in the diplomatic picture so as not to find themselves isolated.

The talks in the spring of 1975 remained in the shadow of the previous autumn's summit resolutions. The king could not forget them. He told the Israelis that he blamed them for taking a tough and uncompromising line on the eve of the Rabat Summit.

The division of diplomatic labor and styles between Hussein and Rifai again came to the fore, as the king remained calm and correct while pointing the finger of blame at the Israelis. Hussein was polite and avoided harsh words. The truly unpleasant words were left to Rifai to utter.

With great irony and bitterness, Jordan's prime minister said, "We are outside the picture. Now go talk to the PLO, and we shall see what happens."[12]

Jordan was not totally out of the picture and had no intention of sliding off to the margins of the Middle East complex. Hussein still hoped to prevent any separate peace between Israel and Egypt, for fear that they would hatch their own plans for a West Bank settlement without regard to Jordan's interests.

The king attempted to undermine whatever confidence the Israelis may have felt in Egypt's President Sadat. Hussein told the Israelis how he had flown to Alexandria and met Sadat there on the eve of the Rabat Summit. Sadat, he said, had promised him that Egypt would take Jordan's side and would prevent the other nations from stripping Jordan of its authority to represent the Palestinians.

Hussein said Sadat had broken his promise, within hours and without hesitation. Hussein challenged Rabin, "How can you believe in Sadat? If he didn't hesitate to double-cross me, and I am an Arab, you think he won't do the same to you, the Jews?"[13]

Despite Hussein's warnings, the Israelis found that they could do business with Sadat. Egypt appeared to be acting quite rationally in the post-Nasser years and especially because a measure of self-confidence was restored by the successful surprise attack on the Israelis in 1973. In September 1975, under heavy American pressure, Israel and Egypt signed a new interim agreement in Geneva. Israeli troops were withdrawn to some 40 kilometers (25 miles) from the Suez Canal, to the Mitla and Gidi Passes through the Sinai Desert mountains. Israel was paying a heavy financial price for the possibility of progress toward peace, because in the land returned to Egypt were the valuable oil fields of Abu Rodeis.

The secret diplomacy between Israel and Jordan continued apace, even though Hussein had no formal authority to act on behalf of the Palestinians. The king was privately ignoring the Rabat declaration in considering various measures touching the West Bank. He also knew that Israel, supported by written pledges from the United States, would never talk to the PLO. The Israelis, at least, would have to deal with him.

The subjects, however, radically changed after the Rabat Summit and the apparent decision by Israel to pursue peace with Egypt as a first step toward a broad settlement with the Arab states. Instead of trading ideas and barbs aimed at a peace treaty, Israel and Jordan began to concentrate on common problems.

Rabin did come up with a new offer, which served at least to show that Israel was not opposed to dealing with Hussein even after the hard knocks he suffered in Morocco. Rabin suggested that Jordan could take over the administration of major cities in the West Bank including Nablus and Ramallah. He also repeated Mrs. Meir's offer of a port in the Gaza Strip, where the Jordanian national flag could fly. If this were not enough, Rabin also said Jordan could use the port of Haifa and enjoy duty-free transport across Israel to get there.

In exchange, Jordan would have to agree—even if not in public—to an accord similar to a nonaggression pact. The military confrontation between Israel and Jordan would have to end.

Hussein must have felt tempted, but he rejected Rabin's new plan, saying Jordan still insisted on a complete withdrawal by Israeli forces from the land captured in 1967. Failing that, he said, a partial accord could feature a limited retreat from the western riverbank, leaving a demilitarized zone for the sake of everyone's security.

The king's reasoning was largely philosophical, touching on his place in Middle East history. He described the region as one filled with logical inconsistencies, with creative and destructive forces rising and falling with cyclical regularity. Hussein added, "The question is whether we have the strength to change the cycles."

He also questioned Israel's desire for peace. Sitting once alongside Amos Eran in a helicopter, Hussein asked the Israeli, "Do your leaders truly want to reach a peace settlement?"

From session to session, it became clear that the importance of the secret talks was simply their existence. The gap between the positions of Israel and Jordan was too great to hope for a peace treaty. Hussein wanted to regain every inch of his land, and the Israelis were not about to return to the thin, constricting and unsafe borders of their state's birth.

There was insufficient will to bridge the gaps and try to solve the Palestinian problem, but agreements and understandings on many secondary issues were still possible.

Another five meetings were held in the next two years, at a rate of one session every four or five months. In July 1976, the Israelis were surprised to hear that Zeid el-Rifai had resigned as Jordan's prime minister. His role as the king's chief adviser in the royal court was unchanged, however, and Rifai—even without holding any formal government post—continued to accompany Hussein to the secret talks with Israel.

The two sides managed to reach understandings on a long chain of subjects that ensured relative peace along the border.

On Arab terrorism, the Israelis were always concerned that Jordan might allow the Palestinian guerrilla organizations to return to their former bases to launch attacks against Israel. Rabin, Peres, and Allon urged Hussein to monitor the PLO closely, and their interest in this regard appeared to be shared by Hussein. He did not want Arafat and the more radical Palestinians walking the streets of Amman again.

To strengthen the common fight against terrorism, the security and intelligence agencies of the two nations stepped up their clandestine cooperation. Direct telex and telephone lines were established between the Mossad headquarters in Tel Aviv and the Jordanian intelligence service in Amman. Israeli intelligence officials visited Jordan from time to time, to exchange information and to coordinate actions against Palestinian guerrillas.

The shared interest could only be expressed secretly on July 5, 1976. In New York, Jordan's ambassador to the UN was condemning the previous day's startling, long-range rescue by Israeli military commandos of hijacked air passengers in Entebbe, Uganda. He called it "air piracy" by the Israelis, saying nothing of the Arab and German terrorists who had seized the Air France flight. Around the same time, the top officials in Jerusalem received a written message from King Hussein in which he congratulated Israel on the successful rescue mission. Hussein wrote that it was "a courageous act" in the war against terrorism.

On ecological matters, Israel and Jordan agreed to cooperate to maintain the cleanliness of the shared waters that they respectively called the Gulf of Eilat and the Gulf of 'Aqaba. A system was established to inform the other nation's authorities immediately if an oil spill occurred at the loading facilities maintained at both ports. Israel warned the Jordanians several times that an oil slick was headed toward 'Aqaba beach.

Concerning water, the two governments assigned experts to look into ways of sharing the Jordan River and its tributary sources without cutting into each other's irrigation needs. Yigal Allon was the senior minister in charge of the Israeli side of the issue. One proposal was that both countries employ an American engineering firm in Chicago to examine possible projects for cooperative use of the river's sources in the north.

On aviation, Israel and Jordan were able to agree on procedures to reduce the danger of midair collisions between aircraft landing at the airports of Eilat and 'Aqaba, separated by only a few miles. It was agreed that the control towers of the two facilities would monitor each other's frequencies to listen for any unusual situations.

Concerning aerial patrols, the two nations had to deal with Hussein's complaints about Israeli aircraft screaming through the skies over the border and beyond it into Jordanian airspace. The king was quite specific, waving a piece of paper and reading that on a certain date at a stated time, aircraft of a specified type flew over a named area for a precisely measured number of minutes. It was all so detailed that the Israeli leaders honestly said they would have to look into the matter. They asked Rifai to repeat the facts and figures, and Amos Eran hurriedly jotted them down. Rabin did promise Hussein that Israeli reconnaissance flights over his palace in Amman would cease.

As for sailing rights, Hussein claimed that Israeli naval vessels close to the 'Aqaba beach were polluting the water with noxious chemicals. He also complained that the Israeli patrol boats were far too noisy, when heard at the king's villa, particularly at night. Hussein suspected that the navy men were intentionally trying to harass the royal family, and if so they were succeeding. Rabin and Peres assured the king that they would stop all unnecessary disturbances off the 'Aqaba shore, and so they did.

On border demarcations, potentially dangerous misunderstandings had to be ironed out after a team of Chinese surveyors in Jordan, planning a new paved road to 'Aqaba, found that the frontier in the Arava was not precisely marked on the ground. Comparing the existing signs with old maps, the Jordanians concluded that Israel had "stolen" a few square miles of territory, and Hussein complained to Rabin about it. An Israeli team examined the area and the documents and concluded that the Jordanians were correct. The prime minister immediately told Hussein that the border markings were being moved a few miles to the west, and Jordan gained a small parcel of land.

Concerning plans for elections in the West Bank, Defense Minister Peres hoped in 1976 that the Palestinians would take part in voting for their own municipal councils. Hussein, however, warned the Israelis that radicals were likely to win most of the seats, and he advised against having an election. He was especially concerned about the future of his veteran supporters, including the mayor of Hebron, Sheikh Jaabri. As a gesture to the king, the Israelis expelled Jaabri's most dangerous rival, a communist organizer named Ahmed Hamze Natshe, on the eve of the balloting.

The expulsion, ordered by Peres, backfired. The elderly sheikh was angry because his townspeople were blaming him for his rival's forced departure from the West Bank. Indeed, Jaabri was defeated overwhelmingly by Natshe's replacement, Fahd Kawasme. Throughout the territory, pro-PLO candidates opposed to the Israeli occupation were victorious.

The king had been correct. His influence in the West Bank was cut by the elections the Israelis had organized. The PLO had received an energizing boost.

There was no progress toward a long-term settlement in the region, and the enemies of peaceful coexistence were gaining strength, but Israel and Jordan continued to discuss and reach understandings on the day-to-day issues that, if unresolved, can make neighbors nasty.

In November 1976, Prime Minister Rabin was advised by his top aides to give Hussein a gift on the occasion of his forty-first birthday. They asked Rifai to test what the king's reaction might be to receiving an Israeli-made Galil assault rifle. Hussein responded, "I would be honored," and Rabin gave him a fine olive-wood box containing the world-famous gun.[14]

As most of the outstanding minor issues had been resolved and there was no prospect of change on the major issue of permanent peace, there were fewer reasons for the leaders of the two nations to meet. Junior officials could handle most matters of cooperation.

Neither side wished to send a hostile message by turning down invitations or otherwise cutting off contact, but the decisive factor was a tragic event on February 9, 1977. Flying through a rainstorm, Hussein's royal helicopter crashed in the southern part of the kingdom. The monarch was not aboard, but his third wife Princess Alia was killed, as was his friend, confidant, and pilot Colonel Baader Zaza. The government's minister of health also perished in the disaster.

Hussein was plunged into depression. As a good Muslim he was a fatalist on such matters, but he appeared to blame himself on the basis that his flights to the west to meet Israel's leaders might have cursed the helicopter. Whatever the reason, diplomats in Amman at the time could see that the king did not have the energy or attention span for politics or diplomacy.

Hussein refused, despite Israeli requests, to carry on with the secret meetings. The king told the U.S. ambassador that until a new royal pilot could be found and fully trusted, flying to a meeting with the nominal enemy would be foolhardy. Abdullah al-Tel had betrayed King Abdullah's secret meetings with the Zionists, and an unreliable pilot could again do terrible damage.

The break in the clandestine talks, in the spring of 1977, fit in neatly with developments in Israel's domestic politics. Rabin had to call early elections, and an unexpected political revolution was the result. In May, the veteran opposition leader, the right-wing Menachem Begin of the Likud bloc, was elected prime minister. The Labor party, after twenty-nine consecutive years in power, was out.

Western governments could hardly hide their dismay, and Arab politicians were positively fearful that a man they expected to be a warmonger, a proud terrorist leader of the pre–1948 Irgun underground in Palestine, was now prime minister of the Middle East's leading power.

No one could guess that within two years, Begin would be making peace with Egypt. Relations with Jordan, however, were nonexistent. And the Palestinians, who expected no good from the Begin administration, got just that.

Chapter 11

Seven Lean Years under Likud

"Mr. Prime Minister, King Hussein says he will be happy to see me in London."
Menachem Begin was pleased by the report from his Foreign Minister Moshe
Dayan. Begin had recently taken office, after decades in the political desert, and
was comfortable with Dayan the war hero, whose strong Jewish nationalism was
enough to outweigh his prior connections with the Labor party.

Begin clung to his heartfelt belief that the Jews had the historic right to hold
the entire land of Israel, including the West Bank, which he called Judea and
Samaria. But he was also out to prove to all who branded him a warmonger that
he could be a peacemaker. Pursuing the secret dialogue with Jordan, about which
he received a full briefing immediately after his election victory, was part of
Begin's strategy. Amman represented a chink in the solid wall of Arab hostility
against Israel.

Dayan was happy to be back in government. After resigning from Mrs. Meir's
cabinet, he had spent three years at home in Zahala, a Tel Aviv suburb, cataloging
his antiques and archaeological artifacts. The Israeli public blamed him for the
mechdal, the "omission," of the Yom Kippur War, and the families of fallen
soldiers labeled Dayan "a murderer." He deeply desired one more chance to
change his public image, to add a positive accomplishment to his already substantial page in history. Dayan was elected to the Knesset on the Labor Alignment
list but barely hesitated to join Begin's Likud when invited to be foreign minister.

Begin declared publicly that his first aim was to bring peace to Israel, and he
assigned the task to Dayan, who immediately renewed old acquaintances who
had proved helpful. He contacted the U.S. State Department and he spoke to
Dr. Emanuel Herbert in London, asking that they arrange a meeting for him
with King Hussein.

Neither Begin nor Dayan believed in the so-called Jordanian option. The new
prime minister had his ideological reasons. Because Judea and Samaria were
justly part of Israel, in his view, why negotiate their future with Jordan? Dayan's

objections were based partially on his emotional attachment to the land of the Bible, but more so on his political analysis. He did not believe that Hussein would ever sign a peace treaty, without Israel's meeting the impossible condition that all captured territories be returned to Jordan.

Still, hoping for a diplomatic breakthrough to start the Likud administration on a positive note, Begin and Dayan wished to explore the Jordanian option. They wanted to see for themselves where the road through Amman might lead.

The meeting with Hussein was set for August 22, 1977, in London, on a Monday so that Dayan would not miss the weekly cabinet meeting on Sunday in Jerusalem. As luck would have it, the El Al Israel Airlines nonstop flight to London's Heathrow Airport had a minor engine problem and had to land in Paris. There, Dayan was delayed a further few hours due to a strike by British air traffic controllers. The foreign minister, traveling in the simple disguise of a hat and sunglasses rather than his customary eye patch, began to fear that he would not get to Dr. Herbert's house in London in time to see the king.

Dayan just made it to 1 Langford Place in St. John's Wood at the appointed hour, 9:30 in the evening. He later wrote, "I had been there some years before, on a similar purpose, and already knew the owner."[1] It was the first time that he met Dr. Herbert's wife, however, and he recalled—without naming the Herberts—that she was tall and elegant and spoke at length about her work "on behalf of the black people in Africa."[2]

This was to be the last secret meeting arranged with the aid of Hussein's Jewish physician in England. Dr. Herbert was certainly willing to help, but he was seventy-nine years old and was beset by bad health. At the end of his fourteen years of service to Israel and Jordan, he no doubt felt a certain sense of satisfaction that the two nations were talking, and no one knows how he personally felt about the Palestinian issue and the failure to resolve it. Emanuel Herbert took his secrets and his opinions to his grave, when he died three years later.

"King Hussein was late, and he apologized as he greeted me with a handshake and a broad smile," Dayan wrote. "I found him greatly changed, not in appearance but in spirit. It was not the same man I had last seen. He was now withdrawn, subdued, without sparkle, and the political topics I raised did not seem to touch him deeply."[3]

Dayan wrote that the king was "depressed," whether by the death of his wife or by his humiliation at the Rabat Summit. The Israeli began to doubt whether Hussein was ruling Jordan, "or was he spending most of his time gallivanting abroad?"

After a ninety-minute talk, Dayan and Hussein parted and there was no indication as to when there would be another meeting, if at all. To his surprise, Dayan was telephoned the next morning by Dr. Herbert, who said the king would like to have another chat. They met at 1 Langford Place at four o'clock in the afternoon for only one hour, but Dayan recalled later that the brief exchange of views finally made it crystal clear that Hussein would not consider any permanent settlement without regaining every inch of the territory he had lost in 1967.

The king said he could not possibly recommend to even a single Arab village that it become Israeli. Territorial compromise would be seen as treachery, he added, because it would appear that he was giving land to the Jews for the sake of expanding his kingdom.

Hussein also told Dayan that while Jordan felt a genuine obligation to help the Palestinians, who comprised over half the Hashemite kingdom's population, the Rabat Summit declaration had made it impossible and useless for him to take any initiatives on their behalf.[4]

This is the Israeli foreign minister's testimony, and there is no version publicly offered by Hussein to set against it. It should be remembered, however, that it would conflict with Dayan's political philosophy to detect any glimmer of hope for progress in what Hussein was saying. Dayan was seeing what he expected and perhaps wanted to see. He always wanted Israel to keep the West Bank, which is steeped in biblical connections to the Jewish people.

When he returned to Jerusalem, Dayan told Prime Minister Begin what he certainly wanted to hear: that there was nothing to discuss with the king. Perhaps Dayan should have thought first about why Hussein had bothered to invite him to a second conversation in London. The foreign minister wrote that "he probably felt that he might not have been sufficiently explicit in our first talk."[5] A bit more meditation might have led Dayan to conclude that Hussein was signaling his willingness to carry forward with his dialogue with Israel, even with a government led by the feared and hated Begin.

The king might, eventually, have been persuaded to be more flexible than his basic position that there could be no formal peace without a complete Israeli withdrawal from the West Bank and East Jerusalem. Throughout his reign, after all, he had hated the notion of being left isolated while others took action. And Hussein had reasons to fear that Israel and Egypt might be working secretly toward peace negotiations.

The connection with Jordan struck Dayan as dry and unfulfilling. He was seeking a breakthrough toward peace to write that new page in the history books, and—as Hussein had feared—Dayan turned his attention toward Egypt. Only two weeks after the last meeting at Dr. Herbert's house, Israel's foreign minister was off on another secret mission to see another Arab king, Hassan II of Morocco, who was helping to bring Egyptians and Israelis together.

By November, President Anwar Sadat would be visiting Jerusalem and calling for "no more war, no more bloodshed." He would be hailed worldwide as the first Arab leader to go to the Jewish state. Hussein's visits were secret, and in any event they seemed meaningless when compared with Sadat's grand gesture.

Dayan met in Morocco with King Hassan, who advised him that "any solution of the Palestine problem within the framework of the Kingdom of Jordan would lead to the loss of the [Hashemite] throne, and so Hussein would assuredly withhold his agreement." A federation linking Jordan and the West Bank would simply make the Palestinians a dominant majority, "and they would soon kick out King Hussein."[6]

The next month, Dayan was back in Rabat and met in the royal palace with Egypt's Deputy Prime Minister Hassan Tuhami. The director of the Mossad secret agency, Yitzhak Hofi, had already been in Morocco to set an agenda with Tuhami,[7] and when Dayan made his secret side trip to North Africa while on official business in Europe he was accompanied to the talks only by the Mossad man representing Israeli interests in Morocco. The espionage agency was again taking a direct and active role in coordinating Israel's clandestine diplomacy.

Tuhami's initial outline of the Egyptian proposal for Middle East peace suggested linking the West Bank with Jordan, and he said Egypt and Saudi Arabia would work together to prevent Palestinian radicals from toppling King Hussein. Tuhami suggested that he and Dayan immediately agree on a peace treaty, based on complete Israeli withdrawal from the occupied territories, and predicted that when Hussein doubtless joined in the peace process, even the radical president of Syria, Hafez al-Assad, would join in.[8]

It was ironic that Begin and Dayan were pursuing the course that King Hussein himself had recommended to Eban and Allon nine years earlier. Make peace first with the largest Arab nation, Egypt, the king had advised, and then all other Arabs would have an easier time accepting Israel. When Rabin was prime minister, he had hoped to separate Egypt from Syria and the Soviet Union, but he had never quite managed to turn the trick.

Begin succeeded where Rabin had failed, in part because the Egyptians saw Begin and Dayan as a formidable team that could be trusted to negotiate seriously and keep its word. Not generally acknowledged was the fact that Rabin and the more traditional Jordan-oriented Labor party politicians of Israel were interested in dealing with Egypt so as to lead to a settlement with Jordan on a final status for the West Bank and Gaza. Begin and Dayan saw Cairo as their only diplomatic destination, because they were not interested in surrendering the West Bank.

President Sadat knew that Begin's intention with regard to the West Bank was simply to keep it. But Egypt had to be seen to be acting for the interests of all Arabs, not only to regain the Sinai Peninsula.

The compromise hammered out at Camp David, Maryland, with U.S. President Jimmy Carter's mediation, was an offer to the Palestinians of "autonomy" over their daily lives. Israeli forces and settlers would remain, but Jordan would be invited to participate in talks to agree on a final status for the occupied territories. The peace treaty signed in Washington on March 26, 1979, had a joint statement by Sadat and Begin attached, which said, "In the event Jordan decides not to take part in the negotiations, the negotiations will be held by Israel and Egypt."

A few rounds of talks were held, but the autonomy discussions led nowhere. The PLO was not interested, local Palestinian residents did not dare defy Arafat by taking part and Hussein simply treated the entire Camp David process as "not good enough."

The Israelis were becoming accustomed to hearing insulting remarks about Hussein from Sadat's lips, just as they had heard their share of anti-Sadat statements uttered by Hussein. The Egyptian president denigrated Hussein's leadership qualities and his reluctance ever to make a decision.

As always, the king was, above all, nervous about being left out of something important. So on September 17, 1978, on the eve of the Camp David Accords, which led to the final peace treaty between Egypt and Israel, Hussein was in London and telephoned Sadat at the U.S. presidential retreat in the Maryland mountains. The king was attempting to invite himself to the talks, but Sadat was not interested in any interloper at this stage. He had been assured of a total Israeli evacuation of the Sinai, including the settlements at Yamit and Sharm ash-shaykh.

Hussein's demands could spoil the deal, so the idea that he fly to Camp David was rejected by Sadat. He instead invited Hussein to meet him in Morocco, where Sadat would stop on his way home to Cairo from Washington. The king was so offended that he did not fly to Morocco. He flew to Baghdad, where he joined Iraq and the other radical Arab states in setting up a new Rejection Front standing against the Egyptian-Israeli accords.[9]

The PLO branded Sadat "a traitor to the Arab peoples," and Palestinian extremists such as Abu Nidal launched a violent campaign of vengeance against Egyptian targets.

King Hussein totally cut the fifteen-year-old secret diplomatic connection between Israel and Jordan. Prime Minister Begin sent requests for a meeting, but at best the Jordanians suggested that the king's brother Prince Hassan might see Deputy Prime Minister Yigael Yadin. Hussein was so angry that he decided to cancel even the low-level talks, and it was Begin's turn to be offended by the king's behavior.[10]

Time appeared to be running against Hussein's interests, however. Under the Likud government, construction of Jewish settlements in the West Bank and Gaza greatly accelerated, and Jews were moving into towns previously recognized as all-Arab. A few days after winning the election in May 1977, Begin visited the West Bank settlement of Elon Moreh, built during the Rabin administration, near the major Arab town of Nablus. The new prime minister celebrated his victory with the ultranationalist settlers and promised there would be "many more Elon Morehs."

Under the authority of Agriculture Minister Ariel Sharon, a hardheaded war hero who spoke of "establishing facts on the ground" so that Israel would never have to leave the West Bank, more than one hundred new settlements were erected in the occupied territories during the seven years of Begin's premiership.

From late 1977 until 1984, however, there were no contacts between the governments of Israel and Jordan. The framework for communications and reaching understandings withered and nearly died. The intelligence agencies of the two nations continued to exchange information aimed at fighting Palestinian terrorists, but to a much more limited degree.

Only a small number of Labor party politicians, now in the unaccustomed role known in parliamentary systems as "the Opposition," still believed in the Jordanian option. One of them was Shimon Peres, the former defense minister who had been impressed by the range of helpful agreements he had been able to arrange with Hussein. Peres was now chairman of the Labor party, and he hoped to be an active leader of the Opposition to pave a route back to government.

Peres visited London in July 1978, naturally meeting Britain's Labor party Prime Minister James Callaghan and Foreign Secretary Dr. David Owen. Peres learned that coincidental with his visit, King Hussein was also in London. The small beacon of an idea was lit in the Israeli's mind, and he asked Callaghan to try and arrange a Peres-Hussein meeting.

Callaghan agreed to try, and messages began flying back and forth across London. The exiled King Constantine of Greece, who lived in England and who was one of Hussein's friends, took part in the secret communications, and the king of Jordan agreed to meet Peres. He was curious to assess Israeli plans after Sadat's surprise visit to Jerusalem the previous November.

Peres realized he should check with Jerusalem and not simply purport to represent Israel without any authority. He telephoned the secretary general of the Labor party in Tel Aviv, Chaim Bar-Lev, and asked him to seek the Begin administration's permission for Peres to meet Hussein.

Bar-Lev made a few telephone calls, and then one more to London. "The answer," he told Peres, "is no." Begin was opposed to such a meeting and would explain his reasons to Peres when the Labor party leader returned home.

Peres called Callaghan, explained his situation and apologized. The British passed the word—and the apology—to Hussein.

When Peres flew back to Jerusalem, he immediately went to see Begin and asked him, "Why did you forbid me to meet with Hussein?"

The two political rivals did not get along personally at all, and Begin scored no points with Peres by portraying the episode as a matter of personal pride. "How could it be that Hussein refuses to meet with us," he asked Peres, as though the concept were painful, "and yet would meet with you? Please understand me. I had to do this. Even your master and mentor, David Ben-Gurion, would not have permitted this meeting."

But Peres did not understand. During the next election campaign in 1981, when public opinion polls indicated the Labor party would topple Begin and return to power, Peres stepped up his efforts to meet clandestinely with Arab leaders. In July 1978, he had met in Salzburg, Austria, with President Sadat, but that was no secret because Sadat had already visited Israel and had begun the negotiating process.

Peres was in Europe again in March 1981, and he no longer cared about having Begin's permission to meet the king of Jordan. Peres sought the assistance of his friends, French businessman Jean Friedman and British retail executive Lord Marcus Sieff, who had personal and political contacts that might lead to Hussein.

The Israeli opposition leader was in Geneva, delivering a speech on March

16 to Switzerland's United Jewish Appeal (UJA) charity. He already had a secret trip to Morocco planned, to meet with King Hassan on March 18. When Peres returned to his hotel after the UJA banquet, Lord Sieff called him from London to say that he had managed to do what he had been asked to do, except "it" was with "the man's brother." Because the conversation was on a normal, insecure telephone line, Peres and Sieff spoke only in vague terms, but the Israeli understood that a meeting had been arranged with King Hussein's brother.

Peres willingly took a detour to London the next day and was driven to Sieff's home. There, at dinnertime, four men assembled around the dining table: Peres, his American-born confidant Al Schwimmer, Marcus Sieff, and King Hussein's brother.

"From the first moment, Peres could not stop staring at the brother," the politician's biographer wrote. "He appeared to be 35 or 40 years old, chubby, with a carefully groomed moustache. The more he kept looking, the greater were the doubts in Peres's mind. The man sitting across from him bore a resemblance to the king, but Peres had never met Prince Hassan. He had studied many photographs of Hassan, and the man sitting across the table and introduced as Hussein's brother did not look like Hassan at all. 'Something strange is happening here,' Peres thought."[11]

It was indeed a very strange meeting. The mystery was solved during the conversation itself, when Peres realized he was meeting "the wrong brother." It was not Crown Prince Hassan, the heir to the throne who was already in charge of economic development, but the other brother who had little or no political influence: Prince Muhammad.

Peres was embarrassed and angry, and the meeting at Sieff's home was a waste of time. Dinner dragged on for some two hours, and Peres then hurried off to be flown by private jet to Paris. There, he entered another small jet and next emerged in Marrakesh, Morocco. This time he knew he was meeting a Hassan—the Moroccan monarch.

Peres's return to Israel was at 8:30 the next evening. The nightly news on Israel Television began, at 9 o'clock, with the dramatic item that the chairman of the Labor party had just had political talks with the king of Morocco and with King Hussein's brother.

The television news and Peres's biographer did not reveal all the details. For instance, Prince Muhammad is said to be mentally unstable. The police in London had detained him several times, once for allegedly entering a casino with a concealed pistol.

The media never reported that Hussein was extremely angry at his brother Muhammad, and the king complained to his friend, British Prime Minister Margaret Thatcher, "Why are the Israelis interfering in my family life?" Muhammad had promised his elder brother long ago not to become involved in politics. The king punished him by cutting his monthly allowance and threatening to take away his two houses in London. According to one private account, Hussein learned that his sister-in-law Princess Fariel was involved in arranging the meeting at Lord Sieff's house, and so he ordered Muhammad to divorce her. Since then, Muhammad and Fariel have lived apart.

The immediate furor in Israel, at the height of an election campaign, was over the incredibly rapid leak to the state-run television station about Peres's secret diplomacy. The opposition leader blamed Begin, saying the prime minister knew of Peres's plans beforehand and arranged the leak to make it appear that Peres was running around the world irresponsibly. Begin's Likud ministers, quite credibly, said Peres had leaked the news through one of his aides in order to seize the image of a dynamic statesman. The Likud accused Labor of a cheap stunt.

Either way, the Hashemite king and his family had become political footballs in the election game as played at its roughest in Israel.

The incident gave Menachem Begin and his party campaigners the opportunity to press on the Israeli public the Likud's claim that "the Jordanian option" was a worthless slogan nurtured only in the minds of Labor politicians.

Leaks to the press were part of the hidden diplomatic process between Israel and Jordan for two decades. The Jordanians privately accused Israeli politicians, trying to inflate their own reputations, of violating the cardinal and mutual pledge of utter secrecy.

A report in *The New York Times* in March 1969, stated that King Hussein had met with Abba Eban. The newspaper added that Israel's military censor had attempted to prevent mention of the talks. Government spokesmen in Jerusalem and Amman immediately denied the story, but in fact the meetings continued. More leaks were to follow.

Rumors abounded in diplomatic circles in 1970 that Hussein was meeting Yigal Allon. The Israeli censor did not simply ban news reports on the subject; he summoned foreign correspondents to remind them of their responsibilities under the censorship rules. The journalists were told that "inaccurate reports" of this type could cause great damage; there would be a political storm in the Arab world, and any Arab politician even considering a peace settlement with Israel would be scared away.

Time magazine published an item in November 1970, reporting that Hussein and Allon had met in both London and the Arava. The king issued a strong denial.

Israeli politician Uri Avneri raised the issue in the Knesset, however, demanding a debate on "the meetings between Minister Allon and King Hussein." The parliamentary speaker immediately ordered that Avneri's remarks be struck from the official record, but word of what he said reached journalists throughout Israel within hours. Three foreign correspondents wrote stories about it, and when the censor banned their transmission abroad, the newsmen protested that the military censor was now engaging in political interference. The journalists sent their stories abroad anyway.[12]

The leaks, then, did not begin with the Begin administration. The difference was that successive Labor party governments did what they could to plug the leaks, appointing committees to investigate who had talked to the press and reminding officials to keep secrets secret. After taking office in 1977, however, Likud bloc ministers themselves were active leakers. In opposition, Labor leaders could only respond in kind.

The Likud ministers simply had a different concept of using the press as a means of promoting party ideology. For relations between Israel and Jordan, Begin's two terms in office were "seven lean years," in the biblical lexicon of Joseph the interpreter of dreams. There were no secret meetings, but the censor was ordered to take an extremely liberal view of the subject, and so an unprecedented flurry of stories about contacts with Jordan appeared in Israeli newspapers between 1978 and 1984.[13]

Before becoming prime minister, Begin himself wrote an article that described in detail but sarcastically a meeting between Labor's Yigal Allon and King Hussein. Then the Opposition leader, Begin told how the Israeli minister used a wooden rod to show Hussein the highlights of the Allon Plan on a map, which had been hung on a wall.[14] Begin was out to ridicule the very notion of dividing the West Bank into Israeli and Jordanian sectors.

On July 18, 1981, Prime Minister Begin was sitting in the Knesset cafeteria surrounded by aides and admirers. He was in a terrific and loud mood, but some of the politicians were surprised to hear him speaking—almost shouting—about issues that were classified as state secrets. Among the topics was Peres's visit to Morocco's King Hassan. "As far as I'm concerned," Begin joked with unusual indiscretion, "he won't be seeing anything more than the earlobe of 'Morocco, shmorocco.' And just because I wouldn't permit him to see Hussein!"[15]

Jordan's king did not like, to put it mildly, any of the leaks. He was extremely sensitive to any mention in the world press that he had had contacts with Israel, and Amman's spokesmen hastened to deny all such reports. Hussein often complained to U.S. and British leaders about "the talkative Israelis."

The king would never confirm publicly that he had met Israeli leaders, but in a strange way his prestige was bolstered by the widespread assumption that he regularly did so. Even in the Arab world, anyone who was pursued and wooed by such figures as Golda Meir and Moshe Dayan could only be considered an important player on the political scene. One Israeli analyst said of Hussein, "It has been good for his ego."

The assumption that he met Israelis was dangerous, too. The PLO, as early as 1968, publicly accused Hussein of maintaining close contacts with the Zionist enemy. The Palestinians even forged documents that purported to prove that the king met with Prime Minister Levi Eshkol.

An Egyptian envoy sent to Amman by President Sadat tried to learn the truth in 1972 by the simple expedient of asking directly. The head of Cairo's military intelligence, General Muhammad Sadeq, simply queried the king, "Have you met with Yigal Allon?" Hussein tried to avoid giving a direct reply, but Sadeq persisted, "Your Majesty, you have not answered my question."

Without blinking an eye, Hussein told the Egyptian: "I did not answer you because I did not go to see him." General Sadeq reported to Sadat, however, that his impression was that Hussein did hold secret meetings with Allon.[16]

Even the radical Syrians felt they knew of Hussein's veiled diplomatic activity, but much as Damascus Radio criticized the king during low points in the two neighbors' relations no emphasis was put on alleged contacts with Israel. On the other hand, Israel's ambassador in London, Gideon Rafael, wrote of an unusual incident touching on Syria and Jordan: "Late one evening in April 1976, I was asked by telephone to go to an urgent meeting that night with a senior Arab personality at the home of a mutual friend."[17] The mutual friend was Dr. Emanuel Herbert and the senior Arab was King Hussein. The brief encounter had a simple purpose: Hussein was handing to the Israeli ambassador a letter from Syria's President Assad, addressed to Prime Minister Rabin.

Assad had at least assumed that Hussein would know how to get a message to the Israelis. The letter was an explanation of Syrian military moves in Lebanon, which were designed to protect the Christian minority from vicious attacks by the PLO for the sake of attempting to preserve the status quo in the troubled neighbor to both Syria and Israel. The message said that Syria's army would not approach Lebanon's border with Israel.

Hussein was not simply a mailman in this regard. He strongly favored the intervention in Lebanon by Syrian troops, hoping in 1976 that they would weaken or wipe out the military might of the PLO. The king said publicly that the Lebanese situation must be controlled and the fighting should not be allowed to spread. What he meant was that the PLO should be smashed.

Hussein told Rafael that he had persuaded Assad to pledge not to send his forces southward toward Israel. The ambassador could not wait for the next El Al flight to Tel Aviv, and so he flew early the next morning to Israel in the private jet of the British Jewish philanthropist Charles Clore. It was not every day, after all, that a letter is sent from the president of Syria to the prime minister of Israel.

A few days after delivering the missive to Rabin, Rafael returned to London holding Israel's response. The ambassador brought the letter to Dr. Herbert, who immediately delivered it to Hussein. The king, in turn, brought Israel's brief acknowledgment to President Assad.

This time, however, Ambassador Rafael took the opportunity to have a three-hour discussion with Hussein. Rafael's memoirs contain much praise for the king, calling him "the magical Houdini of the Middle East" and comparing him with the Bible's Noah because Hussein has survived so many political storms and floods. "By his nature," Rafael wrote, "he is both a dove and a hawk, and he has the sense to know where his sheltered shore is to be found."[18]

The ambassador even shared his assessment of the king with the king himself. Hussein smiled, obviously accepting the notion of being "a great survivor" as a compliment. After all, who would not want to be told that he has a phenomenal ability to walk between the raindrops without getting wet?

The seven lean years for the secret relationship with Jordan, combined with the Likud government's obvious hostility toward Amman, presented a formidable challenge to Hussein's ability to survive most any situation. Throughout his reign, the biggest threats to the Hashemite monarch had come from his fellow Arabs: from Egypt, from his Syrian and Iraqi neighbors, and from the Palestinians of the West Bank. There was never a threat to the kingdom itself from the Israelis. They had even tried to help him at certain times of trouble.

The great uncertainty that Hussein felt about Israel's intentions during Begin's seven years made him feel more vulnerable than ever. Ironically, the Syrian move into Lebanon, which he had so strongly endorsed, eventually resulted in a new threat to Hussein.

Six years after Syria put a temporary halt to the Lebanese factional bloodshed, including arrangements made with Israel through U.S. mediation, which delineated "red lines" that neither Israel nor Syria would cross in Lebanon, Begin sent his army to violate the accords. This was the June 1982 invasion of Lebanon. Israel said the growth of PLO power so close to the border had become intolerable. Under the command of Ariel Sharon, now defense minister, the Israelis seized their first Arab capital by bombing and then occupying much of Beirut.

Sharon called the military move "Operation Peace for Galilee," but his true intention was to establish a broader "new order" in the Middle East. This would include the overthrow of Hussein's government in Jordan.[19]

Sharon's eventual target was not Beirut, but Amman. And the Hashemite king well understood the threat.

Chapter 12

Minimalists and Maximalists in Amman

If there is one snapshot that troubled King Hussein's sleep, it was of Ariel Sharon riding atop an Israeli armored personnel carrier into Beirut. The nightmare was photographed in June 1982, at the climax of Israel's invasion of Lebanon. The Hashemites of Jordan could not help but think that Sharon would redirect his tanks toward Amman.

"We treat Ariel Sharon and his plans with great seriousness," said Crown Prince Hassan, Hussein's brother. "We fear that certain circles in Israel have grandiose ideas of a Greater Israel, including not only the West Bank but also the East Bank. We in Amman could be Sharon's next target."[1]

The official archives in Hussein's royal palace house a complete collection of the slogans and speeches made by right-wing Israeli politicians against Jordan or in favor of persuading Palestinians to leave the West Bank by crossing the river. The Crown Prince is known to keep his collection of Sharon's words of wisdom up to date. To prove his point in warning against Zionist expansionism, Hassan punctuates a political conversation with a visitor by sending an aide to fetch "the Sharon file." One item quotes a Sharon speech in which he says that Israel's security interests extend beyond the conflict with the neighboring Arab states, as far as Pakistan and countries in North Africa.[2]

The image of "*the* Israeli General" became an obsession among government officials and intellectuals in Jordan. They follow Sharon's political fortunes in Israel with great interest, by watching broadcasts and reading newspapers from across the river. They concluded that Sharon was the leading light of Begin's cabinet as defense minister. Even after Sharon left that post, the Jordanians feared that his political star would shine again under the hardline government they expected to follow Israel's Likud-Labor National Unity Coalition.

They hate Sharon, but they respect his abilities as a brilliant, if impulsive, military tactician and a stubborn ideologue who puts the interests of the Jewish people first and foremost. To the Jordanians, he is a dangerous activist and perhaps the only Israeli who could destroy Hussein's kingdom.[3]

The central reason for such alarm was the occasional publicity given to the far-reaching ideas that became known as "the Sharon plan." The veteran general's concept was that Jordan was in fact the Palestinian state—the only state that the Palestinian Arabs deserved, since the Jews had won their state to the west.

The Hashemite kingdom, in Sharon's view, was an artificial entity, of dubious legality, created by British imperialism. He believed that the conflict between Israel and the Palestinians would end, after a few short years, if they were able to establish their own state in Jordan's East Bank.

Outside observers had become accustomed to the existence of Jordan, and it was recognized by the international community, but Sharon's analysis could be supported on historical, geographical, and demographic grounds.

There is no question that turning the controversial concept into reality would make it easier for Likud to make reality of its political platform. The Likud—and especially its central component, the nationalist Herut party of Menachem Begin—did not hide its intention to annex the West Bank and make it part of the State of Israel. The Camp David Accords with Egypt delayed implementation of the plan, as Israel committed itself to granting autonomy to the Palestinians and to negotiating on the future status of the occupied territories.

In Sharon's view, a valuable opportunity was wasted in September 1970, when Israel helped Hussein guard his throne against the PLO onslaught. He believed that Israel should have withheld its support, that Hussein would probably have been toppled, that a Palestinian republic would have been established, and that the Arab-Israeli dispute would have been all but over.[4]

Sharon did not actually articulate such a plan for action, which has been explained and examined by other sources in Israel. At the height of Jordan's civil war, the chief of Israel's military intelligence agency, General Aharon Yariv, received a memorandum that simply shocked him.

"Has he gone mad?" Yariv asked about one of his subordinate officers, Lieutenant General Yoel Ben-Porat, who had written the memo, which could only be described as Machiavellian. Ben-Porat suggested that Israel's army should take advantage of the crisis in Jordan to help overthrow the king. The notion was shocking because it would involve an alliance, in intention if not in deed, with Israel's most implacable enemies, the Palestinian guerrilla organizations.

Ben-Porat's analysis suggested that helping the Palestinian refugees win their own homeland would correct the just and unjust losses they suffered during and since Israel's 1948 War of Independence. Yariv knew, however, that Golda Meir would not even want to hear such an idea and that the United States would totally oppose any move against Hussein that would help Arab radicals. General Yariv did not even pass the Ben-Porat memo on to higher political authorities.[5]

Seven years later, Sharon asked a left-wing Israeli journalist to arrange a meeting for him with PLO leader Yasser Arafat, apparently feeling they would have some points of common interest to discuss.[6] There were other attempts to set up similar meetings, but they all failed.[7]

Jordanian political leaders monitored these developments, to the best of their ability, and they were particularly concerned about more frequent discussion in Israel of the possibility of "transferring" or expelling a large number of Palestinian Arabs from the West Bank or Gaza. Rabbi Meir Kahane, of the Kach party on the fringe of the right wing, openly called for a mass expulsion to separate permanently the Arabs from the Jews. Others in Israeli politics, going as far back as 1967, have considered the possibility of persuading Palestinians to leave, and the Israelis from time to time offered financial incentives to Arabs who would move abroad.[8]

The political and ideological camps in Israel could broadly be divided into "doves" who were prepared to make concessions to win peace, and "hawks" who felt that compromises were too dangerous. In Jordan, the two camps had mirror images in "minimalists" and "maximalists."[9]

Jordan's maximalists, led by King Hussein himself, were interested in regaining complete authority over the West Bank. They believed it was Hashemite duty to rule over a Jordan comprising both sides of the river. And they were deeply pained by the loss of the Temple Mount and its mosques in East Jerusalem. Hussein's proposed federation, which he unveiled in 1972, was aimed at regaining all the lost land in some form.

The maximalists seemed to be guided more by sentiments of history than by political or economic analyses. Hussein spoke publicly of his moral duty to carry forward with his grandfather Abdullah's tasks. He and his group chose to ignore the limitations of Jordan's power, and they were determined to play a central role in the Arab world and the confrontation against Israel. The Hashemites always had a sense of mission, from Hussein's ancestors guarding the holy places in Arabia through Abdullah's dutiful persistence to create and preserve Jordan.

Hussein believed that royal continuity included the inheritance of responsibility. Duty was a large part of his self-image. The capture of all of Jerusalem by Israel weighed heavily on him, and the sense of having to be the guardian of the ancient city's holy sites shaped his perspective on the Jewish state. It was as though the maximalists recognized no other option but to pursue the return to Jordan of all the territory lost in 1967. They were willing to take all the risks of being stubborn.

The minimalists preferred to win what could be won. Their viewpoint crystallized after the bloody civil war of 1970. Against the background of the battle to the death against the Palestinian guerrillas, a strong group was formed in the royal court in Amman that sought to scale down Jordan's ambitions better to match the Middle East's realities.

The leading exponents of the new concept were the heir to the throne, Crown Prince Hassan, and Hussein and Hassan's influential uncle Sharif Nasser. Their supporters included the Queen Mother, Zein, senior army officers and leaders of the security services. Prime Minister Zeid el-Rifai was considered close to this group. They were pragmatists and not slaves to ideology.

The minimalists were extremely aware that Jordan's power and influence were limited by geography and demography, the all important facts that Israel had a perfect defensive line along the Jordan River, and that a majority of Jordan's two million people were Palestinians whose aspirations could not forever be denied. Israel, Syria, and Iraq were militarily more powerful neighbors, and Saudi Arabia to the south continued with its traditional haughtiness, leaving Jordan to sublimate its own interests to the wider consensus of the Arab world.

The demographic factor threatened to worsen for Jordan's Hashemite rulers. The Palestinian proportion of the East Bank population was 60 percent, and in Amman it approached 80 percent. The West Bank issue could not be dismissed as a foreign policy issue, but had to be seen as a matter of reuniting a torn family, a divided nation. Jordan's need to have close ties with the Palestinian nationalist movement repeatedly caused dangerous trouble in the kingdom.

The minimalists wished to avoid repetition of prior mistakes. Crown Prince Hassan and his supporters did not see the West Bank as an asset to be regained, but as a heavy weight without which Jordan could happily live.[10]

They accepted the apparent fact that Jordan could not recover the entire West Bank, and certainly not East Jerusalem, from the Israelis. And even if all the land were handed back by Israel, Jordan would never again be able to exercise all the authority there that it had had before June 1967. The minimalists believed that the long years of Israeli occupation led to formation of new political power centers, a modern outlook among the population and a yearning for independence. The old, established families of the West Bank—who were Jordan's chief supporters—were losing their influence. The younger generation believed more in the PLO than in the Jordanian authorities.

For the minimalists, the oft-renewed attempt by the Hashemite crown to represent the Palestinians put the crown itself in dire danger. Bringing the West Bankers back into Jordan's territory would ruin the delicate demographic balance maintained in the East Bank since 1967. Already in a sense a binational country, Jordan would become much more a Palestinian state. The large majority of citizens would not feel allegiance toward Hussein and his family. The kingdom would be doomed.

It was difficult to predict whether the coexistence of Palestinians and Jordanians in one country would break down. The Hashemite throne, however, could be seen to be depending on a mere 5 percent of the population, one hundred thousand Beduin Arabs, for its firmest bedrock of support. The Beduin comprised some 25 percent, however, of the forces in the army, police and security services.[11] Palestinians were given only minor technical and logistic planning jobs in the armed forces.

King Hussein, his sons, his brother Hassan, and other members of the royal family often visited army bases and spent much time in the company of soldiers. They led traditional ceremonies and took part in the Beduin dances and folklore displays. Such participation encouraged a sense of national identity and unity.

It would be too simple, however, to state that all the Palestinians in the East Bank were enemies of the Hashemite regime. Hussein and his family knew, in fact, how to bring Palestinians into government to give them a sense of belonging. The official policy was equality of opportunity, on the condition that the Palestinians wishing to be active in political life did not demand total political freedom. The sense of shared interests appeared to be built on financial prosperity for the Palestinians, so long as they allowed the Hashemites or "Transjordanians" to rule.[12]

After the loss of the West Bank, Jordan became prosperous, whereas it had been dependent before 1967 on financial assistance from the United States and Great Britain. Economic development continued at an impressive pace. The truly wealthy Arab oil states, Saudi Arabia and Kuwait, helped Jordan with massive loans, sparking a growth in economic output. Compared with 5 percent annually around 1976, Jordan's gross national product doubled in the years between 1978 and 1981 to reach $5 billion. Inflation was extremely low, and the Jordanian dinar held its value in terms of dollars.

After Lebanon became a living hell in the civil war of 1975–1976 and later events, Amman partially took over Beirut's role as a Middle East financial center. The Iran-Iraq war, which began in 1980, also highlighted Jordan's presence as a rock of stability in the region, and foreign investors showed their appreciation with their checkbooks.

Financial prosperity kept political dissidence at bay, and most conveniently for Hussein's government its capital was the chief beneficiary. In the decade following the Six Day War, Amman's population grew from 250,000 to 1 million people.

It was no coincidence that Crown Prince Hassan led the minimalists in Jordan's view of the West Bank, because he was in charge of economic development in Jordan. Carrying the burden of more territory, with the accompanying political challenges, would only hurt the economy.

"The policy of economic legitimacy," which was Hassan's name for the campaign to open opportunities to everyone, including Palestinians, "nourishes the existence of Jordan," he believed.[13] The prince and his bloc hoped to continue to broaden the financial foundations of Jordan. They knew that the economy and its growth were entirely dependent on political stability, and largely dependent on the policies of outside forces.

Jordan had few exports, besides potash mined from the Dead Sea and the many Jordanian citizens who went abroad to find employment. The potash production facilities would be flooded if Israel were to carry out its plan to build a canal from the Mediterranean to the Dead Sea, thus raising the Dead Sea's level. And if the oil states of the Arabian Gulf were either to go broke or to expel foreign workers, the Jordanians sending paychecks from the gulf to their relatives back home would simply become an underclass of the unemployed in Amman.

Only 10 percent of national income came from industrial production, and one-third from agriculture. Earnings from tourism were small, considering the monumental beauty of such sites as Petra in the south and Jarash in the north.

The minimalist camp believed that any political moves that would seriously change Jordan's situation would most likely harm the economy, and that such moves could do little good. Hassan saw himself as a realist, who accepted that the 1967 war and the Rabat Summit decisions seven years later removed Jordan's authority from the West Bank and made it impossible for Jordan to represent the Palestinians. He and the other minimalists believed it better to accept reality and concentrate on developing the remaining kingdom in the East Bank.

Hassan's goal was to make Amman an even greater financial center and the focus for all important economic decision making in the Arab world.

The dispute between the minimalists and the maximalists could be found in all corners of the Jordanian administration. The current state of play could often be seen in King Hussein's mood, in the frequent changes in Jordanian policy toward the PLO and other Arabs, and in the various stages of Jordan's attitude toward the West Bank.

At times divisions in Jordan were sharp. The security forces, in June 1987, launched an investigation into the appearance of dissident posters, signed by an underground group protesting corruption in Hussein's royal palace. The slogans were printed on a simple mimeograph machine, and they were posted in the stairways of apartment houses and office buildings throughout Jordan. They mentioned wasted resources, expensive official parties, and the arrests of political opponents and the destruction of their homes. It was widely believed that Ahmed Obidaat, a former prime minister and chief of the security services, supplied the information, as he was Rifai's strongest rival. Obidaat was also known as a vehement opponent of Jordanian ties with Israel.

Until the right-wing Likud bloc came to power in Israel in 1977, the maximalists of Jordan under Hussein generally had the upper hand, and it was firm policy to seek the return of the entire West Bank to Jordanian rule. After Menachem Begin became prime minister, even maximalists began to have doubts. Begin's government was taking over Arab-owned and so-called empty lands in the West Bank and moving a record number of Jewish settlers into those areas. Viewed from Amman, it seemed to be a gradual annexation of the occupied territory and a worsening of the living conditions of the Palestinians.

Hussein and his closest aides began to realize that the chances of recovering the entire West Bank and East Jerusalem were shrinking each week.

Both schools of thought in Jordan were shaken by "the Sharon Plan" for overthrowing the Hashemite throne, and by the election of Rabbi Kahane to Israel's Parliament, the Knesset.

The effect was not what Sharon and the Likud had planned. By taking a firm line and leaking threats against Hussein, they had hoped to discourage forever his maximalist desires for the West Bank. They hoped to establish a working relationship with Jordan, along the lines of "The East Bank for you, and the West Bank for us."

The Likud concept seemed compatible with that of the minimalists in Amman, who did not want the West Bank anyway. The "soft" side of Jordanian politics seemed to have a shared interest with Israel's "hawks."

Jordanians of the two camps came to realize, however, that the Likud's actions did not always match party ideology. Often, they could not, as the proposed working relationship was built on the fiction that Israel would have no trouble holding on to the West Bank. Demography, it turned out, made the territory hot to handle for the Israelis, too.

A paradox had developed: the minimalists in Jordan had thought that to become the leading political force, they needed the Likud. But the more they understood Begin's party and received its ostensible help, the more firmly they realized that their goals would be only harder to achieve. The minimalists were willing to live without the West Bank because they wanted law and order, calm, and economic development on the East Bank. The Likud might try to keep the West Bank, which was fine for these Jordanians, but to do so Israel might eventually expel hundreds of thousands of Palestinians who would angrily take up residence on the East Bank. Peace and quiet would be gone.

Jordanians fear that when Ariel Sharon speaks of their country as "the Palestinian state," he is interested in sending all the Palestinians to live on the East Bank.

In the seven years of Likud government, then, both minimalists and maximalists concluded that time was running against their interests. It seemed that if they gave up on their continuing demands for return of the West Bank, they could eventually lose the East Bank.

Some analysts maintained that the clash between two schools of thought was extremely minor, and in any event that the minimalist Crown Prince Hassan would never act out of step with his brother King Hussein. The official line was clear: Jordan wanted to regain every inch of territory it had lost.

A basic change had occurred. In deed as well as word, Jordan was again seriously interested in what was happening in the West Bank. It was almost a first line of defense for the East Bank, the heart of the kingdom. With Menachem Begin in power, there may not have been anything to be gained from talking with Israel, but Jordan had to be vigilant so as not to have its own nationhood threatened.

Chapter 13

Return of the Jordanian Option

"I know how to contact Najeeb Halaby," Howard Squadron said.

"Excellent, it is simply an excellent idea," the Israeli prime minister replied. Shimon Peres was playing host to Jewish community leaders and businesspeople in his hotel suite in New York.

It was October 1984, four weeks after Peres was sworn in as Israel's eighth head of government. And what a strange government it was: long days and nights of delicate political negotiations in Tel Aviv after the deadlocked election result in June had finally given birth to the National Unity Coalition, which brought Peres's Labor Alignment and Yitzhak Shamir's Likud bloc into a single, large, and unwieldy cabinet of twenty-five ministers. The Labor leader would be prime minister for twenty-five months, and then Shamir would return to the top office for the coalition's second half.

Knowing his time was limited, Peres threw himself with vigor into the job he had sought for so many years. Among his chief foreign policy goals was to renew the dialogue with Jordan. After all, it had been something of a Labor party tradition. Peres also believed that the seven Likud years without any contact had made peace a more distant prospect for the region.

Peres and the other leading Labor figures feared that annexation of the West Bank, the eventual goal of Shamir's Likud, would be a disastrous error for Israel, endangering its democratic character and alienating the worldwide Jewish community, which provided much of Israel's financial and moral backing.

The seemingly easy alternative, simply continuing with the military occupation, seemed to Peres to be an equally unsavory and dangerous prospect. Far preferable would be negotiations with local Palestinian representatives in the West Bank and Gaza, but with the PLO holding the only real power among Palestinians in the occupied territories and abroad, no talks would be possible anytime soon. In Peres's view, the only realistic alternative—the one which had to be seized as a potentially exciting opportunity—was the Jordanian option.

Shortly after taking office, Peres was busy making telephone calls, sending out dozens of letters and sending diplomatic cables to persons of influence. He arranged meetings with whomever he thought could help reestablish contact with Jordan. He turned to his friends in the Socialist International, including French President François Mitterand. He spoke with Britain's Prime Minister Margaret Thatcher, with American officials, and with private business executives whose travels took them to Amman.[1]

In the United States, successful businesspeople of Jewish and of Arab origins formed an organization aimed at encouraging peace in the Middle East by financing joint development projects in Israel, in Jordan and especially in the West Bank and Gaza Strip. Quite naturally, they called themselves The Business Group for Peace and Development in the Middle East. Among the organizers were Howard Squadron, a lawyer who had been at the head of the Conference of Presidents of Major American Jewish Organizations, and Philip Habib, a former State Department official with experience as a Middle East envoy.

In November 1984, this American group attempted to arrange a meeting between Abba Eban, who had become chairman of a powerful Knesset committee in Jerusalem, and Adnan Abu-Odeh, chief official of the royal court in Amman. Both men were in New York at the time. Apparently no approval was received from King Hussein, so the meeting did not take place. But some good did come of the efforts, because members of the group became acquainted with the king's American father-in-law, Najeeb Halaby.

Halaby was born in 1915 in Dallas, Texas, to parents of Syrian origin. He was educated at Stanford University and then at the law schools of the University of Michigan and Yale University. He was a test pilot for the U.S. navy during World War II and then worked in the Pentagon as an adviser and a deputy assistant secretary of defense. In private industry, he worked with many multinational corporations and helped the American University in Beirut. His fortune was made at Pan American World Airways (Pan Am), where he rose to the posts of president and chief executive officer until his retirement in 1972.

In a sense, his greatest success was that of his daughter, Lisa Najeeb Halaby, who was born in 1951, graduated from Princeton University with a degree in architecture and urban planning in 1974, and married King Hussein in Amman in June 1978. She had been working for Alia, the Royal Jordanian Airline. Now she was Her Majesty Queen Noor. Having divorced two wives and lost a third in a helicopter crash, Hussein had his fourth bride.

Through the American businesspeople seeking to bring peace and prosperity to the Middle East, Shimon Peres made contact with Najeeb Halaby. Not wishing to embarrass his son-in-law, Halaby politely turned down an invitation to come to Israel to see Peres, but the former Pan Am president did agree to use his frequent visits to Amman to pass messages from Peres to Hussein.[2]

Another important channel to reach the king was the U.S. government. Compared with the previous Nixon and Carter administrations, Ronald Reagan's

White House was not active in promoting the Middle East peace process. The Israeli invasion of Lebanon in 1982 called for some American response, however, and Reagan publicly unveiled in September of that year a peace plan for the region to include a Palestinian "homeland" linked with Jordan. American policymakers, largely accepting the Israeli contention that the PLO had been smashed in Lebanon, felt it was time to capitalize on the new situation by moving toward a peace settlement that could reasonably exclude the PLO. Jordan was, to the United States, a friendly nation that could help.

Secretary of State George Shultz, with his background in business and economics, was interested in proposals that could advance the prospects for peace through cooperative economic progress. Several such ideas, including those of The Business Group for Peace and Development in the Middle East, were aimed specifically at Israel and Jordan.

In the first half of the 1980s, the American administration had at least one valuable instrument in the region, and his name was Thomas R. Pickering, veteran U.S. diplomat who had served on both sides of the Jordan River. He was the ambassador in Amman from 1974 to 1978, and in 1985 he took over as U.S. ambassador in Tel Aviv. There was Pickering, sitting in Israel with friendly access to all the top officials, retaining his contacts with Jordan where he had a close relationship with Hussein.

Britain's Mrs. Thatcher also played a decisive role. Hussein the Anglophile always maintained frequent and personal contact with the ruling occupant of Number 10 Downing Street, and he was at the prime minister's official residence in London far more often than his official calendar of state visits would suggest. When he would simply drop into Britain for a few days or a few weeks, he would "pop in" to see Mrs. Thatcher for tea. The king kept in close touch with British prime ministers whether they were Labor socialists or Conservatives, but he seemed to enjoy an exceptionally positive chemistry with the leader dubbed "the Iron Lady."

The various communications channels were only tools to be used for passing messages, although the Israelis hoped the United States and Great Britain would add their own weighty recommendations to Hussein that he meet with Peres. Still, the ultimate decision rested with the king. Why did he agree to renew the series of personal encounters?

Many of Jordan's top officials, and not only the followers of Crown Prince Hassan in the minimalist camp, believed that the status quo was not bad for the Hashemite kingdom. Hussein had taken a hard line in all the secret talks up to 1977, apparently believing that Israel would always be willing to give him the "nonstrategic" sectors of the West Bank as illustrated in the Allon Plan. The king projected that he could receive more, if he continued stubbornly to demand that every inch of territory be returned to him.

Hussein began to realize in or around 1981 that the strategic lineup was changing for the worse, from Jordan's point of view. The PLO's prestige and power had grown in the West Bank. Royalists in the occupied territory were losing strength, and the Israelis were making little progress in attempting superficially to replace their military administrators with cooperative Palestinian mayors and other officials. Added to the fear that right-wing Israelis would continue to search for ways to "transfer" West Bank Arabs to the East Bank, Hussein had powerful reasons to explore a dialogue with the new Prime Minister Peres.[3]

There were also wider strategic factors, suggesting that Hussein need not consider himself a treacherous turncoat to the Arab cause by talking to the Zionists. Egypt had been deeply discomfited by Israel's 1982 invasion of Lebanon but would now be more at ease with the Egypt-Israel peace treaty, because Israel announced in January 1985 that it intended to withdraw its forces, having lost more than six hundred soldiers in Lebanon without a great sense of accomplishment. Hussein's neighbor to the east, Iraq, was less radical in its hatred of the Israelis and on other subjects because of its dependence on moderate Arab states such as Jordan for financial and logistical support in the Gulf War against Iran.

Hussein liked the idea of a moderate, western-aligned Arab axis extending from Egypt through Jordan and Saudi Arabia to the other Gulf states such as Kuwait and the United Arab Emirates. Then there was the pressure, or at least the recommendations, from Reagan, Shultz, Thatcher, Mitterand, and the king's father-in-law Halaby.

There were obstacles, to be sure, making it difficult for Hussein to renew a meaningful dialogue with Israel. First, there was the Rabat Summit of 1974 and its declaration that only the PLO could negotiate on behalf of the Palestinians. The king's solution was to renew first his dialogue with the PLO. Despite the bitterness remaining from the civil war in Black September 1970, Hussein could gain some legitimacy, in considering the future of the West Bank, only from his nemesis Yasser Arafat.

The PLO, at the time, needed Jordan. Arafat had lost his bases and his entire minigovernment in Lebanon in 1982, and Syria had immediately sought to extinguish completely the veteran guerrilla leader and his Fatah central core of the PLO by arming and directing renegade Palestinians who waged a bloody campaign against the mainstream PLO in northern Lebanon and drove Arafat into exile. He was setting up new headquarters in far-off Tunis, and many of his fighting men had been shipped to equally distant Yemen.

Because Arafat was desperate for support from any Arab quarter, and particularly from a "front-line" state bordering Israel, he did not mind bringing Hussein back into the West Bank picture. Theirs was a temporary identity of interests, and while they knew that it was merely tactical it was enough to bring them together.

For the first time in fourteen years, the king permitted the PLO to hold a major conference in November 1984, on Jordanian soil. It was a somewhat stunning event: the Palestine National Council (PNC), known as the "parliament" of nationalist Palestinians, convened in Amman. Hussein came to the opening session, delivered a speech and was applauded warmly. The king, to the surprise of PNC delegates, physically embraced Arafat in the conference hall.

Their formal dialogue continued in February 1985, and "the Hussein-Arafat agreement" was signed in Amman and presented to the world. Few observers could have realized that the pact was the first major breakthrough toward renewing the secret contacts between Jordan and Israel.

The document promised political cooperation and coordination between the PLO and Jordan, but with the two sides having very different desires in the region it was not surprising that each had its own interpretation of the accord and each hoped to profit in a discrepant fashion.

Hussein hoped to cajole the PLO to issue a renunciation of terrorism and a public acceptance of UN Security Council Resolution 242 of 1967, with its call for the right of all states to live within recognized boundaries. The king later claimed that he did receive such a pledge, privately, from Arafat.

A declaration along those lines could have led to formation of a joint Jordanian-Palestinian delegation to peace talks that the United States and other foreign parties would have been eager to sponsor. The king expected that Arafat would recognize that Jordan had the senior role in determining the makeup of a joint delegation. Assuming that negotiations with Israel went well, Hussein expected that the new climate would naturally lead to formation of a federation between the West Bank and Jordan's East Bank. On the basis of his 1972 proposal, the West Bank Palestinians would have a high degree of autonomy but would accept the sovereignty of the Hashemite crown.

Arafat, on the other hand, felt perfectly comfortable signing the cooperation accord with Hussein but had no plans to renounce the Palestinian armed struggle or to recognize Israel through Resolution 242. The PLO's view remained that the basis for peace negotiations would be all the UN resolutions on the Middle East, including those of the General Assembly, which called for "self-determination" for the Palestinians while Resolution 242 spoke only of a "refugee problem." Arafat was willing to meet with "the Butcher," as many Palestinians called Hussein, in the hope that their agreement would lay the groundwork for an Israeli withdrawal from the West Bank in the near future. Nothing, Arafat believed, would then stop the PLO from establishing an independent state.

Arafat never supported Hussein's federal proposal, feeling that the Palestinian people deserved more honor than to live under a Hashemite king. The PLO leader did speak of a future confederation, linking the new Palestine with the Kingdom of Jordan as two equal states.

He continued to move forward on the new, cooperative diplomatic road and within days, in Cairo, Arafat suggested—although in somewhat vague terms—that the PLO was no longer in the business of terrorism. He declared that armed attacks would only take place in Israel and the occupied territories, and not elsewhere in the world or against the citizens of noncombatant nations.

Both Hussein and Arafat knew that their February 1985 accord had merely tactical goals and could not be long lived. Each saw it as an instrument to help achieve his own, separate objectives. The king gained the strength of legitimacy in the eyes of West Bank Palestinians and of the Arab world at large. He could pursue the refurbishment of Jordan's influence in the West Bank and, clandestinely, direct contacts with Israel.

Arafat was also benefiting from legitimacy, especially in the eyes of western nations who would see him as sufficiently moderate to reconcile the PLO with King Hussein, while renouncing international terrorism. And even while Jordan planned to boost its presence and leverage in the West Bank, the PLO had to welcome the opportunity to have offices again just across the river from the cherished, lost land—in part so that the organization could better organize in the very same West Bank. In case the Israelis should withdraw from part of the occupied territories, both Jordan and the PLO had reasons to have their feet in the door to win the inevitable struggle for power.

Jordan and Israel began to have contacts, at a low level at first, in the months after the Hussein-Arafat agreement. Officials of the Israeli military administration in the West Bank exchanged messages with the relevant Jordanian officials through West Bank residents who regularly crossed the Allenby Bridge to and from Amman. The aim of both sides was to allow some involvement by Jordan in technical matters such as financial transactions and water rights.

To underline the importance of the renewed contacts and ensure their continuity, Jordan asked that the Israeli prime minister's bureau appoint a representative to take responsibility for liaison and to focus on the economic aspects of the contacts. Peres appointed his economics adviser, Amnon Neubach, to this sensitive and secret post.

In parallel, a round of indirect diplomatic activity began, with the director general of the Israeli prime minister's bureau Avraham Tamir launching the effort by visiting Cairo in February 1985. He urged Egypt's President Hosni Mubarak to take advantage of the situation emerging in the Middle East, referring both to Israel's newly scheduled withdrawal from Lebanon, and to the Hussein-Arafat agreement in Amman. The objective, as outlined in Cairo by Tamir, would be to bring Jordan and the PLO to the negotiating table with Israel, with the backing of Egypt, Saudi Arabia, and Iraq.

Israel would be willing to bargain with a joint Jordanian-Palestinian delegation, and rather than the PLO itself, Palestinians who lived in the occupied territories and were not connected with terrorist activity could take part in the delegation.

"And why not actual representatives of the PLO?" the Egyptian president asked.

"It would never pass in the Israeli government," Tamir responded. "The Likud and the Labor party are both opposed to negotiating with the PLO. It is a foolish idea, and it has no chance at all."

Mubarak persisted: "And leaders who identify with the PLO would be acceptable to Israel?"

"Yes," said Tamir, who explained that even Menachem Begin, in his days in power, had said he would not closely "examine the forelocks" of any Arab peace negotiators.

Finally, the true breakthrough came in October 1985, when Shimon Peres himself flew off on a secret mission. The Israeli prime minister's schedule for Saturday, October 5, called for no official business, as is the rule on the Jewish Sabbath lest the religious parties in the coalition government suffer deep offense. Peres was to have only an informal chat at his Jerusalem residence with the American woman who had made history the previous year by running unsuccessfully for the vice presidency of the United States.

Peres kept his appointment with Geraldine Ferraro, but with barely minutes to spare. Officials in the protocol department of the foreign ministry had been told by the prime minister's aides that he might be delayed, and the simple statement led to an unintended leak to the press. Ever vigilant for a scoop, Israeli journalists thought it odd to hear that Peres would be away "somewhere" and would have to rush to a Sabbath afternoon meeting in his own home.

An Israeli weekly newsmagazine knew that something had happened and took a guess a few days later, reporting that Peres had "disappeared" that Friday to meet Soviet leader Mikhail Gorbachev in Paris.[4] A government spokesman in Jerusalem immediately denied the story.

Another reporter recalls telephoning the prime minister's office for a daily check on the official timetable, only to be told on Friday, October 4, that Peres would not be coming to work for the usual pre-Sabbath half day because "he has gone with his wife, Sonia, for a private vacation with their grandchildren."[5]

The cover story could not conceal the truth forever, and Peres's inner circle recalls that Friday, in any event, more with pride than embarrassment. The tradition of top-level meetings between Israeli and Jordanian leaders was renewed that day. The venue was the traditional choice, London.

Peres left Jerusalem before the crack of dawn, was driven to an airfield, and boarded an Israeli-made Westwind executive jet along with a few close aides including his military secretary Colonel Azriel Nevo and armed bodyguards of the Shin Bet internal security service.

Peres tried to catch up on his sleep for an hour and so, and he thumbed through the jumbo-size preweekend Israeli newspapers. He read yet again the files drawn up by Mossad and other analysts to prepare for the encounter. A member of the crew served breakfast and noticed that Peres, who was never good at hiding his feelings, was obviously excited.

He had made many clandestine flights in his career. In the 1950s, when he was director general of the defense ministry, Peres had often flown to France to meet leaders of that nation's socialist government. Those contacts had produced the "Bridge over the Mediterranean," an undeclared political and military pact between Jerusalem and Paris, which permitted the Israelis to purchase almost anything they desired—even the atomic research reactor that the French helped them build at Dimona in the Negev Desert. The Israelis also joined France and Britain in invading Nasser's Egypt.[6]

When Peres was defense minister in the 1960s, he flew to secret meetings in the United States, West Germany, and Italy to negotiate arms purchases and the most rapid development in history of a homegrown military industry.[7] It was almost unthinkable that a state so new and tiny as Israel could make its own guns, bombs, and jet fighters. But thanks to Peres and others, Israel did.

He had also been one of the Labor government ministers who met repeatedly with Hussein in the 1970s, but now—at an altitude of 25,000 feet over the Austrian Alps—the situation was completely different for Peres because he was the prime minister. All responsibility for Israel's policies and security rested with him, and he could only hope that the talks awaiting him in London would represent a turning point in Middle East history.

This was the first journey of its kind for Military Secretary Colonel Nevo. He was a career officer, with a military affection for quietly getting to the point. He was not a political appointee, having become military secretary to Prime Minister Shamir in 1983. Nevo was a brilliant organizer and was in charge of liaison with the secret agencies, the Mossad and Shin Bet, which were under the prime minister's sole authority.

After the five-hour flight, the small jet touched down at a Royal Air Force base near London, by arrangement with British authorities, and an ordinary automobile—rather than a flag-bedecked limousine—took the prime minister into town. His destination was not the Israeli Embassy at 2a Palace Green, but King Hussein's main London home just a few doors away. It was a large, three-story house, surrounded by private lawns and a high wall on the street known as a diplomatic enclave.

The king was waiting, and he accorded his guest a polite and even friendly welcome. Although they had exchanged messages and regards, Hussein and Peres had not seen each other in person in ten years.

"I am happy to see you. You look very well," the king said.

"Thank you very much, Your Majesty," Peres replied. "How are your wife and children?"

Hussein escorted Peres to a larger room, with many Middle Eastern carpets covering the floor, where their working discussions began. They were joined by Jordan's Prime Minister Zeid el-Rifai.

The king owned property and several houses in Britain, and he felt quite at home there. On this occasion, in early October 1985, he was enjoying a British break after a short visit to the United States. In New York, he had spoken to the fortieth anniversary session of the UN General Assembly, and Peres had read the copy of the speech he had received from the Israeli delegation.

"I closely studied Your Majesty's speech and praised it in public," Peres said. "Now we should make more progress toward peace."

"I agree with the prime minister," the king replied, "and we are making major efforts in that direction."

Hussein described the renewal of his contacts with PLO leader Arafat and said he hoped eventually to lead a joint Jordanian-Palestinian delegation of peace talks with Israel. The king stressed that the negotiations would have to be part of an international peace conference, and he was hopeful that he could persuade the PLO and Syria to take part.

The United States, at the same time, was launching a new initiative in the person of Richard Murphy, a veteran professional diplomat who was assistant secretary of state for Near East and South Asian affairs. Murphy had a knack for avoiding the publicity limelight, as he simply never spoke to the press and labored quietly, behind closed doors and aboard official U.S. jets. His immediate aim was to gain widespread approval for a joint list of Palestinian and Jordanian negotiators.

In a quiet version of Kissinger's old style, Murphy shuttled between Jerusalem and Amman. King Hussein told Peres that success by Murphy, on the technical task of drawing up lists of participants, would help turn negotiations—and, eventually, a peace settlement—into reality.

As in other encounters over the previous twenty years, the Israeli side heard a general review from Hussein of developments in the Arab world, and of his most recent talks with the leaders of the United States, Britain, France, and other European nations.

Peres then presented a detailed analysis of Israel's complicated domestic politics, explaining how the National Unity Coalition was operating with himself as leader and Shamir as foreign minister. Much of the outline of the differences between Labor and Likud was familiar to Hussein, but he listened patiently and gained some insights that only an inside player can give.

The ultimate insider, Peres advised Hussein to move quickly to negotiate peace with Israel, warning, "My diplomatic time is running out." In almost exactly one year, Peres reminded the king, he would no longer be prime minister. The unique rotation arrangement would have him exchange jobs with Shamir. And then, Peres and Hussein concurred, it would be harder to move toward peace because of the nationalist ideology of Shamir's Likud.

Hussein expressed concern that the government of Israel, by its unusual structure, was paralyzed and unable to reach important decisions.

Peres assured him that if and when the moment of decision came, and the Likud ministers were seen as the final obstacles to peace negotiations with Jordan, he would not hesitate to dismantle the coalition.

The prime minister also consulted his notes to review the situation in the occupied West Bank and Gaza, suggesting that it was important to increase Jordan's involvement in the territories. Peres said Israel would attempt to make the process as easy as possible.

The king agreed to draw up plans for economic development in the occupied lands, and establishment of a new, Arab bank backed by Jordan would be part of the scheme.

In effect, Peres was telling Hussein that the two nations, with the best of will and much hard work, could put the region on the road to peace. He was specifically trying to exclude the PLO. Peres urged the king to minimize his renewed connections with Arafat, to agree that dealing with terrorists only gives them more power and influence.

The Israeli leader said his military commanders were concerned that political rapprochement between Jordan and the PLO might lead to the reappearance of guerrilla bases in Jordan. The message was clear: as always, Israel would not sit idly by if it felt threatened by Palestinian terrorists.

Before their conversation ended, Peres reached into his briefing papers and pulled out a single-spaced, typed sheet, which he gave to Hussein. It was a draft of the speech Peres would deliver, two weeks later, before the UN General Assembly.

The meeting in Hussein's London residence lasted two hours, a bit shorter than the average meeting of the previous decade, but it ended with polite smiles and handshakes and an agreement to meet again "to advance the peace process."

Peres spent the night in London, but on Saturday morning was flown back to Israel aboard the Westwind executive jet, landing in the private airplane on a day when commercial aviation is banned because of the Jewish Sabbath. There were special arrangements for such occasions, however, and Peres once received extraordinary permission from the chief rabbi of Israel to land a cargo aircraft filled with armaments at Ben-Gurion International Airport on a Friday night because it was vital to national security.

The prime minister had to be back in Jerusalem to meet the visiting Geraldine Ferraro, so as not to arouse speculation that he had disappeared for some shadowy purpose. He had, of course, but he was back on time.

Peres left Israel later that month, publicly this time, bound for New York to deliver his UN speech. It was a relatively short discourse, heard by the prime ministers, presidents, and ambassadors gathered for the General Assembly's celebratory session. It was October 21, 1985, and Peres was telling the world that he intended to negotiate peace with Jordan.

"The most complex issue, yet the most promising, involves our neighbor to the East, the Hashemite Kingdom of Jordan," Peres said from the Assembly rostrum. "An issue not confined to borders alone, it reaches across peoples and states. Its settlement should also comprise the resolution of the Palestinian issue."

Talking to Amman, Peres indicated, could solve all ills. Talking to Arafat would be useless. "Nobody has brought more tragedy on the Palestinians than PLO terrorism," the prime minister said.

He called on the UN, not necessarily to sponsor negotiations, but "to fulfill its destiny by ushering the parties to the conflict into a new diplomatic initiative."

He suggested seven principles to be accepted.

First, the objective of these negotiations is to reach peace treaties between Israel and the Arab states, as well as to resolve the Palestinian issue.

Secondly, neither party may impose pre-conditions.

Thirdly, negotiations are to be based on United Nations Security Council resolutions . . .

Fourthly, negotiations are to be conducted directly, between states.

Fifthly, if deemed necessary, those negotiations may be initiated with the support of an international forum . . .

Sixthly, this gathering can take place before the end of this year . . .

Seventhly, negotiations between Israel and Jordan are to be conducted between an Israeli delegation, on the one hand, and a Jordanian or Jordanian-Palestinian delegation on the other, both comprising delegates that represent peace, not terror.

"We know that there is a Palestinian problem," Peres said. "We recognize the need to solve it honorably." It was a long way from Israel's once stubborn denial that such a problem existed, and there was no mention of "the eventual claim of sovereignty over Judea and Samaria" promised by the former Likud prime minister Menachem Begin.

Peres's audience of politicians and diplomats listened intently to hear if any real change might be in the offing in the infuriatingly deadlocked Middle East dispute. Interest peaked, as Peres made an offer in dramatic terms. "I hereby proclaim: the state of war between Israel and Jordan should be terminated immediately," Peres said. "Israel declares this readily, in the hope that King Hussein is willing to reciprocate this step."

There was a more immediate problem in Jerusalem, however, where half of the Peres cabinet declined to support his words. The Likud ministers, led by Shamir, strongly disagreed with the fifth of his seven principles, for they firmly believed that any international forum overseeing peace talks would impose a solution on the parties, and one which would not be beneficial to Israel. They accused Peres of going beyond the united policy of the nominally united government.

Indications from Amman were somewhat more hopeful, as Hussein publicly welcomed the thrust of Peres's UN speech.[8]

Back in Israel, the prime minister was visibly in a good mood. He stubbornly repeated his proposals, including the acceptability of an international forum, in a speech to the Knesset. The parliamentarians then endorsed Peres's actions on the trip abroad, and as is proper etiquette in a coalition even the Likud members voted in favor of the Labor prime minister.

Peres confidently suggested to friends that negotiations between Israel and Jordan could begin, in public, "within six weeks." He felt that he established common ground with Hussein in London, and that he owed it to the king to risk a confrontation with the right-wing half of the government to prove that he, Peres, would stand firm in his willingness to reach a settlement.

The prime minister's office had an unmistakable air of optimism, as policy planners believed that they had reached a turning point in the Middle East conflict.

Peres and his Labor half of the coalition were guilty of wishful thinking. Arranging an international conference would not be easy. And Hussein was insisting that he be given time, before stepping forth into a new and dangerous diplomatic process, to line up support in the Arab world. He would confer with the PLO, of course, and with Syria.

Jordan and Syria had recalled their respective ambassadors, seven years earlier during one of the more vicious inter-Arab disputes, and they had even sent secret agents against each other's governments. Syrian President Assad's secret service worked with the renegade Palestinian terrorist Abu Nidal, while the Jordanians worked with the Islamic Brotherhood group which sought to topple Assad.[9]

On a broader front, choosing the international outsiders who could participate was a matter of dispute. Peres had told the UN that "those who confine their diplomatic relations to one side of the conflict exclude themselves from such a role." In other words, Israel was demanding that the Soviet Union reopen its Tel Aviv embassy, closed in 1967, and that China establish diplomatic links with Israel for the first time. Otherwise, the five permanent members of the UN Security Council would include two ineligible members, from Israel's point of view, for a Middle East peace conference.

The Americans, too, were reluctant to permit the Soviets to restore their prestige and influence in the Middle East, more than eleven years after Russian advisers were expelled from Egypt. The 1979 peace treaty between Egypt and Israel had been a triumph for American diplomacy, establishing the preeminence of the United States over the Russians in the region. Washington had little reason to want to share the glory with Moscow.

In his contacts with Arab leaders and with Israel's prime minister, Hussein raised an idea, which was both new and old: to convene an international conference for peace in the entire Middle East, not only between Israel and Jordan, with the participation of all relevant parties in the region. It would be the perfect cover for the direct talks, which the Israelis so badly wanted, but which Hussein would not dare to enter for fear of being branded a traitor to the Arabs.

Aside from being an umbrella of diplomatic safety, the wider conference might—just might—solve a greater portion of the interlinked Middle East disputes than smaller, direct, bilateral talks could.

The idea was born, in its modern form, less than three years earlier, when Hussein went to Moscow on one of his rare visits designed to remind Washington and Britain that Jordan did not have all of its diplomatic eggs in the western basket. As usual, the king was supposedly considering the purchase of Soviet arms, although he almost always ended up buying weapons and equipment from the United States, Britain, and France instead.

It was early 1983, and Yuri Andropov was the Soviet leader. The former KGB espionage agency chief warned Hussein not to accept the U.S. peace plan announced by President Reagan the previous September. Andropov said it was merely designed to set the Palestinian issue off to one side, and to eliminate Soviet influence from the region. He said the USSR would not allow its friends in the Middle East to go along with the Reagan plan. And because it was therefore a nonstarter, why should Jordan climb aboard the American initiative?[10]

Hussein realized, then, that the Russians would demand to have some role in the peace process. It was necessary for the sake of winning Syrian assent. The United States would, therefore, not be the ideal, sole organizer of an effective conference. The king believed that an international conference, with the UN secretary general sending invitations to all Middle East parties and to the five permanent Security Council members, would be ideal. In a wider forum, he could even negotiate on the future of the West Bank without blatantly violating the Arab Summit resolution of Rabat, which took that right away from him.

The Israelis, however, did not like the idea. Shamir and his Likud ministers bitterly noted that the international conference would most likely take the form of an isolated Israel standing against the harsh demands of nearly a dozen other nations, all demanding that Israel withdraw from the territories it captured in 1967. If Israel refused to make dangerous concessions, as it should in the Likud view, it would be cast in the role of villain in the media worldwide.

Even Peres and his Labor friends spoke out against the wider conference, saying that bilateral, face-to-face talks would make quicker and more effective progress.

It had all been discussed at the secret meeting with Hussein in London. The king persuaded the prime minister that there was no other way to proceed but through an international conference. Hussein said he needed the broad umbrella to enable Jordan to make peace. Peres realized that more than halfway through his twenty-five-month term as prime minister in the coalition rotation, no time could be wasted in the search for a breakthrough.

The two leaders managed to give and take, in their discussion. Peres gave way on the conference, and Hussein modified his stance on Palestinian participation. The king could see that the PLO represented a red line, which the Israelis refused to cross. Arafat's past involvement in bloody terrorism seemed to remind them of Nazi atrocities, the kind of crimes that can never be forgiven.

Hussein was losing patience with Arafat's tricky diplomacy in any event. The PLO leader had promised several times "soon" to declare acceptance of UN Security Council Resolution 242 and to issue an unequivocal condemnation of terrorism. But Arafat did not do so.

Jordan lost all patience in February 1986, when Hussein canceled the agreement he had signed with Arafat a year earlier to coordinate their policies. He did not expel the PLO entirely, however, thus leaving the door open to future talks. Hussein simply could no longer tolerate being seen by the outside world as inextricably linked with the unshaven, brash, and ambiguous Arafat. A proud and elegant king should not be an equal partner—or to some foreign media, a junior partner—with the leader of a guerrilla group.

Peres accepted the notion that Hussein would compile a list of Palestinian dignitaries who were not members of the PLO and who could honestly disavow terrorism. These men and women could be part of a negotiating team at the international conference, which the Israeli prime minister was now reluctantly considering.

In fact, it was Peres who persuaded the Reagan administration to accept the notion of a broad conference, which would make the United States only one of five big-power sponsors. The Americans took sufficient interest in the subject to send Murphy again and again to the region, considering potential schedules, agendas, and lists of participants for a conference.

The secret meeting in London, which revived the tradition of clandestine contacts, led to a host of developments, more of them minor than major. On the Israeli side, Amnon Neubach was in charge of arranging economic cooperation with Jordan in the West Bank and Gaza. Another Peres aide, Yossi Beilin, pursued political cooperation and met in Paris with Jordan's Prime Minister Rifai.

The prime minister's consultant for "special affairs," Adolph ("Al") Schwimmer, had the good fortune to possess American citizenship, and he used his U.S. passport to travel to meetings with Jordanian officials in the United States, in Europe, and even in Jordan. Yet another Peres aide, Avraham Tamir, continued to coordinate political developments with Egypt's President Mubarak, who energetically pushed Jordan and the PLO toward peace.

Peres tried to tell only those who were closest to him about the contacts with Jordan. He had to keep his political rival, Foreign Minister Shamir, fully informed, and former Mossad agent Shamir had thirty years' experience keeping his mouth shut. There were no reports to the full cabinet, nor to the ten ministers of the "inner cabinet," despite the fact that most of them were former army generals or defense ministers who could seemingly be trusted with any and all state secrets. Peres preferred to take no chances, knowing that publicity would frighten Hussein and would prompt the king to cut off all contact.

Hussein, for his part, severely limited the number of confidants who knew of the secret diplomacy. These included his brother Crown Prince Hassan, Prime Minister Rifai, the Royal Court Minister Adnan Abu-Odeh, the military chief of staff General Zeid ibn-Shaker, and a very few additional officials.

Even though Jordan and the PLO made little progress politically, failing to put together a joint delegation that would be accepted by Israel as a negotiating partner, the PLO was making inroads of its own. Having been driven out of Lebanon, on Israel's northern border, it was exhilirating for the guerrilla leaders to be in Jordan—so close to Israel's eastern frontier.

This was part of the price that Hussein had to pay to enjoy the public support of the PLO in efforts to win back the West Bank. The king hoped to regain his land through a political and diplomatic struggle. Some of Arafat's colleagues were apostles of the armed struggle.

Among the PLO officials who manned the newly reopened offices in Amman were the organization's military commanders, Khalil el-Wazir, who was known as Abu Jihad, and Salah Khalaf, who was known as Abu Iyad.

Israeli intelligence reports began to speak of Palestinian military command centers being established in Jordan's East Bank. There was an alarming increase in guerrilla violence in the West Bank, in the Gaza Strip and in Israel itself. Two PLO units in particular caused concern: "the Western Front" group which was responsible for attacks inside the West Bank, and "Force 17" within the mainstream Fatah group, sometimes known as Arafat's bodyguards but focusing on attacking Israeli shores from the sea.

More than mere reports were reaching Israel. Brutal attacks were becoming more frequent throughout 1985, after the Hussein-Arafat agreement was signed in February. The terrorist tactics in Israel and the West Bank were new: simple stabbings of Israelis walking alone and of young lovers hiking through the countryside. Force 17 was active in the Mediterranean, and its members— including a Briton who had joined the PLO—killed three Israelis in September aboard a yacht in the harbor at Larnaca, Cyprus. The orders had come from Jordan.

After the Larnaca murders, the hawkish cabinet minister Ariel Sharon publicly called on Israel to retaliate against "the terrorist headquarters in Amman." Sharon's equally important motive was to spoil any choice of renewing a diplomatic dialogue with King Hussein. Sharon never believed in the Jordanian option, and the accord signed with Arafat provided further evidence that Hussein was not a valid partner for peace talks.

Peres and his Labor ministers had no intention of satisfying Sharon's demand, but they could see that Israeli public opinion was demanding some action by its government. Otherwise, Labor would be seen as "soft" compared with the Likud half of the administration.

Peres and Defense Minister Rabin ordered the Israel air force to launch a long-distance bombing raid on the official PLO headquarters in Tunis. It was, ironically, only a few days before Peres's secret flight to London to renew face-to-face contact with King Hussein.

Five months later, in March 1986, Hussein met in Paris with Rabin. It was their first encounter in nine years. Rabin, no longer prime minister, was now in charge of military affairs as well as of governing the occupied territories. Because of the subjects to be discussed, Hussein was not accompanied this time by Prime Minister Rifai. A senior Jordanian army officer came instead.

At the top of Rabin's agenda was the increase in PLO guerrilla activity. The Israeli said the violence was unacceptable and was being directed from Jordanian soil. Rabin said the PLO was putting any chances for peace in great peril.

Hussein responded that his accord with Arafat had been political and diplomatic in nature, that it was designed to make peace negotiations more likely. The king said there was no intention of allowing the Palestinians to step up their attacks on Israel and the West Bank.

Hussein and Rabin also discussed the beginnings of an idea, which would persist for some years—the "Jordanization" of the West Bank and Gaza, also known as building a "condominium." The territories would remain in Israel's hands, but Jordan would increase its participation in their administration.

The meeting in Paris was a rousing success, from Israel's point of view. Hussein returned home and expelled Abu Jihad, Abu Iyad, and the commander of Force 17, Abu Tayeb. He ordered that PLO offices in Amman be closed.

Israel and Jordan had rediscovered what they had recognized in the early 1970s: that they had a common enemy in the PLO and Palestinian terrorist groups. The security agencies of the two nations were again exchanging information.[11]

A third step in renewing the connection between Hussein and the Israelis was accomplished in the first half of 1986 by the U.S. ambassador in Tel Aviv, Thomas Pickering. He had spent four and a half years as the U.S. ambassador in Amman and earned the trust and respect of the king and his inner circle. Just after arriving in Israel on July 28, 1985, Pickering said publicly, "The peace process will stand at the top of my priority list."

It still came as a surprise on January 19, 1986, when Pickering boarded Peres's official jet to accompany the prime minister on the first leg of an official tour of Western Europe. At the time, Hussein was in London.

Richard Murphy flew from the State Department in Washington to London to confer with the king. Pickering and Murphy both began an unusual bout of shuttle diplomacy between the Hague, the parliamentary capital of the Netherlands where Peres was visiting, and Hussein's house in the Kensington neighborhood of the British capital.

Pickering, an amateur archaeologist who had learned both Arabic and some Hebrew, was using his intimate acquaintances with both Hussein and Peres to narrow the gap between the positions of the two leaders. They had met face-to-face, three months earlier, but still a trusted American broker could succeed where the two principals themselves had failed.

American officials continued to help in the planning of further contacts between leaders of Israel and Jordan. Hussein was willing to return to the secret site used years earlier: the sands of the Arava along the border between the two countries.

On a Friday night, August 30, 1986, the runway lights at Eilat Airport, closed for the Sabbath, were suddenly switched on. An unscheduled domestic flight landed in Israel's southernmost port and popular tourist resort. A few people noted that this was odd, but it was a night for relaxation and recovering from the hot sun of daytime. No one made a fuss over a small airplane coming in.

A minimotorcade of cars had been waiting on the tarmac. A few men alighted from the airplane and entered the cars. The lights went off, and the very important, but secretive, persons were driven away.

At the nearby military section of Eilat's port, they boarded a motorboat, which sped away from the shore, trailed by a white wake of bubbles through the clear, blue water of the Red Sea. It was heading south but then turned sharply left to head northeast toward the Jordanian port of 'Aqaba.

As usual, a patrol boat of Israel's navy was stationed in the middle of the gulf. Its powerful radar detected the speedboat crossing the invisible border and heading for Jordan. The naval crew immediately filed a report, by radio, to the base in Eilat.

The answer came back, from the on-shore commander: "Forget about it."

What the seamen on patrol were not told was that aboard the speedboat were Israel's Prime Minister Peres, Defense Minister Rabin, the military chief of staff General Moshe Levy, two army officers as aides and several bodyguards. They were on their way to another meeting with King Hussein and Prime Minister Rifai.

This was the first encounter since the early 1950s to take place on Jordanian soil. The Israeli speedboat pulled up to a pier just outside 'Aqaba—the king's private wharf where his own yacht and speedboats were tied up.

The talks went on for some four hours, and it was well past midnight when the Israeli speedboat again pulled out into the gulf. General Levy was there because one of the topics was the common fight against Palestinian terrorism.

The discussion focused, however, on political developments. Peres had barely six weeks remaining as prime minister, but he said that as foreign minister after the job rotation he would press on with efforts to begin formal negotiations for peace. Rabin would continue to be defense minister even in the second half of the fifty-month coalition, so he could represent a certain continuity in Israel's policy team.

First, however, Rabin had to be convinced that something good could emerge from the flurry of secret contacts. He had serious doubts about convening an international conference, seeing Shamir's point that foreigners would most likely gang up on Israel. At the late-night 'Aqaba meeting, however, Rabin was persuaded that Hussein intended to engage in direct peace talks with Israel as soon as an international conference began as a broad framework.

King Hussein agreed that there was no sense waiting for the PLO to adopt a single, unified, pro-peace stance. He told the Israelis that he would try to develop an alternative Palestinian leadership in the occupied territories. Hussein told them to leave the matter to him.

It certainly was a time of diplomatic flurry. Peres, two weeks earlier, had been in Morocco for a first, public meeting with an Arab king: Hassan II. Two weeks after the secret 'Aqaba visit, Peres was in Alexandria, Egypt, conferring with President Mubarak.

All these talks were aimed at finding a way to start formal negotiations for peace in the Middle East.

Peres and Shamir swapped jobs, as scheduled in October 1986, despite the suggestions from some senior Labor party figures that "for the good of the country" Peres should abrogate the coalition agreement. As foreign minister, however, he did not give up his hopes, ideals, or secret operations. He kept working toward an international peace conference, although Prime Minister Shamir was opposed to the notion.

In many ways, it was business as usual for the Palestinian issue and for the relationship with Jordan. The United States continued to send Richard Murphy from time to time, and he shuttled between Jerusalem and Amman, as did Ambassador Pickering and a special American envoy named Wat Claverius who worked hard but sought no publicity whatsoever.

The efforts bore fruit on April 11, 1987. Peres and Hussein met in London that day, for five hours of detailed discussion. With senior aides, they considered various draft texts of what could either be a joint, public declaration or a secret memorandum of understanding. Mainly at the king's insistence, they opted for continued secrecy. But the document that emerged was impressive nonetheless.

Typed in English and headed "Secret/Most Sensitive," the text outlined the steps to be taken to invite participants to the international peace conference, under the underlined title, "A Three-Part Understanding between Jordan and Israel." In the lower right corner of the single sheet, it had the date and venue, "11/4/87, London," but it was left unsigned. Hussein and Peres knew it was agreed, and equally importantly they informed the United States that they had agreed totally on the text.

The first part of the document conceived of a UN role in initiating the peace conference. It said, "The Secretary General will issue invitations to the five permanent members of the Security Council and the parties involved in the Arab-Israeli conflict in order to negotiate a peaceful settlement based on Resolutions 242 and 338 with the objects of bringing a comprehensive peace to the area, security to its states, and to respond to the legitimate rights of the Palestinian people."

The second part of the secret "understanding" stated that the conference's aim would be "the peaceful solution of the Arab-Israeli conflict" and "a peaceful solution of the Palestinian problem in all its aspects." To satisfy the Israeli desire for face-to-face, individual pairings to negotiate with Jordan or any other Arab state that agreed to attend, this paragraph also said the conference would contain "geographical bilateral committees to negotiate mutual issues."

The third part of the agreement was more specific and had required mammoth efforts by the American go-betweens and finally had consumed most of the five-hour session in London. It said the negotiations would be conducted in the bilateral committees, and "the International Conference will not impose any solution or veto on any agreement arrived at between the parties."[12] Peres hoped it would be enough to win Prime Minister Shamir's support. No longer could Shamir say that all the foreigners would impose their hostile will on a lone Israel.

Also attractive to both sides of Israeli politics was the provision that "the Palestinians' representatives will be included in the Jordanian-Palestinian delegation." Here was Jordan, not insisting in any way that the PLO be involved in peace negotiations. Peres headed home a happy man, convinced that history had been made and would be made some more.

Shamir and his Likud ministers had no personal regard for Peres and imme-diately suspected that he had given something away. There had to be a secret concession, they believed, because for twenty years King Hussein had rejected repeated requests for direct peace negotiations. He had always insisted on know-ing the outcome of the talks before they could start, because he wanted to hear from the start that he would regain every inch of territory.

Shamir was not easily convinced. Why was Hussein offering more now? And what had Peres promised the Arabs?

Chapter 14

May We Help You, Your Highness?

"My, this is heavy," Ambassador Yitzhak Rabin said in Washington, lifting a thick book in 1971. It was at the end of a meeting with Crown Prince Hassan, Hussein's younger brother who had recently been put in charge of economic development and housing in Jordan.

The king and Prime Minister Golda Meir had arranged the meeting, as part of the vast improvement in the secret relationship after the Hashemite victory over Arafat's PLO. Hussein felt sufficiently confident to begin developing his economy, which had been ruined by the bitter civil war. The focus was on the Jordan River Valley, where agriculture had become a disaster because of the fighting and earlier retaliation raids by Israel and Palestinian guerrillas.

In all the ups and downs of his relationship with the PLO, Hussein would never again permit such a calamity to occur. The guerrillas would not ever be allowed the freedom to have openly armed bases in Jordan, as launching pads for attacks on Israel.

The book that Prince Hassan gave to Rabin was an official government study, published in Amman, reviewing the plans to rehabilitate the river valley. Jordan wished to coordinate the program with Israel, partly so that the Israelis would not interfere with the work—better that they should raise any objections at an early stage—but also to benefit from some of Israel's specialized knowledge in construction, irrigation, and raising finance.

Rabin promised that the book would be closely studied, and that he would transmit Israel's reactions to Jordan.[1]

The architects of the secret relationship between the two nations hoped, from the beginning, to use economic development as a means to promote general understanding. Their hope was based on simple logic. Both countries have similar natural resources: the mineral wealth of the Dead Sea, shale oil in the Arava and the Negev deserts, the waters of the Jordan River and its tributaries, and the valuable Gulf of 'Aqaba-Eilat. What would be more natural than to attempt to develop these resources together?

In the 1930s, King Abdullah hoped to benefit from the investment of Jewish wealth in his kingdom, in exchange for the right to purchase land in Transjordan. In the 1940s, the Jews who ran major industries discussed the possibilities of cooperating with Abdullah's authorities across the river. The 1948 war, however, put a stop to all the plans. In the 1950s, American mediation led to the Johnston Plan for sharing the waters of the Jordan River. And in the 1960s, water rights were discussed in the first years of the secret diplomacy between Jordan and Israel.

But there had been no broad and serious discussion of joint development projects until the meeting in Washington, in 1971, between Hassan and Rabin. Details had still to be worked out, but the two men agreed that their nations should take advantage of the relative quiet, which would follow the PLO's defeat in Jordan. Israel and Jordan would separately develop their respective sides of the Jordan River Valley, secure in the knowledge that the other nation would not raise obstacles.

In May 1973, Mrs. Meir invited her minister for agriculture and development, Chaim Givati, to the prime minister's office. She ordered him to prepare for a meeting on economic matters with "our Jordanian neighbors." King Hussein had requested the meeting, during his last talk with Mrs. Meir. Givati, one of her closest cabinet colleagues, had known for years that there were contacts with Jordan but had never asked his old friend about them. Givati recalls, "I don't like to ask about things which they don't tell me about." He, of course, agreed to the prime minister's request.[2]

In addition to Givati, Israel's team at the meeting included the director-general of the prime minister's bureau, Mordecai Gazit, and the director of farm planning in the ministry of agriculture, Ephraim Shila. The talks with Jordan were held in the official guest house to the north of Tel Aviv, the same residence that King Hussein had visited.

The king sent his top officials, his brother Hassan and Prime Minister Rifai. They arrived by helicopter, following the same route flown by their monarch. The crown prince, resembling the king in being a short man but definitely broader and more solidly built than Hussein, was only twenty-six years old. Hassan, who had earned a degree in Oriental studies at Oxford University, was better educated than his brother. The Jordanian crown prince had learned Hebrew and regularly read the Israeli press.[3]

The meeting went on for four hours as a serious and businesslike discussion, the atmosphere lightening slightly during dinner in the guest house.

Mordecai Gazit began the session by praising Jordan for its cooperative stance and introducing the Israeli team. Prince Hassan impressed the Israelis with his precise, British-accented English and with his command of all the subjects under discussion. He knew all there was to know about the West Bank's economy and about financial matters in general. Hassan did almost all the talking, on the Jordanian side, as Rifai sat and listened with hardly a word passing his lips.

The prince presented, in detail, Jordan's plans for developing the river valley, including a construction program to house tens of thousands of Palestinian refugees, many of whom had been forced to leave their East Bank homes during the civil war. Hassan asked the Israelis how they could help Jordan build homes and create agricultural employment for the refugees. He was not asking *if* they would help, as he hinted that King Hussein had already received a pledge to this effect from Prime Minister Meir.

Givati immediately responded that Israel was not wealthy enough to contribute cash, but could help with advice. The agriculture minister suggested that Jordan send its farming experts to Israel, just as many African nations had done, to learn modern techniques. Givati said, "We are prepared to give you all the knowledge we have."

Prince Hassan expressed his fear that sending Jordanians to Israel on courses could not be kept secret, but Givati suggested several ways in which no one need ever know. The prince appeared to be convinced and promised to take up the matter with the king.

Givati then asked about Jordan's development plans in another area. "What do you intend to do in your part of the Dead Sea?" he asked, even as he passed across the table to Hassan and Rifai a copy of an expansion program for Israel's Dead Sea Works. "It is a big sea and can contain both our programs and yours," Givati said.

The prince said there was a plan to build a new potash plant on the Jordanian side, but he added that the project had run into difficulties. "Would you be able to help us?" Hassan asked.

Various ideas were discussed, and in the end the Israeli officials were asking to be clandestine partners in the Jordanian potash factory, which would export potassium-based chemicals used in agriculture and industry. As partners, the Israelis said they would use their excellent contacts in the United States and Western Europe to raise funding for construction of the plant.

Hassan and Rifai listened attentively to the bold suggestion and even said it was "interesting." They asked the Israelis to check how such a partnership might be formed. It was nearly midnight, and after cordial farewell handshakes the two Jordanians left by helicopter. Both sides promised to meet again soon.

The Israelis followed up on the potentially productive talks with great seriousness. Gazit wrote a detailed report for Prime Minister Meir, and Givati discussed the matters with her in person. Finance Minister Pinhas Sapir was brought into the consultations, and he agreed to find a way to establish a formal, but secret, business partnership. The most likely solution was a company in a third country, with Israeli and Jordanian owners.

In September 1973, Mrs. Meir told Givati that a second meeting with Prince

Hassan was being arranged to make progress in the economic and financial fields. The specific subject, she said, would be exploitation of the Dead Sea's mineral resources.

The selected date was Sunday, October 7, the day after the twenty-four hours of traditional fasting on the holiest day in Judaism, Yom Kippur. And so, there never was a second meeting. Egypt and Syria attacked Israeli military lines on October 6, catching the Israelis by surprise on their holy day. With the Middle East consumed by war, even with the Jordanians staying out of the conflict, they were not about to send their top officials to a fairly routine meeting in Tel Aviv.[4]

Hassan and Rifai simply did not show up at the agreed rendezvous point. The Israelis had been fairly certain they would not be there. In any event, the entire leadership in Jerusalem was busy with the defense of the nation after the initial setbacks of the surprise attack on two fronts.

After the Yom Kippur War, the contacts between Jerusalem and Amman on business, finance, and mineral development were not revived. Israel tried to offer advice, specifically on construction of the potash factory, by sending messages through American officials. Only Israel had an economical method of removing potassium products from water, while other nations—including Canada, the leading producer of potash—dug the material out of mines.

The Jordanians got along without the advice. These were confusing times in the Middle East, and Hussein was in no rush to tighten his contacts with Israel. He turned for finance to his southern neighbors in Saudi Arabia, who were beginning to take great interest in strengthening royalists and other moderates throughout the Arab world.

Construction of Jordan's potash plant on the Dead Sea began in 1976, and within a decade it was producing around a million tons of potash each year. Still, Israel's Dead Sea Works on the western shore of the mineral-rich waters produced three times as much potash.

The attempt to establish a partnership between Israel and Jordan, in exploiting the natural wealth of the Dead Sea, which lay between them, was the biggest economic program considered by the two nations in their clandestine contacts. Both sides made serious efforts, but there was never again anything like it.

Other areas of cooperation were suggested, but they amounted to little of any lasting value.

Shale oil was found in Israel's Negev Desert, and experts from the Technion University worked on ways to produce an alternative form of gasoline. Another idea was to burn shale oil for steam to power industry. Officials considered cooperating with Jordan, which also had shale oil wells, but the notion was not pursued.

Israeli engineers drew up plans for a canal from the Mediterranean to the Dead Sea to take advantage of the hydroelectric power, which could be generated thanks to the huge drop in water level from the coastline of Israel or Gaza to the lowest point on earth, the Dead Sea being a lake nearly 1,300 feet below sea level. The idea had surfaced several times throughout the twentieth century, but Menachem Begin's government seemed to take it especially seriously after 1977.

The Jordanians, however, did not see any potential cooperation in a canal, fearing that an inflow of water would inundate their potash factory and their coastal farms. Jordan asked the American government to intervene, and the United States did elicit a pledge from Israel that a canal would not damage Jordanian facilities. The price of oil on world markets collapsed, meanwhile, and alternative power sources were no longer so important to the Israelis, who shelved the canal program.

Israel and Jordan did cooperate in solving ecological problems, which resulted from development projects on the two sides of the border. Each country used airplanes to spray insecticide to eliminate an onslaught of mosquitoes. And means of communications were arranged to allow each country to inform the other of a pollution alert in the Gulf of 'Aqaba-Eilat.

A dispute concerning ecology was resolved in 1983, when the Jordanians began to activate a waste disposal plant at 'Aqaba, which was aimed at solving the port town's pollution problem by aeration of the refuse. The smell from the facility became intolerable, however, for residents of Eilat, just across the border. U.S. Agency for International Development financed the sewage treatment plant, so it was only natural for Israel to complain to Washington. These were the Begin and Shamir years of Likud government, after all, when there was no direct contact with Jordan.

The message to Washington in July 1984, from the director general of Israel's interior ministry, Chaim Kuberski, was surprisingly sharp. It protested the $15 million AID loan to Jordan, saying the United States should have informed Israel beforehand. The ministry said the unacceptable odor threatened to ruin Eilat's tourist industry. Kuberski and Elyakim Rubinstein, political attaché at the Israeli Embassy in Washington, conducted intensive talks with the United States on the subject of garbage and air pollution. The State Department agreed to ask American experts to assess whether the Jordanian facility constituted an ecological threat to Israeli hotels.[5]

Officials of the U.S. Environmental Protection Agency (EPA) visited 'Aqaba and Eilat in late 1984 and wrote a detailed report on their findings. Based on readings and statistics provided to both sides by the EPA, Jordan agreed to add a scrubbing mechanism that would cleanse the output of the waste treatment process and to control the flow of sewage through the plant while monitoring the air quality. The United States offered to train Jordanian engineers to deal with pollution caused by any serious malfunction.

With so much of it forming the border between them, water was naturally a major concern in the relationship between Israel and Jordan. An Israeli deputy minister for agriculture, Avraham Katz-Oz recalls, ''Throughout human history, but especially in the Middle East, disputes over water sources turned into bitter wars.''[6] To prevent any such calamity, Katz-Oz was put in charge of contacts with Jordan, on issues concerning water, in 1984.

Knowing how serious the subject can be, both Israel and Jordan have taken care—except at the worst of diplomatic times between them—to settle water disputes rapidly whenever possible. Despite general adherence to the principles of the Johnston Plan of 1954, disagreements have appeared, including charges by one side of overuse of Jordan River water by the other. The disputes were usually resolved through face-to-face discussions between Israeli and Jordanian technical experts, brought together through arrangements made by U.S. officials.

In the early 1980s, Jordan began to drill diagonally for water in the northern sector where the borders of Jordan, Israel, and Syria converge. The Israelis complained that Jordan was stealing water from the hidden geological layers on the Israeli side of the frontier. Talks on the subject did not yield agreement, and Israel instead set up its own drilling platform, threatening to launch an underground, revolving retaliation. Perhaps fortunately for all concerned, the ''war of the drills'' was resolved when Jordan's drilling tower collapsed. The Jordanians did not bother to erect a new one.[7]

Another problem surfaced in November 1985, but this one was quickly resolved through direct contacts. Both Jordan and Israel draw water from the Yarmuk River, in the north, using their respective pumping stations. Both share an interest in seeing that the Yarmuk's flow not be impeded. In 1985, the Jordanians pointed out that erosion of the riverbank had formed a small island in the middle of the Yarmuk, obstructing Jordan's pumping operation.

Officials and technical experts from Jordan and Israel, including Prime Minister Peres's aide Amnon Neubach, met several times at the Allenby Bridge to discuss the matter. A rope bridge was strung over the Yarmuk, and a senior Jordanian army officer who was in charge of water planning crossed over into Israel. The two sides agreed on a plan of action.

Half a dozen huge tractors were sent to the scene of the unwanted island—four Israeli tractors on one riverbank, and two Jordanian tractors on the other. They worked together for four days, reducing the buildup of soil in the river, solving the erosion problem and restoring the unimpeded flow of the Yarmuk.[8]

Officials of the two nations met frequently in 1987 to coordinate their positions, in the face of a Syrian plan to use more of the water in the triple-border area. Employing a Soviet construction firm, Syria planned to build a huge network of dams and canals at Shaykh Mishkin on the upper Yarmuk. They would draw water for the irrigation of a new development area on part of the Golan Heights they recaptured from the Israelis in 1973. Tens of thousands of Syrian farmers would settle there.

The greatest threat was to Jordan, the biggest user of Yarmuk water, but Israel's irrigation system would be affected, too. Israeli legal experts said that international law prohibited any action by a state, possessing the upper reaches of a river, which would adversely affect countries using the water downriver.

Israel and Jordan exchanged information on the Syrian plan, which worried both governments. Jordan had the advantage of being able to speak with Syria, and Prime Minister Rifai pleaded privately with Damascus to consider Jordan's interests.[9] The Jordanians might somehow share water with Syria, although Amman would hate to be dependent on its radical neighbor to the north, but Israel would still sustain a loss on the Yarmuk.

All these subjects, related to economics and natural resources, were of secondary interest among the major diplomatic issues and peace-conference plans buzzing back and forth between Jerusalem and Amman. But while water, ecology, shale oil, and Dead Sea minerals seemed mundane, they were the stuff of peaceful coexistence in the Middle East—even without a formal peace treaty.

More importantly, it was good that officials on both sides sought to resolve disputes promptly, because the seemingly mundane issues could lead to hostility and violence in the absence of goodwill or understanding.

On the other hand, anyone who believed the road to peace and normal diplomatic relations would run through economic cooperation must have been disappointed in the Israeli-Jordanian model. It was not a case history of one agreement leading on to another subject, but rather of efforts to cooperate wherever possible without making commitments in related or unrelated fields. Israel and Jordan did not try to use their often-successful handling of these issues to lead to a complete settlement of the official state of war.

A more concentrated and coordinated effort to cooperate economically could be found in the West Bank. Here, both sides acknowledged that while their basic dispute was unresolved, other goals were within their grasp. Here, peace could grow from finance.

When Jordan and Israel made economic plans related to the West Bank and Gaza, they were touching the Palestinian issue more firmly than they did in any other way. High-level contacts between the king and the prime ministers generally ignored the Palestinians as a people with rights and needs. However, cooperation in developing the occupied territories and introducing Jordanian influence was an attempt to design a future for the Palestinians.

Both governments wished to woo the local Arabs away from the PLO to construct a system of interdependence that might lead to a tripartite peace: Israel, Jordan, and the Palestinians. In the first instance, officials spoke of constructing a condominium.

Chapter 15

Building a Condominium

"I spotted a truck crossing the river," the junior officer reported to Colonel Zonik Shacham, an Israeli brigade commander in the West Bank. Israel had just conquered the territory, a few weeks earlier in 1967. And here was a vehicle, being driven through the mud, eastward out of the West Bank.

Shacham recalls, "I was very angry. Here they were violating our authority." He rushed to Umm Suff, another crossing point where the Jordan River runs dry. "And here was the truck returning. We arrested the driver for questioning. He turned out to be a merchant from Jenin, who had a contract to deliver vegetables to the East Bank, and believing in the work ethic he decided to take his chances and honor the contract. I asked him, 'What did you sell?' And he said, 'vegetables.'

" 'And how much did they pay?' I asked. 'More than I thought,' the man answered. And I thought to myself: 'Now this is the solution.' "

Israel's military commanders in the newly occupied territory quickly learned that the 1967 harvest of fruits and vegetables was a bountiful one. There was a huge surplus, and no market was apparent.

The general adds, "I knew that if we did not sell what was left over, the bitterness of the local population would grow. A satisfied population, on the other hand, is never willing to put its satisfaction at risk. A bitter population can turn hostile."

The Israelis studied the seemingly unique and unimportant Umm Suff incident and decided not to stop the commercial traffic. At least for a trial period, if West Bankers wished to continue doing business with the East Bank and honoring previously signed contracts, the Israelis would not stand in their way.

Within a few days, the Jordanian authorities sent powerful tractors to their riverbank, to help trucks from the West Bank get across and up onto the East Bank by towing them over the final stretch if necessary.

For security's sake, the Israeli authorities set up a checkpoint at the most obvious crossing points where the river was all but dry. They had to be sure that no weapons were being brought into the West Bank. An impromptu arrangement was taking on the appearance of something official.

A few weeks later, Defense Minister Moshe Dayan went to the river and saw that two hundred trucks a day were crossing the Jordan. Dayan liked what he saw and gave the arrangement his official approval.[1]

It was the beginning of the "Open Bridges Policy" distinctly identified with Dayan. It had started with an unplanned event, but it continued in light of Israel's view of the occupied territories immediately after the Six Day War.

1. Israel, until 1977, saw the occupation as a temporary phenomenon, and the territories themselves—or at least, most of them—as bargaining chips in negotiating peace treaties.

2. Even after 1977, when Prime Minister Begin opposed the return of the territories to Arab rule, Israel still did not wish to govern over one million Palestinians.

3. Jordan, through all the internal disturbances and policy adjustments, consistently wished to maintain close connections with the West Bank.

4. Both Israel and Jordan knew that a permanent settlement of their dispute would have to include a lasting arrangement for the Palestinian Arabs.

The only logical solution to the triangular problem of the Israelis, the Jordanians, and the Palestinians was for all three to be involved in administering the West Bank. The concept, at various stages, had various names: "functional compromise," "condominium," and even "Jordanization."

The notion of a "functional compromise" was the product of official Israeli thinking at the end of the 1960s, during Dayan's time as defense minister and thus ruler of the occupied territories.

The "condominium" proposal, by that name, was made in 1985, by Prime Minister Peres's senior aides. It referred to a shared administration for the West Bank, with Israelis and Jordanians working together.

"Jordanization" was a term in vogue around the same time, as Peres and his officials encouraged King Hussein to become more deeply involved in West Bank affairs.[2]

Israel captured the West Bank from Jordan in 1967 but annexed only East Jerusalem. The term for "annexation," in Hebrew, refers specifically to extending the authority of Israeli law over an area. In the West Bank, Jordanian law continued to be the basis of the legal system, although the Israelis did exercise some of the "Emergency Powers" left behind by the British mandate when imprisoning or expelling alleged Palestinian terrorists. Courts and judges were Jordanian, for disputes between West Bankers and many criminal cases not involving Israel itself.

West Bank residents, and even the Palestinians of East Jerusalem—unless they chose otherwise—remained citizens of the Hashemite Kingdom of Jordan.

The schools continued to be under the official authority of the Ministry of Education in Amman, which supplied books and curricula to the West Bank teachers. Israel's military censors checked, however, that the material contained no anti-Semitic or anti-Zionist material.

The men and women who worked for municipalities and public health and education agencies were all employees of the Jordanian government and continued to receive their salaries from Amman.

Within several years, the Israeli pound—later replaced by the shekel—was used throughout the occupied territories, as many thousands of Arabs had jobs within Israel, but the official currency in the West Bank was still the Jordanian dinar.

Jordan continued to play a role in planning the West Bank's agriculture, and the Israelis saw this area as a fruitful one for cooperation between Jerusalem and Amman. Exporting farm produce was the key to prosperity for the West Bankers, who annually grew over 700,000 tons of olives and half a million tons of other produce. At the beginning of each planting season—for one crop or another—a delegation from Amman would arrive to inspect the fields and to offer advice.

Some of the officials from Jordan's agriculture ministry met their Israeli counterparts, to discuss the West Bank harvest and where to sell it. Israel did not want the crops to be sold in Israel, because the prices charged by the communal kibbutzim and other farms would decline due to oversupply. Only when there were shortages of specific fruits or vegetables did the Agriculture Ministry in Jerusalem allow the sale of West Bank produce within Israel's pre–1967 borders.

Israel, therefore, encouraged and helped the farmers to send their produce, by truck, across the river to the huge outdoor markets of Amman. From there, the fruits and vegetables were often sold to Syria, Kuwait, Iraq, and Saudi Arabia, which would never have anything to do with Israel. Jordan's agriculture officials, meanwhile, sought to protect the interests of East Bank farmers while not cheating the West Bankers who officially were just as Jordanian.

The men from Amman were often reluctant to grant permission to farmers to sell their products to East Bank buyers. The fine balance was discussed almost every year by the two sides, with the Israeli officials using aerial photographs of West Bank fields while the Jordanians said they did not believe the high crop projections.[3]

Israel and Jordan also cooperated in the power supply to East Jerusalem, where the Electricity Company was seen since 1967 as an important relic of Jordanian rule. Israel trusted the company sufficiently to depend on it to supply electricity to the new Jewish neighborhoods built in and around the ancient city. The Electricity Company, however, had old equipment, already stretched to full capacity, and the new houses suffered occasional outages. Their residents demanded to be hooked up to the Israeli electricity grid.

An agreement was reached in December 1986, after lengthy negotiations including a visit to Jerusalem by Jordanian Senator Hazem Zaki Nuseibeh, the brother of the late chairman of the Electricity Company, Anwar Nuseibeh—both former government ministers in Amman and personal friends of King Hussein. The senator, who also had served as Jordan's ambassador to the United Nations, led a team that met with Israel's Energy Minister Moshe Shahal. The Arab-owned company was to have its franchise extended for ten years. The agreement collapsed, however, because the pro-Jordanian management could not impose it on the pro-PLO work force. After maddening delays, Israel's parliament passed a law canceling the company's right to supply Jewish neighborhoods, and they and the Jewish settlements of the West Bank were connected to Israel's electricity grid by technicians in a midnight "raid" near the end of 1987.

Cooperation in tourism, to market visits by foreigners to the two nations of the Holy Land together, was often considered. Jordan's national airline, Alia, looked into the possibility of opening offices in the West Bank to serve Palestinians who flew to destinations in the Arab world by way of Amman. Alia officials also inquired about cooperation with Israel in encouraging Christian tourists to widen their pilgrimage route beyond Jerusalem, Nazareth, and Bethlehem by crossing the Jordan River and seeing such marvels as the rose-colored city of stone, Petra.

The Israelis regularly allowed East Bankers to visit their West Bank relatives during the summer months. Traveling from Jordan and occasionally from other Arab countries, up to a million Palestinians a year, who would never want the fact to appear in their passports or any other official records, crossed the Allenby Bridge. And once in the West Bank, they could travel freely into Israel itself.

In 1987, for instance, a leading Israeli newspaper reported on "the children of several Jordanian government ministers, who crossed the bridges over the Jordan to visit relatives and visited luxury shops on Dizengoff Street in Tel Aviv, some even swimming in the Mediterranean Sea."[4]

Israel and Jordan could not simply act as enemies in a state of war—or at least they chose not to do so—in dealing with the desire by Muslims to gain immunity from their sins by making pilgrimage to the holy shrines in Mecca. The authorities of all three states concerned permitted Arabs from Israel, the West Bank, and Gaza Strip to travel to Saudi Arabia, by way of Jordan.

The strong but wholly unpublicized relationship between Israeli and Jordanian officials focused on the bridges over the Jordan River. Allowing trucks to drive through the extremely shallow water in 1967 proved to be a temporary arrangement, as much greater flows of traffic could be accommodated on the bridges once they were repaired after the Six Day War. Israel's air force had struck them all, fearing that Jordanian and Iraqi reinforcements might otherwise pour into the West Bank during the fighting. Several Israeli units crossed over what remained of the spans, pursuing Hussein's Arab Legion onto the East Bank, but when Defense Minister Dayan learned of the crossings he ordered his troops to withdraw and to blow up the bridges. At the time, Dayan remarked that he aimed to separate the two banks of the Jordan.

The defense minister was also directing a hint at Hussein, that he need not fear an invasion of Amman by the Israelis. The destruction of the bridges was ironic, considering that shortly afterward Dayan formulated his "open bridges" policy.[5]

It was some time later, after the trucks laden with produce had already begun crossing into the East Bank, that Israel and Jordan decided jointly, but secretly, to repair the ruined bridges. They became the most obvious example of the strange relationship between the two nations, which were officially at war, but which maintained an open border between them.

Both armies had inspection posts, defended by sandbags and machine guns at their respective ends of the Allenby Bridge, which was by far the busiest crossing point. The small military bases were not linked in any official way, but the needs of simple administration required daily contacts between the two commanders. A million tourists and travelers, and millions of tons of produce, crossed the Allenby Bridge each year.

The fact that the two nations kept the border open was more important for its political significance than the value of the vegetables or the revenues from tourism.

When Shimon Peres became Israel's prime minister, in 1984, he asked his closest aides to assess the chances of achieving peace with Jordan. The director general of his office, Avraham Tamir, set up a "think tank," which included academics, on the subject. Peres received several reports from the group, which pointed out that in the framework of the various attempts to find a diplomatic solution since 1967, Israel had found itself confronting the Arab world on two levels—one political, the other territorial.

The team of advisers suggested that the lesson to be learned from the successful negotiations with Egypt was that a formal peace treaty could not be reached without territorial concessions by Israel. However, there was no consensus in Israel in favor of conceding territory to Jordan and certainly no hint of an agreement on how much land to give up.

The think tank added that King Hussein had failed to receive the Palestinians' endorsement of his right to represent them.

In all, the chances of a territorial settlement seemed hardly to exist. The advisers said that the notion of a "trade off" of land, in exchange for setting aside the Palestinians' political demands, had been tried but had failed in the talks with Egypt. President Sadat had not been willing to recover the Sinai Peninsula without winning concessions for the Palestinians, too. The reports also pointed out that Israel could not obtain the type of peace treaty that it would want with Syria.

The think tank concluded, however, that the status quo was dangerous for Israel in the long run. The demographic factor gained the recognition it deserved in this analysis, which pointed out that the rate of growth of the Arab population was considerably greater than that of Israel's Jews.

The advisers suggested that because a political settlement, a territorial compromise, or a combination of the two were all unlikely, an interim arrangement would be the appropriate goal. Some suggested it was the only possible goal, and one which must be achieved.[6]

Until such time as a permanent settlement could be possible, an interim arrangement—or an officially designated period of transition—could help lay the groundwork for peace. This analysis produced the Peres view of the Middle East peace process, in two parallel stages: political and economic.

The political aspect would involve a period meant to produce the conditions needed for a final peace settlement, including agreement on permanent borders. This would take time, simply because these conditions did not exist in the mid–1980s. When the stage was set, negotiations could best be held through an international process to gain foreign sponsorship for the process.

The administration of President Ronald Reagan in the United States, after much reluctance to bring the Soviet Union into Middle East affairs, finally in 1987 endorsed the notion of an international peace conference. All efforts by U.S. and European diplomats to promote the idea ran into a wall of opposition in Jerusalem put up by Prime Minister Yitzhak Shamir.

The United States privately applied pressure on both Jordan and Israel, and the Americans persuaded King Hussein to deviate from his lifelong avoidance of the hard-line Likud bloc by meeting clandestinely with Shamir.

The historic meeting, never publicly confirmed by either side, took place in London during the final weekend of September 1987. On the Israeli side, the prime minister shared the details with only two senior aides and the director of the Mossad, where Shamir had served as European operations chief.

According to fragmentary accounts leaked in Jerusalem, Shamir suggested to the king that they meet in public in Washington in December, at the invitation—which could surely be arranged—of President Reagan and the Soviet leader Mikhail Gorbachev, who would be holding their fourth summit. The superpower chiefs were understood to be interested in jointly achieving a breakthrough in the Middle East.

Shamir said that Hussein would thus have the international umbrella he seemed to require to engage in peace negotiations. The Israeli leader said he would not agree to a wider conference, which Hussein was demanding, on the grounds that outside parties would attempt to impose a regional settlement.

The king said he recognized that Shamir was offering a concession, but Hussein said he strongly preferred, and would insist on, the format he had agreed in London a half a year earlier with Peres. Hussein said the participation of more Arab delegations would open the possibility of a comprehensive settlement.

From the king's point of view, the meeting was a failure. His major step in agreeing to see Shamir, Hussein felt, had not been met by a suitable Israeli gesture.

There were a few minor achievements at the meeting, however, as the Israelis and Jordanians exchanged intelligence that included the latest on the Syrian threat to divert Yarmuk River water from both Israel and Jordan.

Less than three weeks later, in October 1987, the United States sent Secretary of State George Shultz to the Middle East on one of his whirlwind tours. In four days, Shultz held discussions with the leaders of Israel, Jordan, Saudi Arabia, and Egypt. Shamir again expressed a willingness to have the two superpowers sponsor peace talks with Jordan. Hussein stood his ground, however, in calling for an international peace conference.

Shultz returned to Washington from a region in deadlock. His aides suggested that with barely a year until the U.S. and Israeli elections, there was no point in pursuing ideas that were making no headway. The United States was expected to drop the Middle East from its agenda for a while.

The secretary of state was back, however, within four months on an ambitious shuttle diplomacy mission prompted by the *intifadda*, the Palestinian uprising that Israel seemed unable to control. Some Arab officials commented bitterly that the United States was only interested in the region when its Israeli allies were in trouble. But Shultz seemed sincere in his contention that the search for a settlement had become far more urgent for the good of all.

Shultz went to the Middle East on February 25, 1988, for six days, and again on April 3 for four days. Jerusalem's King David Hotel was the base to which he returned every night, but he spent the days flying back and forth among Israeli, Jordanian, Syrian, Egyptian, and Saudi leaders. He was proposing an international peace conference, where face-to-face bilateral negotiations could take place between Israel and each of its neighbors.

To demonstrate further that he meant business, Shultz met in Washington with two Palestinians who were open supporters of the PLO. The United States insisted that it was still not talking to the PLO itself. Later, Shultz invited two members of the Palestine National Council to see him at the State Department. U.S. officials pointed out that both Edward Said and Ibrahim Abu Lughod were American university professors and U.S. citizens. It was thus perfectly natural, it was said, that they should be consulted.

It was, in fact, an extraordinary event and a barely veiled warning to Israel's Prime Minister Shamir that he should talk peace before the United States lost its patience.

Shultz was also consulting with the Russians. His frequent meetings with Soviet Foreign Minister Eduard Shevardnadze were dominated by issues of nuclear arms control, but regional conflicts including the Middle East were also discussed. Joint positions seemed possible for the first time in many years. The Soviet agreement to withdraw troops from Afghanistan contributed to the atmosphere of superpower cooperation.

An international peace conference appeared to be inching closer to becoming a reality. In the meantime, Israel did what it could to work together with Jordan for the secret coordination of West Bank affairs.

The economic aspect of building peace would take place "in the field," as the Israeli analysts put it. Actual problems affecting the lives of people could be resolved by the appropriate experts, if political disputes were left to politicians.

Contacts between Israel and Jordan on both aspects continued until the *intifadda* began in December 1987. The talks and the joint work were directed at establishing a unique form of administration in the West Bank. Israel's goal would be to withdraw from governing the daily lives of Arab citizens going about their peaceful business, but Israel would have to maintain its military presence for the foreseeable future. The new administration could lead to a simultaneous Jordanian-Palestinian solution, from Israel's point of view, and could naturally fit in with King Hussein's proposal of 1972 for a federation linking the East and West Banks.

The first stage, politically, would be the formation of Israeli-Jordanian-Palestinian administration—an arrangement that came to be known as the "condominium."[7]

The meetings with Hussein during the Peres administration—with the prime minister in October 1985, in London; with Yitzhak Rabin in March 1986, in Paris; and with both Israelis in August 1986—made significant progress in building the condominium that could help create the necessary conditions for lasting peace.

Four months after the first meeting, the king delivered an important speech to his parliament in Amman on February 19, 1986. He spoke of his disappointment with the PLO and of his decision to end the coordination talks with Arafat, but also of his renewed sense of responsibility toward the Palestinian problem.

Declaring that the PLO was unable to fulfill its duty, Hussein said that he would henceforth concern himself with the welfare of the West Bank's Arabs. He stressed the importance of helping them with economic development, and he included the West Bank in a new five-year plan for prosperity in Jordan.

The speech in Parliament conflicted completely with Hussein's previous policy and with the dictates of the Rabat Summit of 1974, and it signaled a major change in Jordan's intentions: accepting the notion that had been put forward by Peres's Israeli advisers, that economic progress and cooperation could help the political aspect of the peace process.[8]

The West Bank had four open sources of revenue and a few which were kept secret.

The first public source was the funding from Jordan's Ministry of Occupied Lands, which was established in 1972 and poured some $12 million a year into the West Bank. Most of the money was for the salaries of three thousand officials in the municipalities, courts, schools, and health facilities and for pension payments to thousands of retired government employees. Around one-third of the money from Amman went to the Waqf, the Islamic authority in Jerusalem.

After Hussein's speech in February 1986, Jordan announced that the salaries of West Bank employees would be doubled, and that Arabs hired by the Israeli authorities would be added to Jordan's payroll. It was a dual signal: that Jordan would become more active in the West Bank, and that the door was opened even wider to cooperation with the Israelis.

The second public source was the Arab world. The summit that convened in

Baghdad in 1978, to reject the Camp David Accords between Israel and Egypt, decided to establish a fund to help Jordan and the PLO and "the firm resistance and opposition of the people of the West Bank and Gaza, against the Israeli occupation." The fund had its headquarters in Amman and made payments of around $70 million a year, most of it spent on housing, municipal office buildings, and institutions of learning in the West Bank. The money was contributed mainly by the wealthy oil-producing states, including Saudi Arabia and Kuwait, and when the price of petroleum declined in the mid–1980s, so did the activities of the Arab fund.

The third source of funding to the West Bank was the wider, international community. Organizations such as the United Nations Relief and Works Agency (UNRWA) spend around $70 million a year in the West Bank. Aid organizations and other charities in the United States and Western Europe contributed another $25 million annually.

The fourth source was open but somewhat secret, too. It was known that Israel provided financial aid, despite a decision made in the early days of the military occupation in 1967 that the captured territories should not become an economic burden on Israel. The military-run Civil Administration refused, however, to publish any budget.[9]

In the absence of any banks in the occupied territories that could receive formal transfers, most of the money sent in from outside Israel was brought, in cash, over the Jordan River bridges by couriers.

The secret sources of finance were similarly delivered by hand. These included payments from Palestinian organizations, even as the Israeli authorities attempted to prevent guerrilla groups from paying their supporters and operatives in the West Bank. Some of the money financed acts of terrorism, underground purchases of weapons, or payments to the families of guerrillas who were imprisoned or killed.

There were some complications. For security reasons, Israel would not allow industrial raw materials to be imported by way of the Jordan River bridges. It would be too easy to smuggle arms and ammunition as part of the truck cargoes. The Israelis insisted that raw materials arrive by sea, at Israeli ports. The Jordanians, however, had commercial regulations that prohibited the entry—by bridge into the East Bank—of any finished goods not made of raw materials that passed through Jordan.

Prime Minister Peres enlisted the support of U.S. Secretary of State Shultz for plans to develop the economies of the West Bank and Gaza toward a political and economic "condominium." Shultz also believed that financial incentives could speed the path toward peace, and his favorite phrase in this regard was "the need to improve the quality of life." Likud leader Yitzhak Shamir was also comfortable with the slogan.

The shared Israeli and U.S. hope was that economic assistance would weaken the PLO and strengthen political moderates in the occupied territories. The Palestinians had a low standard of living, especially compared with the average

Israelis living a short distance away, and America, Israel, and all Jordan agreed that poverty fueled terrorism.

The United States assigned the subject to the "Israel Desk" at the State Department, which proposed that the West Bank and Gaza be turned into a "free trade zone," similar to the tariff-free status enjoyed by Israel in its trade with America. Israeli officials moved quickly to kill the proposal, explaining that with the lack of an industrial base in the occupied territories, combined with low average wages, a free-trade arrangement would simply be an economic distortion causing more damage than good.[10]

The Israelis could be accused of putting their own economic interests first, fearing perhaps that if Palestinians were more fully employed in their own industries, finding it easy to export thanks to American arrangements, they would be less willing to work for Israeli employers. West Bank and Gaza products could even pose competition to Israel's exports.

Israel persuaded the United States instead to press Jordan to contribute more direct aid to the West Bank. The Jordanians were also asked by Washington to help establish homegrown financial institutions in the occupied areas, to grant loans and make other business decisions that could boost economic development.

From 1985 onward, Israeli officials came to the conclusion that of all alternatives, allowing the Palestinians to have their own bank branches—not their own bank, because that might appear too much to involve separate sovereignty— would be the most acceptable way of encouraging, but monitoring, economic progress in the West Bank. All the Arab banks had closed during the Six Day War in 1967 and none had reopened, largely because of arguments over which government or banking authority would supervise their operations.

The Jordanian and other Arab owners of the banks rejected Israel's insistence that its central bank would have authority over branches in the occupied territories. Hussein's secret meetings with Peres and Rabin, however, led to a change of heart, and technical talks began between junior officials of Jordan and Israel. The Israelis were Amnon Neubach, governing coordinator of the territories, Shmuel Goren, and Galia Maor, the official inspector of banks. The Jordanians included the deputy governor of the central bank and members of the Shasha family, which owned the Cairo-Amman Bank.

The Shashas and their bank became the linchpin in the efforts to make progress on the economic and financial front. It had branches in Egypt, Jordan, and the United Arab Emirates. Before 1967, five of its Jordanian branches had been in the West Bank. Most of the shares were in the hands of Jordanian investors, led by the Shasha family, which had its origins in the West Bank town of Jericho. Fifteen percent of the shares were held by Egyptians, and Egypt's ambassador in Tel Aviv became involved in the secret negotiations, as did U.S. officials.

The president of the bank, Juwadad Shasha, visited Israel several times, holding talks in Jerusalem's elegant King David Hotel, at the Bank of Israel offices in Jerusalem, and even in the defense ministry in Tel Aviv, the planning center for the military occupation.

The negotiations achieved success in London. The three Israeli officials most directly concerned, Neubach, Goren, and Maor, arrived there in August 1986, identifying themselves merely as tourists to the British passport control officers at Heathrow Airport. They checked into a central London hotel, and the Jordanian negotiators stayed nearby. Their talks took place in the conference room of a third hotel near Oxford Street, taking three full days to draw up and sign an agreement.

Concessions had been made by both sides. Israel agreed that the Cairo-Amman Bank could conduct business in Jordanian dinars as well as Israeli shekels. A system of double regulation would be in force: the Central Bank in Jerusalem would enforce the usual strictures imposed on Israeli banks, but Israel would also permit an inspector from Jordan's central bank to base himself in Nablus to oversee banking operations in the West Bank. The Jordanians would set the level of reserves, in dinars, which the bank would be required to maintain. The bank would be allowed to maintain savings accounts up to a total equivalent of $75 million.

A final obstacle was Israel's insistence on a clear antiterrorism clause in the banking agreement: "The bank will not be used as an instrument for the transfer of funds for purposes hostile to the State of Israel." Jordan, in the end, demanded that a parallel statement about anti-Jordanian purposes be inserted. The Israelis readily agreed.

Neubach and his team knew they had achieved an historic breakthrough: the first signed agreement directly negotiated between Israel and Jordan. Even King Abdullah's nonaggression pact with the Israelis in 1950 had only been initialed and never signed or ratified. The four-page banking accord, in black and white and in multiple copies, was signed in London by representatives of "the Hashemite Kingdom of Jordan" and officials of "the State of Israel." Rare, direct talks had yielded complete success.

The three Israelis returned home, for reasons of safety and secrecy, on three separate El Al flights. They reported their success only to Prime Minister Peres and Defense Minister Rabin, who in turn informed Foreign Minister Shamir. The unique and secret pact with Jordan was kept, for a time, in Neubach's personal safe at the prime minister's office, until foreign ministry officials learned of it and demanded that, as protocol dictated, the signed accord should be stored by them with Israel's other treaties.[11]

The Cairo-Amman Bank reopened its first West Bank branch in Nablus and rapidly was considered a success story. Its one thousand customers were mainly Palestinian exporters and importers. The government of Jordan provided business by paying the salaries of public service employees through the new bank. A second branch was planned for Ram Allah.

Jordan took other steps, during the twenty-five-month Peres administration, to emphasize the historic connection between the West and East Banks, and the Israeli authorities—concerned above all with restraining the PLO's power base in the occupied territories—seemed to approve fully the Jordanian steps. Some of these were minor, although they still had symbolic value.

Jordan's state television service, after more than a decade of not doing so, resumed broadcasting weather forecasts for the West Bank as part of the local, Jordanian news. The television station also covered more news concerning the area, even before the Palestinian uprising began in late 1987, by hiring the British-based television agency Visnews to record interviews—even with dovish members of the Israeli Parliament, such as Abba Eban and Yossi Sarid—that were then broadcast on Jordanian television.[12]

The many aspects of cooperation—in agriculture, tourism, energy, and especially banking—helped strengthen the economy of the occupied territories. Without Jordan's involvement, it had seemed that the Palestinians under occupation were wholly dependent on the Israeli economy for their income. Tens of thousands of them continued to travel daily into Israel to work, mainly at jobs involving physical labor, such as construction and hotel and restaurant services. The Palestinians still found it difficult to do any long-term financial planning, but here, too, Jordan's government was becoming more involved in doing it for them.

Officials in Amman, especially the senior individuals who knew about the burgeoning cooperation with the Israeli government under Peres, decided that giving new impetus to the West Bank's economy would require a major push. That is what Jordan promised in August 1986, when Crown Prince Hassan announced a new five-year plan that would help both banks of the Jordan River develop through the end of the decade. Interestingly, the Gaza Strip was included in the plan, too, because while it had been captured by the Israelis from Egypt it was Palestinian Arab land.

Hassan's program was ambitious, involving $3 billion to be invested in the Israeli-occupied territories. A deep-water port would be built at Gaza. Twenty-three thousand housing units and eighty-five new schools would be built. More financial institutions, such as credit unions to offer loans for further development, would be established.[13]

Prince Hassan met, that same month, with U.S. Vice President George Bush, who was on a tour of the Middle East. Bush later flew to Jerusalem, bringing the Israelis a transcript of his detailed discussion with Hassan, which had focused on the five-year plan and the potential role of foreign aid.

Israeli officials, seeing for the first time details that Hassan had not publicly announced, were surprised to see how grandiose were the prince's plans. He wanted to build ultramodern industrial plants in the West Bank, including computer and electronics factories. The Israelis knew that Palestinians were relatively well educated, certainly compared with the people of other Arab nations, but the infrastructure for such schemes seemed lacking. "This plan is divorced from reality," Amnon Neubach said.

It was ironic. The more Jordan tried to prove to the watching Israelis and Americans that it was serious about renewing the intimate Jordanian role in the West Bank, the greater were the doubts felt—at least by the Israelis.

Officials in both Israel and the United States were skeptical about the five-year plan. They knew that Jordan was seeking finance from Saudi Arabia, and King Fahd had already been generous in funding specific Jordanian projects. But the Americans, who would also be called on to contribute, were not convinced that King Hussein and his brother would know how to spend billions wisely, even if they could obtain billions.

No one wanted to give up entirely on such plans, however, because the notion of a "condominium" for sharing administration of the West Bank and Gaza depended on sharing the responsibilities and benefits of a healthier economy, too. More than twenty years of discussions between Israel and Jordan had failed to bring a political and a full treaty any closer, and the Camp David Accords' offer of autonomy to the Palestinians had led nowhere. The economic route was vital—almost a last chance for Israel and Jordan to make peace on their own terms, but in a manner that could give the Palestinians trapped between them some incentive to keep the peace.

The hopes harbored by Israel, Jordan, and their American supporters were severely damaged by the Palestinian uprising, or *intifadda*, in 1988 and beyond. The Israeli economy itself suffered an estimated 15 percent decline in output due to the unrest. Minister of Economy and Planning Gad Yaacobi estimated that in the first six months alone, the uprising cost Israel $600 million in lost tourism and the cost of additional security. Men serving in the army reserves saw their periods of duty lengthened during the *intifadda*, and their industrial production was lost.

The economic losses to the Palestinians, in the occupied territories, were even worse. Some economists estimated that nearly half of all agricultural and industrial production was lost in the first six months of the uprising. It was obvious that the retail trade was at a standstill, with shopkeepers unable to open their businesses at all when faced with the underground *intifadda* leadership calling for strikes at certain hours, while Israeli troops insisted that they be open in those hours and close down in other time periods.

The Israelis living in the southern half of the country, who used to bring their cars and trucks for cheaper, but excellent, servicing and repairs to the Gaza Strip garages, were no longer doing so—afraid their vehicles would be doubly damaged by stone-throwing mobs.

Israeli authorities applied economic pressure to fight the uprising, but in so doing they undid much of the progress made in cooperation with Jordan in recent years. The Israelis punished entire towns and refugee camps by imposing curfews that prevented any economic activities. Towns and villages that did not "behave" saw their licenses to export goods across the bridges into the Jordan's East Bank canceled by the Israelis.

Palestinian industries in the West Bank were not allowed to import their raw materials from Jordan and sometimes not even from the outside world, unless they proved that they had paid all their Israeli taxes. The *intifadda* organizers, meanwhile, threatened violence against the Palestinians who "collaborated" by paying taxes.

If the uprising were to wind down in its intensity, as Israeli officials were optimistically predicting, then they and their Jordanian counterparts could have one last chance to resuscitate the economic path to peace.

The so-called Palestinian economy was lying in relative tatters, and aid would be required from somewhere to repair the damage. The strike's organizers were vehemently anti-Jordanian, charging that King Hussein had betrayed Palestinian interests for years, but the need for financial aid could still lead the general public in the West Bank and Gaza to look to Amman for support.

It would be in Israeli interests to encourage a renewed link between Jordan and the occupied territories. The alternative would be a hostile form of "economic self-sufficiency," which was named as the first goal in the underground leaflets of the United National Command of the Uprising. The leaders of the unrest wished to cut off the West Bank and Gaza from both Israel and Jordan—first economically, and then politically.

As a first step toward crushing the occupation, they were out to kill the "condominium."

Chapter 16

Breaking the Deadlock?

A tale is told of the young King Hussein, asking one of his elderly Beduin advisers, "Tell me, what is the secret of living a long life?"

"It is simple, Your Majesty," the wrinkled Arab is said to have replied. "Never set out on a journey through the desert, unless you are certain your camel can bear its burden."[1]

Hussein appears to have heeded whatever good advice he was given, for no leader but he survived through four decades of turmoil in the Middle East. While still a young man, he was the Arab world's senior statesman. Considering the few natural resources at his command, Hussein ibn-Talal could be proud of his performance.

On the other hand, he was ruler of a relatively small and unimportant nation, and the obvious lack of democratic values was further sullied by the regime's reputation for being corrupt. Hussein himself spent nearly half of every year outside his kingdom.

Being abroad so much made him a man of the world, unlike other Arab dictators who knew little more than the intrigues of their own domestic politics. He was well acquainted with foreign capitals and welcome in most of them. In London, Hussein was one of the family. In Washington, he was a friend to be protected. He could feel sincerely wanted in Moscow, where the authorities constantly offered to sell him arms.

Since losing the most productive sector of his kingdom, the West Bank, in 1967, he became even more appreciated in the west as a moderate and balanced leader.

Israeli politicians consistently sought his company, and despite the rumors and evidence of his contacts with Israel, Hussein continued to be welcome in Cairo and Damascus, in Baghdad and Riyadh. The Israelis who met Hussein praised him, and the negative words came only from politicians who refused to meet him. He was a "humane" or "positive" figure to the Israelis, while the

PLO's Yasser Arafat kissed both Hussein's cheeks when meeting him at Arab conferences.

Jordan received financial aid both from the oil-rich Arab states of the Gulf and from the United States. Rumors abounded in Washington, meanwhile, that he was personally on the CIA's payroll.

The secret of a long life, Hussein learned, had little to do with camels and the sands of the desert. Life was a balancing act, and the king was an expert at sitting on the fence: one foot about to step in one political direction, while the other was ready to stride in the opposite direction.

He exploited his position with precision:

* Israel's military superiority in the region proved itself to be Hussein's protector against Arab plots against him.
* His good relations with Israel allowed Jordan to develop its agricultural production, planting on every centimeter right up to the border.
* Israel was helping him rebuild his influence in the West Bank he had lost.

Hussein was also in the diplomatic driver's seat. Only his judgment would determine whether there would ever be open negotiations for peace between Jordan and Israel. He may have been walking on a tightrope between his image as an Arab and his other image as a pro-western moderate. But his policy was clearly inscribed on that tightrope, ever since the first days after the Six Day War of 1967; he would sign a peace treaty with Israel, only in exchange for all his lost territory including East Jerusalem. In this, he was consistent—for, after all, stepping to the left or to the right would only lead to his falling from his tightrope.

A peace treaty was never very close, with any positive developments through the years more than negated by negative events in the region. Hussein continued to meet with Israel's leaders, except in the years of Menachem Begin and Yitzhak Shamir's first term, when the king believed that dialogue would do no good at all. The Israelis tried, from time to time, to bring the talks out into the open, but Hussein always insisted on keeping them secret. It was a huge, even ridiculous fiction, for all other Arab leaders knew that Hussein was in touch with Israel.

It was a matter of pride. Even if most Arabs knew most of the truth, the king would never have to admit that he had a long and valuable dialogue with the Zionists. The secrecy may also have reflected Hussein's doubts that the contacts were helping, for he came to the conclusion that the passage of time was working against his interests. The Israeli occupation was becoming better and more firmly established. The construction of Jewish settlements signaled the possibility of eventual annexation. Israeli politicians increasingly called for "transfer" or "expulsion" or "encouraging" the Palestinians of the West Bank to leave. Jordan's population, already with a Palestinian majority, might lose whatever Hashemite character it had. Hussein feared that Ariel Sharon might put on his general's uniform again and lead an invasion of Amman.

After the Begin-Shamir-Sharon years, Peres and his Labor party came to power in Israel—albeit sharing power with Shamir, Sharon, and the rest of the Likud. Hussein could not do nothing in the face of his fears and the ticking clock of history. In his contacts with Peres, the king seriously considered negotiating openly with Israel. They even set the ground rules in their London agreement of April 1987.

The old clock was shattered on December 8 of that year. Its hands were not turned back. History was not repeating itself. A new history was being made, as the Palestinians launched their uprising.

The PLO may have been caught by surprise by the rapid and violent events, but Yasser Arafat quickly seized the role of spokesman for the revolt. The young Palestinian protesters carried his picture. And Hussein was pushed out of the picture. He had to put aside any pretensions of representing the Palestinians, and in their new mood he did not want any close involvement with them in any event. The PLO had risen again from its ashes. Similar to a seesaw, when Arafat was up, Hussein was down.

King Hussein could only reduce his expectation of returning triumphantly to the West Bank as sovereign, and now he would instead have to worry about keeping the Palestinian uprising away from the East Bank.

In April 1988, the sound of ambulance sirens pierced the calm of an Amman morning. They were rushing to the national center for drivers' licenses, where dozens of people had been wounded by a terrorist bombing. It was a most unusual event in the Jordanian capital, and the royal palace had much that was worrying to consider when a man claiming to represent ''Black September'' telephoned the press in Beirut to say that the organization had planted the bomb and would launch a new wave of attacks.

Hussein had already been quicker than the Israelis to interpret the *intifadda*. He knew how to read the political map, and he understood what the ''children of the stones'' were saying as they braved bullets to confront Israel's troops. The king rapidly tightened his grip on Jordan's Palestinians, particularly those in the crowded refugee camps around Amman. Jordanian security agents surrounded the camps, day and night to prevent the fire of the West Bank uprising from spreading eastward. Hundreds of Palestinian activists linked with leftist, radical groups were arrested in Jordan.

Hussein faced another threat to his fragile regime in April 1989, when his usually loyal Beduin subjects went on the rampage to protest price rises. The king was away in the United States, but his brother Crown Prince Hassan efficiently sent security forces to quell the disturbances. In sharp contrast with 1970, the PLO did not stir up the trouble. Arafat had no desire to divert attention from the *intifadda* or the West Bank and he did not want the United States to brand the PLO as troublemakers.

At the same time, Hussein returned to the conclusion he had reached in 1975 that he would never again be able to pray at the holy mosques of Jerusalem without the cooperation of the PLO. Much as the Israelis might refuse to accept the fact, the king believed, they would have to speak with Arafat. Hussein had had his doubts before, and had tried as hard as anyone to avoid Arafat and negotiate around him. But by 1989, Jordan's message to Israel and the United States was, "We are ready to talk peace, but we must include the PLO, too."

The United States eventually accepted the reality of the Middle East, that there was no way to ignore the PLO as representative of the Palestinian people and their desire for a political entity of their own. The message, though, was not getting through to the Israeli leadership. Both the Likud and Labor halves of the government, in their new National Unity Coalition led by Yitzhak Shamir after the 1988 election, refused to consider any form of negotiations in which Israel might be pressed to reciprocate the PLO's new recognition of the Jewish state.

The Israelis, in a sense, believed in the Jordanian option more than Jordan did. They were more Hussein-oriented than was Hussein himself.

The Likud, under Shamir, was willing to pursue the "Jordanization" of the West Bank because it seemed to be a useful weapon in the fight against the Palestinians' hope of establishing their own state there. There was no real intention of reaching a compromise on the issue of sovereignty over the territory.

Jordan was being used, in effect, as a fig leaf by both major political parties in Israel. The Likud was committed to the old, right-wing aim of annexing the West Bank, but party leaders were aware of the demographic dangers of absorbing over one million Arabs whose descendants would outnumber the Jews of Israel in around twenty years. Perhaps they would leave for Jordan. Perhaps Jordan would keep them as citizens, even if they lived under Israeli sovereignty. If there were no Jordan to hide behind, Israel's leaders might be forced to make the crucial decisions that combined politics with ideology and conscience.

Many Labor party politicians knew in their hearts that the PLO, and not Jordan, was the real representative of the Palestinians, and that a serious effort to establish peace should include Arafat. The Israeli public, however, was not ready for such a shift, not even at the end of the 1980s when the Jewish state was over forty years old and the military occupation over two decades long. Labor's leaders would continue to use Jordan as a temporary address for their peace proposals.

There were some Labor party figures who supported the Jordanian option as a tactical move. In their rather Machiavellian calculations, either Israel's democratic society would eventually be swamped by a Palestinian Arab majority, or the Hashemite Kingdom of Jordan would be inundated by a similar Palestinian multitude. The choice, for Israel, was clear: establishment of a Jordanian-Palestinian confederation should be encouraged; and with some regret, but little alternative, Israel would be helping King Hussein to self-destruct.

Israel made the mistake, however, of concentrating on what to do with the occupied West Bank, rather than on what was happening inside the West Bank.

The conceptual failure was seen, again, in a speech given by a senior Israeli general soon after the uprising began, in which he gave eleven reasons for the *intifadda*. They included: the difficult economic situation in the territories, high unemployment among the Palestinian intelligentsia, religious fundamentalism, the fact that the Arab states had ignored the Palestinian problem as seen at the Amman summit, and the indifference toward the Middle East shown by Mikhail Gorbachev and Ronald Reagan at the Soviet-American summits.[2]

He gave many interesting reasons for the trouble, but he failed to mention the simplest and strongest fact: that the Palestinians did not want to live under the authority of the Jewish state. Israel's leaders seemed to have a mental block against seeing the heart of the matter. They refused to see the Palestinians as an active element in the complex political picture. It is not quite so serious as the oft-quoted comment by Golda Meir that there never was a Palestinian people. But as a political player, the Palestinians did not exist for the Israelis, and if they did not exist they did not have legitimate aspirations.

In the Israeli view, the only known organization of Palestinians, the PLO, was a known terrorist group. Israel was prepared to discuss the Palestinians with everybody: the United States, the Soviet Union under certain conditions, Jordan, Egypt, and even Syria. But not with the Palestinians themselves. Several Israeli politicians said that it was "impossible" for the PLO to change its line and renounce violence. "It would no longer be the PLO," one said. Even after the PLO, according to this concept, shed its identity and did renounce terrorism, Israel's leaders refused to accept the new realities.

There was the extreme danger that history was being repeated in an unexpected, reversed fashion. From 1948 to 1967, the Arabs had refused to speak with Israel. The only identifiable Palestinian leadership rejected Israel's right to exist. The Arab governments erased Israel's name from their maps. They referred to the country only as "the Zionist entity" or "the Tel Aviv puppet regime," as though such labels would lead to the state's abolition. The ridiculous and unrealistic stand taken by the Arabs led to their disastrous defeat in the Six Day War.

After the war, in the glow of victory and even the eventual burden of military occupation, Israel was suffering a similar blindness in regard to the Palestinians. They had come a long way. The mainstream leaders of the PLO were speaking of peace, and while there were occasional, brutal acts of violence against Jews within and without the Middle East, it could be argued that these were the actions of isolated hotheads.

Avowedly good intentions would have to be tested, to be sure, and Arafat's claimed conversion into an apostle of peace seemed too extreme to be true. After so many years of armed struggle and terrorism, there was still a long road to be traveled by Arafat, and his words would have to be matched by deeds.

His political body, the PLO, certainly was modifying its stated policies and exploring the possibility of settling the bloody Middle East dispute by peaceful means. Israel chose to fight the PLO, however, sending warplanes to bomb Palestinian bases while calling for negotiations only with Arab governments.

Again turning to history, when the United Nations voted in 1947 in favor of the partition of Palestine into two states, the world community was declaring that it was not fair to place a minority consisting of 600,000 Jews under Arab rule. The Zionists were delighted, of course, that their right to a homeland and a state was recognized.

Twenty, thirty, and forty years later, however, the Israelis were denying that one million Palestinians had similar rights. The Arabs were now a minority in the land once called Palestine, but they were living under Jewish rule.

Israel was beginning to find, as the *intifadda* indicated, that the occupied territories were a bone in its throat. The captured land could not be swallowed, nor could it be spit out.

One of Israel's leading experts on the West Bank, Meron Benvenisti, wrote in the early 1980s—at the height of the Likud's power—that the situation in the occupied territories had passed the point of no return. The clock could not be turned back. "On the seventh day of the Six Day War, the Second Republic of Israel was founded," in Benvenisti's words.[3] "Its government, social, economic and political establishments were formed in a long process. The Israeli government rules over all of Eretz Israel [Palestine]. . . . The differentiation between Israel's sovereign territory and the area she governs by military administration has lost its significance."

Benvenisti, a former deputy mayor of Jerusalem, believed that without making an intentional decision, Israel had practically annexed the West Bank and Gaza Strip.

Emmanuel Sivan of the Hebrew University in Jerusalem, an expert on the Middle East and the French experience in Algeria, said the West Bank and Gaza were in "a colonial situation." He wrote,

Some three and a half million Jews are holding a military and political monopoly on territories in which one and a half million Arabs live without rights. These Arabs are separate in their housing and employment, and they are at the bottom of the ladder of prestige. The main encounter with them is the necessary one in the employment market, and there is almost no social interaction. These Arabs are not described as a nation, and so "naturally" they have no right to self-government above the municipal level. A large part of the land and water are not in their control. From an economic point of view, they provide a cheap supply of labor to the ruling society. As is standard in colonialism, the territories do not enjoy equal economic rights. This is, without doubt, a colonial situation on the Algerian model, but still very far from the South African model. But the direction of further developments is clear.[4]

The Zionists and the Hashemites have come a long way together—through many years of clandestine cooperation—working to prevent establishment of a Palestinian state. They have used every possible means of statecraft, ranging from war to diplomacy and beyond. Their leaders met secretly. They collaborated economically. They even found themselves in the battlefield, at war when their self-perceived interests would have dictated otherwise.

Almost everything was sacrificed for the sake of the ultimate ideal: not to allow the Palestinians to have their own country. Jordan and Israel, in their talks, have tested all the ideas, proposals, and definitions—from territorial compromise, through autonomy, to condominium. All those models failed, because they were on a collision course with the Palestinians who displayed dedication and a readiness to suffer as a people and as a nation.

It would seem only logical for both the Jordanians and Israelis to try a different way: perhaps instead of fighting the Palestinians, attempt to accommodate them between the existing borders. The choices confronting all three corners in the troubled triangle of Israel, Jordan, and the Palestinians were matters of life and death, questions of national existence.

However often they might be delayed, Israel still faced, after the 1988 election and in the years to come, decisions that could be the most dramatic in the history of the state and of the Jewish people. The Israelis would have to choose whether to annex the West Bank and Gaza Strip. And if they did so, they would have to decide whether to grant full civil rights to the Palestinians, in light of the projections by statisticians that they would constitute an Arab majority in the Jewish state early in the twenty-first century.

What had seemed a problem of ''the territories'' threatened to become a crisis for the very existence of Israel and Zionism. It seemed that Israel was losing the power to decide whether to absorb the occupied lands, because they were absorbing Israel.

It is quite possible that with superior military force, Israel could suppress the *intifadda* and retain the territories. But Israel, in securing that achievement, would lose others that had been hard won. A ''Complete Land of Israel,'' as sought by the Likud and most of the Jewish settlers, would in due course cease to be a Jewish, democratic state. Extending from the Mediterranean to the Jordan River, an enlarged Israel would lack social cohesion at home and certainly would not enjoy peace with its neighbors.

The alternative of not granting civil rights to the West Bank and Gaza residents would lead to an equally dangerous distasteful situation resembling that of South Africa. A Jewish minority, eventually, would be ruling by force over an Arab majority denied its rights. An even worse scenario would see Israel converted into a combination of South African racism, the sectarian violence of Northern Ireland, and the endless terrorism of Lebanon.

Hussein had plainly become disgusted with the lack of progress in the Middle East. As part of his withdrawal from the intense center of the dispute, he publicly renounced his claim to the West Bank, canceled his five-year development plan for the territory, and took other steps designed to signal that he was standing aside. The *intifadda*, which he publicly hailed, could eventually become a threat to the stability of Jordan.

The proposals for an international conference, put forward by Shultz and others, were gathering dust on the shelves of all the region's capitals. The five-year plan and the salaries for West Bank civil servants were expensive symbols that the king could do without. He would simply concentrate, for a while, on administering his East Bank, at least until new developments emerged. Known for his tightrope-walking cautiousness, Hussein had not said good-bye to the

West Bank, still harboring some hopes to have it, but his immediate plans were to sit on his traditional fence.

As for the PLO, its gradual trend toward moderation stood just a chance of interesting the Israeli people and their leaders. There was still a long path to tread, and Arafat's public acceptance of Israel as "a reality" was not enough to persuade the Israelis that he could eliminate the uncompromising killers in the PLO's midst.

Arafat himself seemed to have learned King Hussein's masterful trick of tiptoeing through the political raindrops without getting wet. The PLO leader was quick to shift policies and difficult to pin down. He had an overriding determination to retain his position in the face of stiff opposition. Arafat was reminiscent of Hussein in more ways than one.

Arafat deserved a place at the negotiating table, whether leading an independent Palestinian delegation or as part of a joint Jordanian-Palestinian one. The aim was to achieve a peace treaty in the Middle East.

A treaty would have to be just as solid and verifiable as any arms-control pact between the superpowers. Similar breakthroughs would have to be achieved. And as the Americans and Soviets had done, the Israelis, Palestinians, and Jordanians would have to start somewhere.

It was no good standing by the old concept of a zero sum game in which "anything that is good for you is bad for me." The three sides of the triangle had long been coping with shared interests, but they had yet to attempt seriously to find shared solutions. The interests of each side, however, would have to be promoted and preserved: the security of Israel, the continued existence of Jordan, and the right of the Palestinians to determine their own future so long as it was not warlike.

The chances for a rapid breakthrough, at this writing, appeared poor. But all three sides of the Israeli-Jordanian-Palestinian triangle knew that the alternative was another round of bloodshed. And with modern weapons and deepening bitterness, the next war could be the most lethal and tragic in Middle East history.

Appendix 1

Draft Agreement between Israel and Jordan

February 24, 1950

A special agreement will be signed, pursuant to the Armistice Agreement, bound to the latter and reinforcing it. The agreement will include the following principles:

(1) Non-aggression for a period of 5 years.

(2) Maintenance of the existing armistice borders and a search for acceptable solutions for the abolishment of areas of no-man's-land by their division, wherever possible, between both parties.

(3) In order to reach a comprehensive agreement between the two parties, Special Joint Committees will be appointed to study and discuss each of the fundamental issues. These will include territorial and economic problems as well as other issues to be included in the agreement, with a view to replacing the temporary lines and arrangements comprised in the Armistice Agreement by permanent lines and arrangements, including Jerusalem and the question of a port and access to the sea for Jordan, under her full sovereignty.

(4) Measures are to be taken by both sides to safeguard the Holy Places and to ensure freedom of prayer and access, while elminating the possibility of military disputes between the parties over those sites, and providing the U.N. authorities with satisfactory guarantees in this matter.

(5) One of the first tasks to be imposed on one of the Committees mentioned in Paragraph 3, will be to devise arrangements for payment of monetary compensation to owners of property in Jerusalem without affecting the territorial settlement in the city of Jerusalem referred to in Paragraph 3.

(6) Measures are to be taken to grant to Jordan a free zone in the port of Haifa in order to implement the principle of commercial cooperation between the two parties for the duration of this agreement.

(7) Measures are to be discussed to settle matters pertaining to Arab property in Israel territory by allowing the owners of such property either to enter Israel themselves or to send their representatives in order to sell such property or to deal with it as they see fit. And this is in order that they will have the right, if such solutions prove difficult to implement, to authorize the parties to the agreement to resolve the difficulties. This would apply also to Jewish property in Jordan territory.

(8) The Special Committee will discuss measures to facilitate Israeli access to the institutions on Mt. Scopus and Arab access to Bethlehem, in accordance with Article 8 of the Armistice Agreement.

Addenda to this agreement will be drawn up to determine ways and means of implementing the above resolutions.

R[euven] S[hiloah]
M[oshe] D[ayan]
F[awzi al-] M[ulqi]
S[amir al-] R[ifa'i]

Source: Israel State Archives, Documents on the Foreign Policy of Israel.

Appendix 2

United Nations Security Council Resolution 242

November 22, 1967

The Security Council,

Expressing its continuing concern with the grave situation in the Middle East,

Emphasizing the inadmissibility of the acquisition of territory by war and the need to work for a just and lasting peace in which every State in the area can live in security,

Emphasizing further that all Member States in their acceptance of the Charter of the United Nations have undertaken a commitment to act in accordance with Article 2 of the Charter,

1. *Affirms* that the fulfillment of Charter principles requires the establishment of a just and lasting peace in the Middle East which should include the application of both the following principles:

   (i) Withdrawal of Israel armed forces from territories occupied in the recent conflict;

   (ii) Termination of all claims or states of belligerency and respect for and acknowledgement of the sovereignty, territorial integrity and political independence of every State in the area and their right to live in peace within secure and recognized boundaries free from threats or acts of force;

2. *Affirms further* the necessity

   (a) For guaranteeing freedom of navigation through international waterways in the area;

   (b) For achieving a just settlement of the refugee problem;

   (c) For guaranteeing the territorial inviolability and political independence of every State in the area, through measures including the establishment of demilitarized zones;

3. *Requests* the Secretary-General to designate a Special Representative to proceed to the Middle East to establish and maintain contacts with the States concerned in order to promote agreement and assist efforts to achieve a peaceful and accepted settlement in accordance with the provisions and principles in this resolution;

4. *Requests* the Secretary-General to report to the Security Council on the progress of the efforts of the Special Representative as soon as possible.

Source: United Nations

Appendix 3

Excerpt from the Camp David Accords between Israel and Egypt Calling for Palestinian Autonomy

September 17, 1978

West Bank and Gaza:

1. Egypt, Israel, Jordan and the representatives of the Palestinian People should participate in negotiations on the resolution of the Palestinian problem in all its aspects. To achieve that objective, negotiations relating to the West Bank and Gaza should proceed in three stages.

(A) Egypt and Israel agree that, in order to ensure a peaceful and orderly transfer of authority, and taking into account the security concerns of all the parties, there should be transitional arrangements for the West Bank and Gaza for a period not exceeding five years. In order to provide full autonomy to the inhabitants, under these arrangements the Israeli military government and its civilian administration will be withdrawn as soon as a self-governing authority has been freely elected by the inhabitants of these areas to replace the existing military government.

To negotiate the details of a transitional arrangement, the government of Jordan will be invited to join the negotiations on the basis of this framework. These new arrangements should give due consideration to both the principle of self-government by the inhabitants of these territories and to the legitimate security concerns of the parties involved.

(B) Egypt, Israel, and Jordan will agree on the modalities for establishing the elected self-governing authority in the West Bank and Gaza. The delegations of Egypt and Jordan may include Palestinians from the West Bank and Gaza or other Palestinians as mutually agreed. The parties will negotiate an agreement which will define the powers and responsibilities of the self-governing authority to be exercised in the West Bank and Gaza. A withdrawal of Israeli armed forces will take place and there will be a redeployment of the remaining Israeli forces into specified security locations.

The agreement will also include arrangements for assuring internal and external security and public order. A strong local police force will be established, which may include Jordanian citizens. In addition, Israeli and Jordanian forces will participate in joint patrols and in the manning of control posts to assure the security of the borders.

(C) When the self-governing authority (administration council) in the West Bank and Gaza is established and inaugurated, the transitional period of five years will begin. As soon as possible, but not later than the third year after the beginning of the transitional period, negotiations will take place to determine the final status of the West Bank and Gaza and its relationship with its neighbours, and to conclude a peace treaty between Israel and Jordan by the end of the transitional period.

These negotiations will be conducted among Egypt, Israel, Jordan, and the elected representatives of the inhabitants of the West Bank and Gaza. Two separate representatives of Israel and representatives of Jordan to be joined by the elected representatives of the inhabitants of the West Bank and Gaza, to negotiate the peace treaty between Israel and Jordan, taking into account the agreement reached on the final status of the West Bank and Gaza.

The negotiations shall be based on all the provisions and principles of U.N. Security Council Resolution 242. The negotiations will resolve, among other matters, the location of the boundaries and the nature of the security arrangements.

The solution from the negotiations must also recognize the legitimate rights of the Palestinian people and their just requirements. In this way, the Palestinians will participate in the determination of their own future through:

—1) The negotiations among Egypt, Israel, Jordan and the representatives of the inhabitants of the West Bank and Gaza to agree on the final status of the West Bank and Gaza and other outstanding issues by the end of the transitional period.

—2) Submitting their agreement to a vote by the elected representatives of the inhabitants of the West Bank and Gaza.

—3) Providing for the elected representatives of the inhabitants of the West Bank and Gaza to decide how they shall govern themselves consistent with the provisions of their agreement.

—4) Participating as stated above in the work of the committee negotiating the peace treaty between Israel and Jordan.

2. All necessary measures will be taken and provisions made to assure the security of Israel and its neighbours during the transitional period and beyond. To assist in providing such security, a strong local police force will be constituted by the self-governing authority. It will be composed of inhabitants of the West Bank and Gaza. The police will maintain continuing liaison on internal security matters with the designated Israeli, Jordanian and Egyptian officers.

3. During the transitional period, the representatives of Egypt, Israel, Jordan and the self-governing authority will constitute a continuing committee to decide by agreement on the modalities of admission of persons displaced from the West Bank and Gaza in 1967, together with necessary measures to prevent disruption and disorder. Other matters of common concern may also be dealt with by this committee.

4. Egypt and Israel will work with each other and with other interested parties to establish agreed procedures for a prompt, just and permanent implementation of the resolution of the refugee problem.

Source: Israeli Foreign Ministry.

Appendix 4

Secret Agreement Reached by King Hussein and Israel's Foreign Minister Shimon Peres in London
April 11, 1987

SECRET/MOST SENSITIVE

(Accord between the Government of Jordan, which has confirmed it to the United States, and the Foreign Minister of Israel, ad referendum to the Government of Israel. Parts "A" and "B", which when they become public upon agreement of the parties, will be treated as U.S. proposals to which Jordan and Israel have agreed. Part "C" is to be treated, in great confidentiality, as commitments to the U.S. from the Government of Jordan to be transmitted to the Government of Israel.)

A Three-Part Understanding Between Jordan and Israel

A. Invitation by UN Secretary General
B. Resolutions of the International Conference
C. The Modalities Agreed Upon by Jordan-Israel

A. The Secretary General will issue invitations to the five permanent members of the Security Council and the Parties involved in the Arab-Israeli conflict in order to negotiate a peaceful settlement based on Resolutions 242 and 338 with the objects of bringing a comprehensive peace to the area, security to its states and to respond to the legitimate rights of the Palestinian people.

B. The Participants in the Conference agree that the purpose of the negotiations is the peaceful solution of the Arab-Israeli conflict based on Resolutions 242 and 338 and a peaceful solution of the Palestinian problem in all its aspects. The Conference invites the Parties to form geographical bilateral committees to negotiate mutual issues.

C. Jordan and Israel have agreed that: (I) the International Conference will not impose any solution or veto any Agreement arrived at between the Parties; (II) the negotiations will be conducted in bilateral committees directly; (III) the Palestinian issue will be dealt with in the committee of the Jordanian-Palestinian and Israeli delegations; (IV) the Palestinians' representatives will be included in the Jordanian-Palestinian delegation; (V) participation in the Conference will be based on the Parties' acceptance of Resolutions 242 and 338 and the renunciation of violence and terrorism; (VI) each committee will negotiate independently; (VII) other issues will be decided by mutual agreement between Jordan and Israel.

The above understanding is subject to approval of the respective Governments of Israel and Jordan. The text of this paper will be shown and suggested to the U.S.A.

11/4/87
London

Source: Confidential.

Appendix 5

The "Shultz Peace Plan," as Presented to Israel's Prime Minister Yitzhak Shamir
March 4, 1988

The Secretary of State
Washington

March 4, 1988

His Excellency
Yitzhak Shamir,
Prime Minister of Israel.

Dear Mr. Prime Minister:

I set forth below the statement of understandings which I am convinced is necessary to achieve the prompt opening of negotiations on a comprehensive peace. This statement of understandings emerges from discussions held with you and other regional leaders. I look forward to the letter of reply of the Government of Israel in confirmation of this statement.

The agreed objective is a comprehensive peace providing for the security of all the States in the region and for the legitimate rights of the Palestinian people.

Negotiations will start on an early date certain between Israel and each of its neighbors which is willing to do so. These negotiations could begin by May 1, 1988. Each of these negotiations will be based on United Nations Security Council Resolutions 242 and 338, in all their parts. The parties to each bilateral negotiation will determine the procedure and agenda of their negotiation. All participants in the negotiations must state their willingness to negotiate with one another.

As concerns negotiations between the Israeli delegation and the Jordanian-Palestinian delegation, negotiations will begin on arrangements for a transitional period, with the objective of completing them within six months. Seven months after transitional negotiations begin, final status negotiations will begin, with the objective of completing them within one year. These negotiations will be based on all the provisions and principles of United Nations Security Council Resolution 242. Final status talks will start before the transitional period begins. The transitional period will begin three months after the conclusion of the transitional agreement and will last for three years. The United States will participate in both negotiations and will promote their rapid conclusion. In particular, the United States will submit a draft agreement for the parties' consideration at the outset of the negotiations on transitional arrangements.

Two weeks before the opening of negotiations, an international conference will be held. The Secretary General of the United Nations will be asked to issue invitations to the parties involved in the Arab-Israeli conflict and the five permanent members of the United Nations Security Council. All participants in the conference must accept United Nations Security Council Resolutions 242 and 338, and renounce violence and terrorism. The parties to each bilateral negotiation may refer reports on the status of their negotiations to the conference, in a manner to be agreed. The conference will not be able to impose solutions or veto agreements reached.

Palestinian representation will be within the Jordanian-Palestinian delegation. The Palestinian issue will be addressed in the negotiations between the Jordanian-Palestinian and Israeli delegations. Negotiations between the Israeli delegation and the Jordanian-Palestinian delegation will proceed independently of any other negotiations.

This statement of understandings is an integral whole. The United States understands that your acceptance is dependent on the implementation of each element in good faith.

Sincerely yours,
George P. Shultz

Source: Confidential.

Notes

Chapter 1

1. *Yediot Aharonot* devoted an investigative issue on April 1, 1988, to the *intifadda*; also, *Koteret Rashit* (magazine), April 29, 1988.

Chapter 2

1. Peter Snow, *Hussein: A Biography* (Washington: Robert B. Luce, 1972), p. 17; also, Avi Shlaim, *Collusion across the Jordan: King Abdullah, the Zionist Movement, and the Partition of Palestine* (Oxford: Clarendon, 1988), pp. 20–23.
2. Nasser H. Aruri, *Jordan: A Study in Political Development 1921–1965* (The Hague: Martinus Nijhoff, 1972), p. 14.
3. Aruri, *Jordan*, pp. 15–16.
4. Howard M. Sachar, *A History of Israel* (New York: Alfred A. Knopf, 1985), p. 95.
5. Sachar, *History*, p. 92.
6. Snow, *Hussein*, p. 17.
7. Snow, *Hussein*, p. 17.
8. Snow, *Hussein*, p. 19.
9. Sachar, *History*, p. 126.
10. Snow, *Hussein*, p. 20.
11. Snow, *Hussein*, p. 55, quoting Sir Alec Kirkbride's memoirs.
12. Sachar, *History*, p. 126.
13. Aruri, *Jordan*, p. 21.
14. Uriel Dann, *Emirut Ever-HaYarden [The Trans-Jordan Emirate] 1921–1946* (Tel Aviv: Shiloah Center for Middle East Studies, 1982), p. 4.
15. Quoted in Sachar, *History*, p. 127.
16. Dann, *Emirut*, p. 4.
17. Snow, *Hussein*, p. 21.

18. Snow, *Hussein*, p. 22.

19. Dann, *Emirut*, pp. 7, 8, 14, 15.

Chapter 3

1. Aharon Klieman, *Du-Kiyum L'lo Shalom [Coexistence without Peace]* (Tel Aviv: Ma'ariv, 1986), p. 17.

2. Dan Schueftan, *Optzia Yardenit [Jordanian Option]* (Tel Aviv: Kibbutz Meuchad, 1987), pp. 23–25.

3. Sachar, *History*, p. 120.

4. Sachar, *History*, p. 120.

5. Sachar, *History*, p. 121.

6. Sachar, *History*, p. 121.

7. General Staff History Department, *Toldot Milhemet HaKomemiyut [War of Independence: The Official History]* (Tel Aviv: Israel Defense Forces, 1962), p. 12.

8. Schueftan, *Optzia*, p. 41.

9. Sachar, *History*, p. 122.

10. Schueftan, *Optzia*, p. 41.

11. Schueftan, *Optzia*, p. 41.

12. Schueftan, *Optzia*, p. 42; and Klieman, *Du-Kiyum*, p. 123.

13. Avraham Sela, *Mi-Maga'im L'Massa Umatan (From Contacts to Negotiation)* (Tel Aviv: Shiloah Center, Tel Aviv University, 1985), p. 11.

14. Klieman, *Du-Kiyum*, pp. 123–130.

15. Sela, *Mi-Magaim*, p. 11.

16. Shlaim, *Collusion*, p. 78, quoting report from Sassoon in the Central Zionist Archives; and Schueftan, *Optzia*, p. 42.

17. Sachar, *History*, p. 321.

18. Schueftan, *Optzia*, pp. 46–48.

19. Sela, *Mi-Magaim*, p. 22; Schueftan, *Optzia*, p. 57.

20. Schueftan, *Optzia*, p. 57.

21. As told to the authors by sources close to the late Yigal Allon.

22. Published in London in 1956 as *A Crackle of Thorns*, according to Snow, *Hussein*.

23. Yehoshua Palmon, interviewed by the authors in June 1987.

24. Sir John Bagot Glubb, *Soldier with the Arabs* (London: Hodder and Stoughton, 1957), p. 420.

25. Moshe Dayan, *Evnei Derekh* [his Hebrew autobiography] (Tel Aviv: Dvir, 1976), p. 80.

26. Sachar, *History*, p. 349.

27. Sachar, *History*, p. 350.

28. Schueftan, *Optzia*, p. 206.

29. Snow, *Hussein*, pp. 33–34.

Chapter 4

1. Snow, *Hussein*, p. 34.

2. Snow, *Hussein*, p. 35.

3. Snow, *Hussein*, p. 36.

4. Snow, *Hussein*, pp. 58–59.

5. Snow, *Hussein*, p. 24.

6. Snow, *Hussein*, p. 25.

7. Snow, *Hussein*, p. 39.

8. Snow, *Hussein*, p. 42.

9. *Al-Hamishmar* [newspaper], May 8, 1987; and interview with Yoel Ben-Porat, who served in the 1970s as deputy director of the IDF Intelligence Corps, chief military spokesman, and Israeli military attaché in the United States.

10. Snow, *Hussein*, p. 45.

11. Snow, *Hussein*, p. 50.

12. Snow, *Hussein*, p. 52.

13. Snow, *Hussein*, p. 62.

14. Snow, *Hussein*, p. 54.

15. Snow, *Hussein*, p. 55.

16. Snow, *Hussein*, p. 90.

17. Snow, *Hussein*, p. 95.

18. Snow, *Hussein*, p. 96.

19. King Hussein, *Uneasy Lies the Head* (London: Heinemann, 1962), p. 127.

20. Snow, *Hussein*, p. 100.

21. Palmon interview.

22. President Chaim Herzog, interviewed by author Melman in February 1987.

23. Snow, *Hussein*, p. 57.

24. Ben-Porat interview.

25. Palmon interview.

26. Dayan, *Evnei*, p. 89; and Schueftan, *Optzia*, pp. 87, 91, 217.

27. Palmon interview.

28. Foreign Office documents of 1957, released thirty years later by the British Government's Public Records Office.

29. Snow, *Hussein*, p. 101.

30. Snow, *Hussein*, p. 77.

31. Schueftan, *Optzia*, pp. 257–263; and Klieman, *Du-Kiyum*, p. 162.

32. Snow, *Hussein*, p. 106.

33. Snow, *Hussein*, p. 111.

34. Ben-Porat interview.

35. Klieman, *Du-Kiyum*, p. 162; and interview with Yuval Ne'eman, member of Knesset, February 1987.

36. Snow, *Hussein*, p. 132.

37. Snow, *Hussein*, pp. 133–134.

38. Snow, *Hussein*, p. 135.

39. Herzog interview.

40. Interview with Foreign Minister Shimon Peres in May 1987.

Chapter 5

1. Interview with Dr. Peter Collier, who shared his practice with the late Dr. Herbert, in June 1987.

2. *Sunday Telegraph* (London), May 3, 1987.

3. Foreign Office documents of 1957.

4. Nadav Safran, *Ha-Imut HaYisraeli-Aravi [The Israeli-Arab Conflict] 1949–1967* (Tel Aviv: Keter, 1969), pp. 77–78.

5. Tom Segev, *HaYisraelim HaRishonim [The First Israelis]* (Jerusalem: Domino, 1984), p. 33.

6. Walter Laqueur, *A World of Secrets: The Uses and Limits of Intelligence* (New York: Basic Books, 1985); and Yossi Melman *Doh Ha-CIA [The CIA Report]* (Tel Aviv: Erez, 1982), p. 44.

7. Melman, *Doh Ha-CIA*, p. 57.

8. Snow, *Hussein*, pp. 66, 147, 148.

9. Snow, *Hussein*, pp. 154–155.

10. Bernard Reich and Arnon Gutfeld, *Arhab Ve-HaSichsuch HaYisraeli-Aravi [USA and the Israeli-Arab Conflict]* (Tel Aviv: Israel Defense Forces, 1977), pp. 35–36.

11. Snow, *Hussein*, p. 137.

12. Michael Breecher, *The Foreign Policy System of Israel* (London: Oxford University Press, 1972), pp. 45–46.

13. Moshe Zak, "Israeli-Jordanian Negotiations," *Washington Quarterly* (Winter 1985): 167–168.

Chapter 6

1. The full name was *Mifleget Poalei Eretz Yisrael*, Hebrew for "the Workers' Party of the Land of Israel."

2. Yaakov Herzog, *Am L'Vaded Yishkun [A People Living Alone]* (Tel Aviv: Ma'ariv, 1976), p. 16.

3. Herzog, *Am L'Vaded*, pp. 21, 52; interview with Lord Sieff of Brimpton, August 1987.

4. Interview with Meir Avidan, researcher at Ben-Gurion University, June 1987.

5. Gideon Rafael, *30 Shnot Mediniut Hutz: Mabat M'Bifnim [Three Decades of Foreign Policy: An Inside View]* (Jerusalem: Edanim, 1981), pp. 74–75.

6. Zak, "Israeli-Jordanian," p. 168.

7. Snow, *Hussein*, p. 157.

8. Snow, *Hussein*, p. 164.

9. Schueftan, *Optzia*, pp. 266–267.

10. Michael Breecher, *Decisions in Israel's Foreign Policy* (London: Oxford University Press, 1974), pp. 188–215.

11. Sachar, *History*, p. 618.

12. Asher Susser, *Ben Yarden L'Falastin: Biographia Politit shel Wasfi el-Tell [Between Jordan and Palestine: Political Biography of Wasfi el-Tell]* (Tel Aviv: Kibbutz Meuhad, 1983), pp. 73–74.

13. Interview with Walter Eytan, February 1987; and Robert Slater, *Golda: Uncrowned Queen of Israel* (Middle Village, N.Y.: Jonathan David, 1981), p. 266.

14. Snow, *Hussein*, p. 168.

15. Snow, *Hussein*, p. 168.

16. *The Guardian*'s Peter Mansfield, quoted in Snow, *Hussein*, p. 166.

17. Susser, *Ben Yarden*, p. 85.

18. Interview with Mordecai Gazit, January 1987.

19. Zak, "Israeli-Jordanian," pp. 168–169.

20. Snow, *Hussein*, p. 183.

21. Snow, *Hussein*, p. 183.

22. Snow, *Hussein*, p. 183.

23. Schueftan, *Optzia*, pp. 277–278.

24. Schueftan, *Optzia*, p. 278; and *Haaretz* [Tel Aviv newspaper], quoting Yitzhak Rabin on June 25, 1987.

Chapter 7

1. Snow, *Hussein*, pp. 190–195.

2. Snow, *Hussein*, p. 187.

3. Zeev Schiff, *A History of the Israeli Army* (New York: Macmillan, 1985), p. 142.

4. Miriam Eshkol, interviewed by Israeli Television, June 6, 1987.

5. Interview with Azariah Arnan, former assistant to Allon, April 1987; also, Moshe Zak in *Ma'ariv*, April 19, 1989.

6. Interview with David Kimche, former Mossad operative, August 1988.

7. Avidan interview; Dayan, *Evnei*, pp. 488–492; and Yossi Beilin, *Mehiro shel Ihud [The Price of Unity]* (Tel Aviv: Revivim Books, 1985), p. 42.

8. *Ma'ariv*, April 19, 1989.

9. Snow, *Hussein*, pp. 198–199.

10. *The Washington Post*, April 10, 1988.

11. Interviews with Abba Eban, December 1986 and February 1987; and authors' interview with Miriam Eshkol based on her diaries, June 1987.

12. Susser, *Ben Yarden*, pp. 31–51, 63–64, 158.

13. Beilin, *Mehiro*, p. 50.

14. Avidan and Eshkol interviews.

15. Avidan interview; and *Davar* [Tel Aviv newspaper], June 2–5, 1987.

16. Beilin, *Mehiro*, p. 49.

17. Beilin, *Mehiro*, p. 49.

18. *Davar*, June 2 and 5, 1987.

19. *Davar*, June 2 and 5, 1987.

Chapter 8

1. Interview with Chaim Bar-Lev, January 1987.

2. Ehud Yaari, *Fatah* [in Hebrew] (Tel Aviv: A. Levin Epstein, 1970), pp. 83–84.

3. Snow, *Hussein*, p. 205.

4. Bar-Lev interview.

5. Peres interview.

6. Yossi Melman, *Dyokano shel Irgun Terror [A Profile of a Terrorist Organization]* (Tel Aviv: Hadar, 1984), pp. 50–80.

7. Gazit interview.

8. Zak, "Israeli-Jordanian," p. 169.

9. Interview with Rehavam Amir, former consul general in New York who discussed the issue with Yaakov Herzog, May 1987.

10. Gazit interview.

11. Zak, "Israeli-Jordanian," pp. 170–171; and Bar-Lev and Eban interviews.

12. Snow, *Hussein*, p. 207.

13. *The Times* [London], February 17, 1970.

14. Eban interview.

15. Zak, "Israeli-Jordanian," p. 170.

16. Snow, *Hussein*, p. 216.

17. Snow, *Hussein*, p. 219.

18. Susser, *Ben Yarden*, pp. 97, 152, 156; and Schueftan, *Optzia*, p. 306.

19. Snow, *Hussein*, p. 224.

20. Interview with an American official who had access to the messages but preferred anonymity.

21. Schueftan, *Optzia*, p. 306.

Chapter 9

1. Interviews with Simcha Dinitz, November 1986, and Gazit interview.

2. Dinitz interview.

3. Dinitz and Gazit interviews.

4. Interview with Sara Rehavi, daughter of Golda Meir, June 1987.

5. *Haaretz* reported, on February 22, 1987, that King Hussein gave the Israelis expensive Swiss watches.

6. *Yediot Aharonot* [Tel Aviv newspaper], June 14, 1985; and Eban interview.

7. Zak, "Israeli-Jordanian," p. 170; and Klieman, *Du-Kiyum*, p. 161.

8. Dayan, *Evnei*, pp. 542–543.

9. Dayan, *Evnei*, pp. 171–172, 542; and Zak, "Israeli-Jordanian," p. 170.

10. Henry Kissinger, *Years of Upheaval* (Boston: Little, Brown, 1982), pp. 846, 976.

11. Schueftan, *Optzia*, p. 308.

Chapter 10

1. Sachar, *History*, pp. 801–802.

2. King Hussein spoke of his impressions with an American diplomat, who asked to remain anonymous but spoke with the authors, March 1987.

3. Zak, "Israeli-Jordanian," p. 171; and Kissinger, *Years*, pp. 787, 847.

4. Gazit interview; Kissinger, *Years*, pp. 787, 847; and interview with Yitzhak Rabin, May 1987.

5. Kissinger, *Years*, p. 976.

6. Rabin interview; and Klieman, *Du-Kiyum*, p. 163.

7. *Yediot Aharonot*, June 14, 1985; and *L'Express* [a French weekly], February 27, 1981.

8. *Al-Hamishmar* [Tel Aviv newspaper], May 8, 1987.

9. Matti Golan, *Peres* [in Hebrew] (Tel Aviv: Schocken, 1982), p. 161; and Zak, "Israeli-Jordanian," p. 173.

10. Zak, "Israeli-Jordanian," p. 173; Golan, *Peres*, p. 161; Schueftan, *Optzia*, p. 322; and interview with Moshe Zak, January 1987.

11. Schueftan, *Optzia*, pp. 340–342.

12. Interview with Amos Eran, November 1986; Gazit interview; and Golan, *Peres*, p. 162.

13. Eran and Gazit interviews.

14. Eran interview; and Zak, "Israeli-Jordanian," p. 167.

Chapter 11

1. Moshe Dayan, *Breakthrough* (New York: Alfred A. Knopf, 1981), pp. 35–37.

2. Parts of this account are based on the Hebrew version of Dayan's memoirs, *Ha-L'Netzach Tochal Herev? [Shall the Sword Devour Forever?: Breakthrough]* (Jerusalem: Edanim, 1981), pp. 36–37.

3. Dayan, *Breakthrough*, p. 35.

4. Dayan, *Breakthrough*, p. 36.

5. Dayan, *Breakthrough*, p. 36.

6. Dayan, *Breakthrough*, p. 42.

7. *Monitin* [Israeli magazine], September 1986, p. 46.

8. Dayan, *Breakthrough*, p. 48.

9. Zak, "Israeli-Jordanian," p. 175.

10. Golan, *Peres*, p. 232.

11. Golan, *Peres*, p. 260.

12. Walter Bar-On, *HaSippurim sh'Lo Supru [The Untold Stories]* (Jerusalem: Eidanim, 1981).

13. Noteworthy articles were by Shmuel Segev and Moshe Zak in the newspaper *Ma'ariv* and Shlomo Nakdimon in *Yediot Aharonot*.

14. *Ma'ariv*, October 1, 1978.

15. Golan, *Peres*, p. 232.

16. Zak, "Israeli-Jordanian," p. 171.

17. Rafael, *30 Shnot*, p. 322.

18. Interview with Gideon Raphael, January 1987.

19. Arye Naor, *Memshala B'Milhama [Cabinet at War]* (Tel Aviv: Lahav, 1986).

Chapter 12

1. Milton Viorst, in *Haaretz*, August 15, 1982.

2. Viorst, in *Haaretz*.

3. Viorst, in *Haaretz*; and speech by Ariel Sharon to the Center for Strategic Studies at Tel Aviv University, December 1981.

4. *Ma'ariv*, November 29, 1974; *Haaretz*, July 14, 1978; and Klieman, *Du-Kiyum*, pp. 219–223.

5. *Davar*, April 30, 1987.

6. Interview with Israeli politician and publisher Uri Avineri, November 1986, who said Sharon asked him to arrange a meeting with Yasser Arafat, but the PLO leader declined.

7. Dayan, *Evnei*, pp. 510–511.

8. Yossi Melman and Dan Raviv, "Expelling Palestinians," *The Washington Post*, February 7, 1988, "Outlook," p. 1.

9. Klieman, *Du-Kiyum*, p. 35.

10. Klieman, *Du-Kiyum*, p. 37; and Ian Lustick, *Israel and Jordan: The Implications of an Adversarial Partnership* (Berkeley, Calif.: University of California, 1978).

11. Lustick, *Israel and Jordan*.

12. Bernard Avishai, in *The New York Review of Books*, April 28, 1983.

13. Avishai, in *Review*.

Chapter 13

1. Peres interview.

2. Interview with Nimrod Novick, political adviser to Peres, May 1987; and *Newsweek*, November 28, 1984.

3. Novick and Tamir interviews.

4. *Koteret Rashit* [Israeli magazine], October 9, 1985.

5. Interview with Rafi Mann, diplomatic correspondent of *Ma'ariv*, December 1986.

6. Michael Bar-Zohar, *Gesher Al-Pnei HaYam HaTichon: Israel-Tzarfat 1947–1973 [Bridge Over the Mediterranean: Israel-France Relations]* (Tel Aviv: Am HaSefer, 1965).

7. Briefing for reporters by Prime Minister Peres, February 8, 1985; and Golan, *Peres*.

8. *The New York Times*, October 24, 1985; text of Peres's UN speech obtained from his office.

9. Yossi Melman, *The Master Terrorist: The True Story behind Abu Nidal* (London: Sidgwick and Jackson, 1987), pp. 107–108.

10. *Ma'ariv*, January 13, 1984.

11. *Newsweek*, November 11, 1986.

12. Text of secret agreement obtained by authors from anonymous source.

Chapter 14

1. Interview with Chaim Givati, February 1987.

2. Givati interview.

3. Givati interview; and *Ma'ariv*, January 13 and June 17, 1984.

4. Interview with Givati.

5. Interviews with Chaim Kuberski, December 1986, and with Eli Rubinstein, June 1987.

6. Interview with Avraham Katz-Oz, December 1986.

7. Interviews with Israeli officials who were involved, January–February 1987.

8. Interviews with officials; and report on Israeli Television, November 1985.

9. *Financial Times* [London], December 15, 1987; and Israeli Television, June 26, 1987.

Chapter 15

1. *Hadashot* [Tel Aviv newspaper], May 29, 1987.

2. Tamir interview.

3. Katz-Oz interview.

4. *Yediot Aharonot*, June 30, 1987.

5. Shlomo Gazit, *HaMakel V'HaGezer: HaMimshal HaYisraeli B'Yehuda V'Shomron [The Stick and the Carrot: The Israeli Administration in Judea and Samaria]* (Tel Aviv: Zmora Bitan, 1985), p. 204.

6. Tamir interview.

7. Tamir interview.

8. *Davar*, February 20, 1986.

9. Gazit, *HaMakel*, pp. 250–251.

10. Interview with Amnon Neubach, January 1987.
11. Tamir, Neubach, and Goren interviews.
12. *Yediot Aharonot*, February 8, 1987.
13. *Jerusalem Post*, February 12, 1987.

Chapter 16

1. Aaron D. Miller, "Jordan and the Arab Israeli Conflict: The Hashemite Predicament," *Orbis* 29, no. 4 (Winter 1986): 795.
2. *Haaretz*, April 1, 1988.
3. *Davar*, December 26, 1986.
4. *Haaretz*, May 13, 1987.

Bibliography

Sources in English

Abdullah, King of Jordan (1978) *My Memoirs Completed*. London and New York: Longman.

Aruri, Nasser H. (1972) *Jordan: A Study in Political Development 1921–1965*. The Hague: Martinus Nijhoff.

Breecher, Michael (1974) *Decisions in Israel's Foreign Policy*. London: Oxford University Press.

———— (1972) *The Foreign Policy System of Israel*. London: Oxford University Press.

Cobban, Helen (1984) *The Palestinian Liberation Organization: People, Power and Politics*. London: Cambridge University Press.

Dayan, Moshe (1981) *Breakthrough: A Personal Account of the Egypt-Israel Peace Negotiations*. New York: Alfred A. Knopf.

Financial Times (London), December 15, 1987.

Foreign Office Documents (1957) London: British Public Records Office.

Glubb, Sir John Bagot (1957) *Soldier with the Arabs*. London: Hodder and Stoughton.

Hart, Alan (1984) *Arafat: Terrorist or Peacemaker?*. London: Sidgwick and Jackson.

Hussein, King of Jordan (1962) *Uneasy Lies the Head*. London: Heinemann.

Kissinger, Henry (1982) *Years of Upheaval*. Boston: Little, Brown and Company.

Laqueur, Walter (1985) *A World of Secrets: The Uses and Limits of Intelligence*. New York: Basic Book Publishers.

Lustick, Ian (1978) *Israel and Jordan: The Implications of an Adversarial Partnership*. Berkeley, Calif.: Institute of International Studies, University of California.

Melman, Yossi (1987) *The Master Terrorist: The True Story behind Abu Nidal*. London: Sidgwick and Jackson.

Miller, Aaron D. (1986) "Jordan and the Arab-Israeli Conflict: The Hashemite Predicament." *Orbis* 29, no. 4 (Winter): 795–820.

Newsweek, November 28, 1984; November 11, 1986.

The New York Times, October 24, 1985.

Pincher, Chapman (1987) *Traitors: The Labyrinth of Treason*. London: Sidgwick and Jackson.

Rhodes, Robert James (1986) *Anthony Eden*. London: Weidenfeld and Nicholson.

Sachar, Howard M. (1985) *A History of Israel: From the Rise of Zionism to Our Time*. New York: Alfred A. Knopf.

Safran, Nadav (1969) *From War to War: The Arab-Israeli Confrontation 1948–1967*. New York: Pegasus; Bobbs-Merrill.

Schelling, Thomas C. (1973) *Strategy of Conflict*. London: Oxford University Press.

Schiff, Zeev (1985) *A History of the Israeli Army*. New York: Macmillan.

Shlaim, Avi (1988) *Collusion across the Jordan: King Abdullah, the Zionist Movement, and the Partition of Palestine*. Oxford: Clarendon Press.

Slater, Robert (1981) *Golda: The Uncrowned Queen of Israel*. Middle Village, N.Y.: Jonathan David.

Snow, Peter (1972) *Hussein, a Biography*. Washington and New York: Robert B. Luce.

Steven, Stewart (1980) *The Spymasters of Israel*. London: Hodder and Stoughton.

Sunday Telegraph (London), May 3, 1987.

The Times (London), February 17, 1970.

The Washington Post, February 7 and April 10, 1988.

Zak, Moshe (1985) "Israeli-Jordanian Negotiations." *Washington Quarterly* (Winter): 167–176.

Books in Hebrew—Titles as Provided By Publishers

Bar-On, Avner (Walter) (1981) *The Untold Stories: The Diary of the Chief Censor*. Jerusalem: Edanim Publishers-Yediot Aharonot Edition.

Bar-Zohar, Michael (1965) *Bridge over the Mediterranean: Israeli-French Relations 1947–1963*. Tel Aviv: Am HaSefer.

Beilin, Yossi (1985) *The Price of Unity: The Israeli Labor Party until the Yom Kippur War 1973*. Tel Aviv: Revivim Books.

Dann, Uriel (1982) *The Emirate of Trans-Jordan: 1921–1946*. Tel Aviv: Shiloah Center, Tel Aviv University.

Dayan, Moshe (1981) *Shall the Sword Devour Forever?: Breakthrough*. Jerusalem: Edanim Publishers-Yediot Aharonot Edition.

——— (1976) *Story of My Life*. Jerusalem: Edanim Publishers with Dvir Publishers.

Gazit, Shlomo (1985) *The Stick and the Carrot: The Israeli Administration in Judea and Samaria*. Tel Aviv: Zmora Bitan Publishers.

General Staff History Department (1962) *War of Independence: The Official History*. Tel Aviv: Maarachot Publishers, Israel Defense Forces.

Golan, Matti (1982) *Peres*. Tel Aviv: Schocken Publishing.

Herzog, Yaakov (1976) *A People Living Alone*. Tel Aviv: Maariv Library.

Klieman, Aharon (1986) *Unpeaceful Coexistence: Israel, Jordan and the Palestinians*. Tel Aviv: Maariv Library.

Melman, Yossi (1984) *A Profile of a Terrorist Organization*. Tel Aviv: Hadar Publishers.

——— (1982) *The CIA Report on the Israeli Intelligence Community*. Tel Aviv: Erez Books, Zmora Bitan Publishers.

Naor, Arye (1986) *Cabinet of War: Functioning of the Israeli Cabinet During the Lebanon War 1982*. Tel Aviv: Lahav Publishers.

Rafael, Gideon (1981) *Destination Peace: Three Decades of Israeli Foreign Policy*. Jerusalem: Edanim Publishers-Yediot Aharonot Editor.

Reich, Bernard and Arnon Gutfeld (1977) *USA and the Israeli-Arab Conflict*. Tel Aviv: Maarachot Publishers, Israel Defense Forces.

Safran, Nadav (1969) *From War to War: The Israeli-Arab Conflict 1949–1967*. Tel Aviv: Keter Books.

Schueftan, Dan (1987) *A Jordanian Option: The "Yishuv" and the State of Israel Vis-à-Vis the Hashemite Regime and the Palestinian National Movement*. Tel Aviv: Kibbutz Meuhad.

Segev, Tom (1984) *The First Israelis*. Jerusalem: Domino Books.

Sela, Avraham (1985) *From Contacts to Negotiation: the Relations of the Jewish Agency and the State of Israel with King Abdullah 1946–1950*. Tel Aviv: Shiloah Center, Tel Aviv University.

Susser, Asher (1983) *Between Jordan and Palestine: A Political Biography of Wasfi el-Tell*. Tel Aviv: Kibbutz Meuhad.

Yaari, Ehud (1970) *Fatah*. Tel Aviv: A. Levin Epstein Publishing.

Israeli Newspapers and Magazines

Al-Hamishmar, May 8, 1987.

Davar, February 20 and December 26, 1986; April 30, June 2, and 5, 1987.

Haaretz, July 14, 1978; August 15, 1982; February 22, May 13, and June 25, 1987; April 1, 1988.

Hadashot, May 29, 1987.

Jerusalem Post, February 12, 1987.

Koteret Rashit, October 9, 1985; April 29, 1988.

Ma'ariv, April 19, 1989.

Monitin, September 1986.

Yediot Aharonot, June 14, 1985; February 8 and June 30, 1987; April 1, 1988.

Interviews

Ali, Kamal Hassan; former head of Egyptian intelligence service and prime minister of Egypt.

Allon, Yiftach; son of the late Israeli foreign minister Yigal Allon.

Amir, Rehavam; former Israeli consul-general in New York.

Arnan, Azariah; former assistant to Israeli minister Yigal Allon.

Avidan, Meir; researcher in *Moreshet* Institute, Ben-Gurion College, Sde-Boker, Israel.

Avneri, Uri; former member of Israeli Knesset, editor of *Ha-Olam ha-Zeh* magazine.

Aweidah, Faisal; representative of the PLO in London.

Bar-Lev, Chaim; former chief of staff of Israeli army and cabinet minister.

Bassiouny, Muhammad; former brigadier general in Egyptian military intelligence and Egypt's ambassador to Israel.

Ben-Porat, Yoel; retired brigadier general in Israeli military intelligence.

Berger, Arthur; State Department official.

Claverius, Wat; special U.S. envoy to the Middle East.

Collier, Dr. Peter; partner of the late Emanuel Herbert, King Hussein's physician.

Daraushe, Abdel Wahab; Israeli Arab member of the Knesset.

Dinitz, Simcha; former assistant to Israeli prime minister Golda Meir.

Eban, Abba; former foreign minister of Israel.

Eden, Motti; Israeli television correspondent.

Eran, Amos; former director general of the Israeli prime minister's office.

Eshkol, Miriam; widow of Israeli prime minister Levi Eshkol.

Eytan, Walter; former director general of Israeli foreign ministry and ambassador in France.

Gazit, Mordecai; former aide to Israeli prime ministers Golda Meir and Yitzhak Rabin.

Goren, Shmuel; former Mossad operative and ministry of defense coordinator of the occupied territories.

Herbert, Dr. Peter; son of the late Emanuel Herbert, King Hussein's physician.

Herzog, Chaim; former chief of Israeli military intelligence, president of Israel.

Katz-Oz, Avraham; minister of agriculture in Israeli cabinet.

Kimche, David; former Mossad operative and director general of Israeli foreign ministry.

Kuberski, Chaim; former director general of the Israeli interior ministry.

Ne'eman, Yuval; former colonel in Israeli military intelligence.

Neubach, Amnon; economic aide to former Israeli prime minister Shimon Peres.

Novick, Nimrod; diplomatic aide to former Israeli prime minister Peres.

Palmon, Yehoshua; former official in Jewish Agency and Israeli foreign ministry.

Peres, Shimon; former prime minister and foreign minister of Israel.

Rabin, Yitzhak; former chief of staff of the Israeli army, former prime minister and Israeli minister of defense.

Rafael, Gideon; former director general of the Israeli foreign ministry.

Rehavi, Sara; daughter of the late prime minister Golda Meir.

Rubinstein, Elyakim; secretary of the Israeli cabinet.

Said, Edward, professor of Columbia University, New York, and member of Palestine National Council.

Sartawi, Issam; late diplomatic assistant to PLO chariman Yasser Arafat.

Shamir, Yitzhak; prime minister of Israel.

Sieff, Lord of Brimpton; former president of Marks and Spencers, London.

Siniora, Hana; newspaper editor in East Jerusalem.

Sneh, Ephraim; retired brigadier general in Israeli army and head of civil administration in the West Bank.

Tamir, Avraham; retired major general in Israeli army and former director general of the prime minister's office.

Tsur, Yaakov; minister in Israeli cabinet.

Vardi, Yaakov; deputy director general of Tahal, Israel's water development authority.

Yaacobi, Gad; minister in Israeli cabinet.

Yaakobovitch, Mordecai; senior official of Mekorot, Israel's water supply company.

Zak, Moshe; author and columnist for *Maariv* newspaper.

Index

About the Authors

YOSSI MELMAN, currently a Nieman Fellow at Harvard University, is an Israeli newspaper columnist and a graduate of Hebrew University, Jerusalem. He is the author of *The Master Terrorist* as well as several articles concerning foreign policy and relations and secret intelligence.

DAN RAVIV, a CBS News correspondent in London, graduated from Harvard University, won two Overseas Press Club of America awards, and is currently coauthoring a second book with Yossi Melman on Israeli intelligence.